T0255537

Lecture Notes in Computer Science

Lecture Notes in Artificial Intelligence   **13448**

Founding Editor

Jörg Siekmann

Series Editors

Randy Goebel, *University of Alberta, Edmonton, Canada*
Wolfgang Wahlster, *DFKI, Berlin, Germany*
Zhi-Hua Zhou, *Nanjing University, Nanjing, China*

The series Lecture Notes in Artificial Intelligence (LNAI) was established in 1988 as a topical subseries of LNCS devoted to artificial intelligence.

The series publishes state-of-the-art research results at a high level. As with the LNCS mother series, the mission of the series is to serve the international R & D community by providing an invaluable service, mainly focused on the publication of conference and workshop proceedings and postproceedings.

Randy Goebel · Han Yu · Boi Faltings ·
Lixin Fan · Zehui Xiong
Editors

Trustworthy Federated Learning

First International Workshop, FL 2022
Held in Conjunction with IJCAI 2022
Vienna, Austria, July 23, 2022
Revised Selected Papers

 Springer

Editors
Randy Goebel ⓘ
University of Alberta
Edmonton, AB, Canada

Han Yu ⓘ
Nanyang Technological University
Singapore, Singapore

Boi Faltings
École polytechnique fédérale de Lausanne
Lausanne, Switzerland

Lixin Fan
WeBank
Shenzhen, China

Zehui Xiong
Singapore University of Technology
and Design
Singapore, Singapore

ISSN 0302-9743   ISSN 1611-3349 (electronic)
Lecture Notes in Artificial Intelligence
ISBN 978-3-031-28995-8   ISBN 978-3-031-28996-5 (eBook)
https://doi.org/10.1007/978-3-031-28996-5

LNCS Sublibrary: SL7 – Artificial Intelligence

This Springer imprint is published by the registered company Springer Nature Switzerland AG
The registered company address is: Gewerbestrasse 11, 6330 Cham, Switzerland

Preface

Federated Learning (FL) is a learning paradigm that enables collaborative training of machine learning models in which data reside and remain in distributed data silos during the training process. FL is a necessary framework to ensure AI methods remain compliant in the privacy-focused regulatory environment. As FL allows self-interested data owners to collaboratively train and share machine learning models, end-users can become co-creators of AI solutions. To enable open collaboration among FL co-creators and enhance the adoption of the federated learning paradigm, we envision that communities of data owners can self-organize during FL model training, when provided with tools to support diverse notions of trustworthy federated learning, which include, but are not limited to, security and robustness, privacy-preservation, interpretability, fairness, verifiability, transparency, auditability, incremental aggregation of shared learned models, and creating healthy market mechanisms to enable open dynamic collaboration among data owners under the FL paradigm.

This proceedings includes latest advances in the field of trustworthy federated learning presented during the International Workshop on Trustworthy Federated Learning in Conjunction with the International Joint Conference on AI (IJCAI 2022, workshop FL-IJCAI'22). Selected chapters focus on diverse topics including enhancing the personalization aspect of FL in the presence of non-IID data, enhancing the robustness and security of FL in the face of threats and misbehaviours, enhancing the efficiency of FL model training in the face of resource limitations, as well as real-world applications of trustworthy federated learning in industrial domains such as energy and recommender systems. Each paper has received at least 2 reviewers and has gone through several rounds of revisions to ensure that the issues raised by the reviewers have been completely resolved. With this special volume, we aim to spark discussions and collaborations among researchers and practitioners to further advance the field of trustworthy federated learning. This volume is edited by Randy Goebel, Han Yu, Boi Faltings, Lixin Fan and Zehui Xiong.

Randy Goebel
Han Yu
Boi Faltings
Lixin Fan
Zehui Xiong

Organization

Steering Committee Chair

Qiang Yang — The Hong Kong University of Science and Technology, and WeBank, China

Organizing Committee

General Co-chairs

Boi Faltings — EPFL, Switzerland
Randy Goebel — University of Alberta, Canada

Program Co-chairs

Han Yu — Nanyang Technological University, Singapore
Lixin Fan — WeBank, China
Zhiwei Xiong — Singapore University of Technology and Design, Singapore

Local Arrangements Chair

Guodong Long — University of Technology Sydney, Australia

Publicity Co-chairs

Sin G. Teo — Institute for Infocomm Research, A*STAR, Singapore
Le Zhang — University of Electronic Science and Technology, China
Zengxiang Li — Digital Research Institute, ENN Group, China

Contents

Adaptive Expert Models for Federated Learning

Martin Isaksson[1,3](✉)(iD), Edvin Listo Zec[3,5](iD), Rickard Cöster[2](iD),
Daniel Gillblad[4,7](iD), and Sarunas Girdzijauskas[3,6](iD)

[1] Ericsson Research, Stockholm, Sweden
martin.isaksson@ericsson.com
[2] Ericsson Global AI Accelerator, Stockholm, Sweden
[3] KTH Royal Institute of Technology, Stockholm, Sweden
[4] Chalmers AI Research Center, Chalmers University of Technology,
Göteborg, Sweden
[5] RISE Research Institutes of Sweden, Göteborg, Sweden
[6] RISE Research Institutes of Sweden, Stockholm, Sweden
[7] AI Sweden, Stockholm, Sweden

Abstract. Federated Learning (FL) is a promising framework for distributed learning when data is private and sensitive. However, the state-of-the-art solutions in this framework are not optimal when data is heterogeneous and non-IID. We propose a practical and robust approach to personalization in FL that adjusts to heterogeneous and non-IID data by balancing exploration and exploitation of several global models. To achieve our aim of personalization, we use a Mixture of Experts (MoE) that learns to group clients that are similar to each other, while using the global models more efficiently. We show that our approach achieves an accuracy up to 29.78% better than the state-of-the-art and up to 4.38% better compared to a local model in a pathological non-IID setting, even though we tune our approach in the IID setting.

Keywords: Federated learning · Personalization · Privacy preserving

1 Introduction

In many real-world scenarios, data is distributed over organizations or devices and is difficult to centralize. Due to legal reasons, data might have to remain and be processed where it is generated, and in many cases may not be allowed to be transferred [10]. Furthermore, due to communication limitations it can be practically impossible to send data to a central point of processing. In many applications of Machine Learning (ML) these challenges are becoming increasingly important to address. For example, sensors, cars, radio base stations and mobile devices are capable of generating more relevant training data than can be practically communicated to the cloud [8] and datasets in healthcare and industry cannot legally be moved between hospitals or countries of origin.

R. Goebel et al. (Eds.): FL 2022, LNAI 13448, pp. 1–16, 2023.
https://doi.org/10.1007/978-3-031-28996-5_1

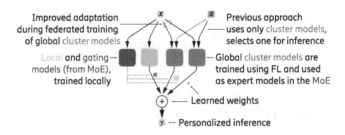

Fig. 1. Our approach adjusts to non-Independent and Identically Distributed (IID) data distributions by adaptively training a Mixture of Experts (MoE) for clients that share similar data distributions.

Federated Learning (FL) [1,27] shows promise to leveraging data that cannot easily be centralized. It has the potential to utilize compute and storage resources of clients to scale towards large, decentralized datasets while enhancing privacy. However, current approaches fall short when data is heterogeneous as well as non-Independent and Identically Distributed (non-IID), where stark differences between clients and groups of clients can be found. Therefore, personalization of collectively learned models will in practice often be critical to adapt to differences between regions, organizations and individuals to achieve the required performance [11,18]. This is the problem we address in this chapter.

Our approach adjusts to non-IID data distributions by adaptively training a Mixture of Experts (MoE) for clients that share similar data distributions.We explore a wide spectrum of data distribution settings: ranging from the same distribution for all clients, all the way to different distributions for each client. Our aim is an end-to-end framework that performs comparable or better than vanilla FL and is *robust* in all of these settings.

In order to achieve personalization, the authors of [11] introduce a method for training cluster models using FL. We show that their solution does not perform well in our settings, where only one or a few of the cluster models converge. To solve this, inspired by the Multi-Armed Bandit (MAB) field, we employ an efficient and effective way of balancing exploration and exploitation of these cluster models. As proposed by the authors of [24,29], we add a local model and use a MoE that learns to weigh, and make use of, all of the available models to produce a better personalized inference, see Fig. 1.

In summary, our main contributions are:

1. We devise an FL algorithm which improve upon [11] by balancing exploration and exploitation to produce better adapted cluster models, see Sect. 3.1;
2. We use said cluster models as expert models in an MoE to improve performance, described in Sect. 3.1;
3. An extensive analysis[1] of our approach with respect to different non-IID aspects that also considers the distribution of client performance, see Sect. 4.5.

---

[1] The source code for the experiments can be found at https://github.com/Ericsson Research/fl-moe.

2   Background

2.1   Problem Formulation

Consider a distributed and decentralized ML setting with clients $k \in \{1, 2, \ldots, K\}$. Each client k has access to a local data partition P^k that never leaves the client where $n_k = |P^k|$ is the number of local data samples. In this chapter we are considering a multi-class classification problem where we have $n = \sum_{k=1}^{K} n_k$ data samples x_i, indexed $i \in \{1, 2, \ldots, n_k\}$, and output class label y_i is in a finite set. We further divide each client partition P^k into local training and test sets. We are interested in performance on the local test set in a non-IID setting, see Sect. 2.2.

2.2   Regimes of Non-IID Data

In any decentralized setting it is common to have non-IID data that can be of non-identical client distributions [14,18], and which can be characterized as:

- *Feature distribution skew* (covariate-shift). The feature distributions vary between clients. Marginal distributions $\mathcal{P}(x)$ varies, but $\mathcal{P}(y \mid x)$ is shared;
- *Label distribution skew* (prior probability shift, or class imbalance). The distribution of class labels are different between clients, so that $\mathcal{P}(y)$ varies but $\mathcal{P}(x \mid y)$ is shared;
- *Same label, different features*. The conditional distributions $\mathcal{P}(x \mid y)$ varies between clients but $\mathcal{P}(y)$ is shared;
- *Same features, different label* (concept shift). The conditional distribution $\mathcal{P}(y \mid x)$ varies between clients, but $\mathcal{P}(x)$ is shared;
- *Quantity skew* (unbalancedness). Clients have different amounts of data.

Furthermore, the data independence between clients and between data samples within a client can also be violated.

2.3   Federated Learning

In a centralized ML solution data that may be potentially privacy-sensitive is collected to a central location. One way of improving privacy is to use a collaborative ML algorithm such as Federated Averaging (FEDAVG) [27]. In FEDAVG training of a global model $f_g(x, w_g)$ is distributed, decentralized and synchronous. A parameter server coordinates training on many clients over several communication rounds until convergence.

In communication round t, the parameter server selects a fraction C out of K clients as the set S_t. Each selected client $k \in S_t$ will train locally on n_k data samples $(x_i, y_i), i \in P^k$, for E epochs before an update is sent to the parameter server. The parameter server performs aggregation of all received updates and updates the global model parameters w_g. Finally, the new global model parameters are distributed to all clients.

We can now define our objective as

$$\min_{\boldsymbol{w}_g \in \mathbb{R}^d} \mathcal{L}(\boldsymbol{w}_g) \triangleq \min_{\boldsymbol{w}_g \in \mathbb{R}^d} \underbrace{\sum_{k=1}^{K} \frac{n_k}{n} \overbrace{\frac{1}{n_k} \sum_{i \in P^k} \underbrace{l(\boldsymbol{x}_i, y_i, \boldsymbol{w}_g)}_{\text{sample } i \text{ loss}}}^{\text{client } k \text{ average loss}}}_{\text{population average loss}}, \tag{1}$$

where $l(\boldsymbol{x}_i, y_i, \boldsymbol{w}_g)$ is the loss for $y_i, \hat{y}_g = f_g(\boldsymbol{x}_i, \boldsymbol{w}_g)$. In other words, we aim to minimize the average loss of the global model over all clients in the population.

2.4   Iterative Federated Clustering

In many real distributed use-cases, data is naturally non-IID and clients form clusters of *similar* clients. A possible improvement over FEDAVG is to introduce cluster models that map to these clusters, but the problem of identifying clients that belong to these clusters remains. We aim to find clusters, subsets of the population of clients, that benefit more from training together within the subset, as opposed to training with the entire population.

Using Iterative Federated Clustering Algorithm (IFCA) [11] we set the expected largest number of clusters to be J and initialize one cluster model with weights $\boldsymbol{w}_g^j$ per cluster $j \in \{1, 2, \ldots, J\}$. At communication round t each selected client k performs a cluster identity estimation, where it selects the cluster model $\hat{j}^k$ that has the lowest estimated loss on the local training set. This is similar to [26].

The cluster model parameters $\boldsymbol{w}_g^j$ at time $t+1$ are then updated by using only updates from clients the jth selected cluster model, so that (using model averaging [11,27])

$$n_j \leftarrow \sum_{k \in \{S_t \mid \hat{j}^k = j\}} n_k, \tag{2}$$

$$\boldsymbol{w}_g^j(t+1) \leftarrow \sum_{k \in \{S_t \mid \hat{j}^k = j\}} \frac{n_k}{n_j} \boldsymbol{w}^k(t+1). \tag{3}$$

2.5   Federated Learning Using a Mixture of Experts

In order to construct a personalized model for each client, [24] first add a local expert model $f_l^k(\boldsymbol{x}, \boldsymbol{w}_l^k)$ that is trained only on local data. Recall the global model $f_g(\boldsymbol{x}, \boldsymbol{w}_g)$ from Sect. 2.3. The authors of [24] then *learn to weigh* the local expert model and the global model using a gating function from MoE [12, 15,29]. The gating function takes the same input $\boldsymbol{x}$ and outputs a weight for each of the expert models. It uses a Softmax in the output layer so that these weights sum to 1. We define $f_h^k(\boldsymbol{x}, \boldsymbol{w}_h^k)$ as the gating function for client k. The same model architectures are used for all local models, so $f_h^k(\boldsymbol{x}, \boldsymbol{w}) = f_h^{k'}(\boldsymbol{x}, \boldsymbol{w})$ and $f_l^k(\boldsymbol{x}, \boldsymbol{w}) = f_l^{k'}(\boldsymbol{x}, \boldsymbol{w})$ for all pairs of clients k, k'. For simplicity, we write $f_l(\boldsymbol{x}) = f_l^k(\boldsymbol{x}, \boldsymbol{w}_l^k)$ and $f_h(\boldsymbol{x}) = f_h^k(\boldsymbol{x}, \boldsymbol{w}_h^k)$ for each client k. Parameters $\boldsymbol{w}_l^k$ and $\boldsymbol{w}_h^k$ are local to client k and not shared. Finally, the personalized inference is

$$\hat{y}_h = f_h(\boldsymbol{x}) f_l(\boldsymbol{x}) + [1 - f_h(\boldsymbol{x})] f_g(\boldsymbol{x}). \tag{4}$$

3 Adaptive Expert Models for Personalization

3.1 Framework Overview and Motivation

In IFCA, after the training phase, the cluster model with the lowest loss on the validation set is used for all future inferences. All other cluster models are discarded in the clients. A drawback of IFCA is therefore that it does not use all the information available in the clients in form of unused cluster models. Each client has access to the full set of cluster models, and our hypothesis is that if a client can make use of *all* of these models we can increase performance.

It is sometimes advantageous to incorporate a local model, as in Sect. 2.5, especially when the local data distribution is very different from other clients. We therefore modify the MoE [24] to incorporate *all* the cluster models from IFCA [11] *and* the local model as expert models in the mixture, see Fig. 2. We revise (4) to

$$\hat{y}_h = g_l f_l^k (\boldsymbol{x}) + \sum_{j=0}^{J-1} g_j^k f_g^j (\boldsymbol{x}), \tag{5}$$

where g_l is the local model expert weight, and g_j^k is the cluster model expert weight for cluster j from $f_h^k (\boldsymbol{x})$, see Fig. 2.

However, importantly, we note that setting J in [11] to a large value produces few cluster models that actually converge, which lowers performance when used in a MoE. The authors of [34] note that this method is difficult to train in practice and that the performance is worse than FEDAVG together with fine-tuning. We differ from [11] in the cluster estimation step in that we select the same number of clients $K_s = \lceil CK \rceil$ in every communication round, regardless of J. This spreads out more evenly over the global cluster models. Since cluster models are randomly initialized we can end up updating one cluster model more than the others by chance. In following communication rounds, a client is more likely to select this cluster model, purely because it has been updated more. This also has the effect that as J increases, the quality of the updates are reduced as they are averaged from a smaller set of clients. In turn, this means that we needed more iterations to converge. Therefore, we make use of the ε-greedy algorithm [31] in order to allow each client to prioritize gathering information (*exploration*) of the cluster models or use the estimated best cluster model (*exploitation*). In each iteration a client selects a random cluster model with probability ε and the currently best otherwise, see Algorithm 3.

By using the ε-greedy algorithm we make more expert models converge and avoid a mode collapse. We can then use the gating function f_h^k from MoE to adapt to the underlying data distributions and weigh the different expert models. We outline our setup in Fig. 1 and provide details in Fig. 2 and Algorithms 1 to 4.

When a cluster model has converged it is not cost-effective to transmit this cluster model to every client, so by using per-model early stopping we can reduce communication in both uplink and downlink. Specifically, before training we initialize $\mathcal{J} = \{1, 2, \ldots, J\}$. When early stopping is triggered for a cluster model we remove that cluster model from the set $\mathcal{J}$. The early-stopping algorithm is described in Algorithm 1.

Algorithm 1. Adaptive Expert Models for FL — server

1: **procedure** SERVER(C, K)
2:    initialize $\mathcal{J} \leftarrow \{1, 2, \ldots, J\}, \{\boldsymbol{w}_g^j(0) \mid j \in \mathcal{J}\}$ ▷ Initialize J global cluster models
3:    $K_s \leftarrow \lceil CK \rceil$ ▷ Number of clients to select per communication round
4:    **for** $t \in \{1, 2, \ldots\}$ **do**   ▷ Until convergence
5:       $S_t \subseteq \{1, 2, \ldots, K\}, |S_t| = K_s$ ▷ Random sampling of K_s clients
6:       **for all** $k \in S_t$ **do**   ▷ For all clients, in parallel
7:          $\boldsymbol{w}^k(t+1), n_k, \hat{j}^k \leftarrow k.\text{CLIENT}\left(\{\boldsymbol{w}_g^j \mid j \in \mathcal{J}\}\right)$ ▷ Local training (Alg. 2)
8:       **for all** $j \in \{1, 2, \ldots, J\}$ **do**   ▷ For all cluster models
9:          $n_j \leftarrow \sum_{k \in \{S_t \mid \hat{j}^k = j\}} n_k$ ▷ Total number of samples for cluster model j from clients where $j = \hat{j}$
10:          $\boldsymbol{w}_g^j(t+1) \leftarrow \sum_{k \in \{S_t \mid \hat{j}^k = j\}} \frac{n_k}{n_j} \boldsymbol{w}^k(t+1)$ ▷ Update cluster model j with clients where $j = \hat{j}$
11:       **if** early stopping triggered for model j **then**
12:          $\mathcal{J} \leftarrow \mathcal{J} \setminus j$ ▷ *Optional:* Remove j from the set of selectable cluster models $\mathcal{J}$

Algorithm 2. Adaptive Expert Models for FL — client

13: **procedure** CLIENT($\{\boldsymbol{w}_g^j \mid j \in \mathcal{J}\}$)
14:    $\hat{j} \leftarrow \text{CL.-EST.}\left(\varepsilon, \{\boldsymbol{w}_g^j \mid j \in \mathcal{J}\}\right), n_k \leftarrow |P^k|$ ▷ Estimate best cluster (Alg. 3)
15:    $\boldsymbol{w}^k(t+1) \leftarrow \text{UPDATE}\left(\boldsymbol{w}_g^{\hat{j}}(t), n_k\right)$ ▷ Perform local training using cluster model $\hat{j}$ (Alg. 4)
16:    **return** $(\boldsymbol{w}^k(t+1), n_k, \hat{j})$

---

4   Experiments

4.1   Datasets

We use three different datasets, with different non-IID characteristics, in which the task is an image multi-class classification task with varying number of classes. We summarize these datasets in Table 1.

- **CIFAR-10** [20], where we use a technique from [24] to create client partitions with a controlled *Label distribution skew*, see Sect. 4.2;
- **Rotated CIFAR-10** [11], where the client feature distributions are controlled by rotating CIFAR-10 images—an example of *same label, different features*;
- **Federated Extended MNIST (FEMNIST)** [4,5] with handwritten characters written by many writers, exhibiting many of the non-IID characteristics outlined in Sect. 2.2.

Algorithm 3. Adaptive Expert Models for FL — cluster assignment

---
17: **procedure** CL.-EST.($\varepsilon, \{\boldsymbol{w}_g^j \mid j \in \mathcal{J}\}$)
18:    **return** $\begin{cases} \operatorname{argmin}_{j \in \mathcal{J}} \sum_{i \in P^k} l\left(\boldsymbol{x}_i, y_i, \boldsymbol{w}_g^j\right) & \text{prob. } 1 - \varepsilon \quad \triangleright \text{ Lowest loss model} \\ \mathcal{U}\{1, J\} & \text{prob. } \varepsilon \quad \triangleright \text{ Random assignment} \end{cases}$

Algorithm 4. Adaptive Expert Models for FL—local update

19: **procedure** UPDATE($\boldsymbol{w}^k(t+1), n_k$)   ▷ Mini-batch gradient descent
20:     **for** $e \in \{1, 2, \ldots, E\}$ **do**   ▷ For a few epochs
21:         **for all** batches of size B **do**   ▷ Batch update
22:             $\boldsymbol{w}^k(t+1) \leftarrow \boldsymbol{w}^k(t+1) -$
        $\frac{\eta}{B}\nabla_{\boldsymbol{w}^k(t+1)} \sum_{i=1}^{B} l_i\left(\boldsymbol{x}_i, y_i, \boldsymbol{w}^k(t+1)\right)$ ▷ Local parameter update
23:     **return** $\boldsymbol{w}^k(t+1)$

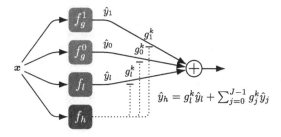

Fig. 2. Our solution with 2 global cluster models. Each client k has one local expert model $f_l(\boldsymbol{x}, \boldsymbol{w}_l^k)$ and share $J = 2$ expert cluster models $f_g^j(\boldsymbol{x}, \boldsymbol{w}_g^j)$ with all other clients. A gating model $f_h(\boldsymbol{x}, \boldsymbol{w}_h^k)$ is used to weigh the expert cluster models and produce a personalized inference $\hat{y}_h$ from the input $\boldsymbol{x}$.

Table 1. Dataset summary statistics — number of samples per client.

Dataset	Classes	K	C	Samples, training set			Samples, test set		
				Mean	Min	Max	Mean	Min	Max
CIFAR-10	10	50	0.1	500.0	500	500	100.0	100	100
Rot. CIFAR-10	10	200	0.1	500.0	500	500	100.0	100	100
FEMNIST	62	182	0.07	199.7	98	387	22.7	11	44

4.2   Non-IID Sampling

In order to construct a non-IID dataset from the CIFAR-10 dataset [20] with the properties of class imbalance that we are interested in we first look at [27]. A *pathological non-IID* dataset is constructed by sorting the dataset by label, dividing it into shards of 300 data samples and giving each client 2 shards.

However, as in [24], we are interested in varying the degree of *non-IIDness* and therefore we assign two majority classes to each client which make up a fraction p of the data samples of the client. The remainder fraction $(1 - p)$ is sampled uniformly from the other 8 classes. When $p = 0.2$ each class has an equal probability of being sampled. A similar case to the *pathological non-IID* above is represented by $p = 1$. In reality, p is unknown.

4.3 Model Architecture

We start with the benchmark model defined in [4] which is a Convolutional Neural Network (CNN) model with two convolutional layers and one fully connected layer with fixed hyperparameters. However, in our case where n_k is small, the local model is prone to over-fitting, so it is desirable to have a model with lower capacity. Similarly, the gating model is also prone to overfitting due to both a small local dataset and the fact that it aims to solve a multi-label classification problem with fewer classes (expert models), than in the original multi-class classification problem. The local model, gating model and cluster models share the same underlying architecture, but therefore have hyperparameter such as number of filters in a hidden layer individually tuned, see Sect. 4.4. The AdamW [25] optimizer is used to train the local model and the gating model, while Stochastic Gradient Descent (SGD) [2] is used to train the cluster models to avoid issues related to momentum parameters when averaging. We use negative log-likelihood loss in (1).

4.4 Hyperparameter Tuning

Hyperparameters are tuned using [23] in four stages and used for all clients. For each model we tune the learning rate η, the number of filters in two convolutional layers, the number of hidden units in the fully connected layer, dropout, and weight decay. For the ε-greedy exploration method we also tune ε.

First, we tune the hyperparameters for a local model and for a single global model. Thereafter, we tune the hyperparameters for the gating model using the best hyperparameters found in the earlier steps. Lastly, we tune ε with two cluster models $J = 2$. For the no exploration experiments we set $\varepsilon = 0$.

Hyperparameters depend on p and J but we tune the hyperparameters for a fixed majority class fraction $p = 0.2$, which corresponds to the IID case. The tuned hyperparameters are then used for all experiments. We show that our method is still robust in the fully non-IID case when $p = 1$. See Table 2 for tuned hyperparameters in the CIFAR-10 experiment.

4.5 Results

We summarize our results for the class imbalance case exemplified with the CIFAR-10 dataset in Table 3. In Fig. 3, we see an example of how the performance varies when we increase the non-IID-ness factor p for the case when $J = 3$. In Fig. 3a we see the performance of IFCA [11] compared to our solution in Fig. 3b. We also compare to: a local model fine-tuned from the best cluster model, an entirely local model, and an ensemble model where we include *all* cluster models as well as the local model with equal weights. In Fig. 4 we vary the number of cluster models J for different values of the majority class fraction p.

Table 2. Tuned hyper-parameters in the CIFAR-10 experiment for the global cluster models, the local models and the gating model.

Model	η	Conv1	Conv2	FC	Dropout	Weight Dec.	E	ε
Global	5.86×10^{-3}	128	32	1024	0.80	1.10×10^{-3}	3	0.33
Local	2.69×10^{-4}	32	256	256	0.76	9.89×10^{-3}		
Gate	3×10^{-6}	12	12	8	0.78	6.88×10^{-4}		

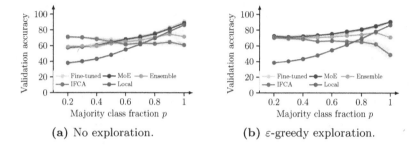

(a) No exploration.   **(b)** ε-greedy exploration.

Fig. 3. Results for CIFAR-10. Comparison between no exploration and our ε-greedy exploration method for $J = 6$. Our proposed MoE solution with ε-greedy exploration is superior in all cases from IID to pathological non-IID class distributions, here shown by varying the majority class fraction p.

Table 3. Results for CIFAR-10 and $p \in \{0.2, 0.4, \ldots, 1\}$ when $J = 6$. Mean μ and standard deviation σ for our exploration method ε-greedy and without exploration. We compare our proposed MoE solution to the baseline from IFCA [11]. Our proposed solution is superior in all but one case, indicated by **bold** numbers.

			MoE		IFCA		Ensemble		Fine-tuned		Local	
p	Exp. strategy	# trials	μ	σ	μ	σ	μ	σ	μ	σ	μ	σ
0.2	ε-greedy (ours)	7	**72.39**	1.26	70.38	0.74	70.82	1.87	70.16	0.61	38.52	0.75
	No exploration	6	57.73	1.95	71.25	0.86	58.58	1.96	70.13	1.04	38.06	0.87
0.4	ε-greedy (ours)	6	**72.05**	1.79	68.59	1.00	69.96	2.33	70.28	1.05	43.36	0.47
	No exploration	9	60.12	2.37	68.29	1.56	59.54	1.31	69.42	1.54	43.16	0.71
0.6	ε-greedy (ours)	8	**75.22**	0.75	66.53	0.98	71.44	1.17	72.50	0.54	54.63	0.33
	No exploration	9	67.94	0.75	61.47	2.27	65.15	0.87	68.27	1.71	55.04	0.45
0.8	ε-greedy (ours)	14	**81.09**	1.18	65.23	2.40	74.44	0.76	80.13	1.02	69.49	0.58
	No exploration	15	75.04	0.93	62.59	1.95	70.82	1.56	76.49	1.27	69.55	0.70
1.0	ε-greedy (ours)	14	90.76	0.82	48.79	5.35	71.06	4.03	90.26	1.02	86.65	0.39
	No exploration	6	88.79	0.52	60.97	2.07	71.56	9.12	**91.11**	0.33	86.37	0.31

An often overlooked aspect of performance in FL is the inter-client variance. We achieve a smaller inter-client variance, shown for CIFAR-10 in Fig. 6a and Table 3.

We see that for CIFAR-10 our ε-greedy exploration method achieves better results for lower values of p by allowing more of the cluster models to converge—thereby more cluster models are useful as experts in the MoE, even though the models are similar, see Fig. 5a. For higher values of p we see that the cluster models are adapting to existing clusters in the data, see Fig. 5c. The most interesting result is seen in between these extremes, see Fig. 5b. We note that the same number of clients pick each cluster model as in IFCA, but we manage to make a better selection and achieve higher performance.

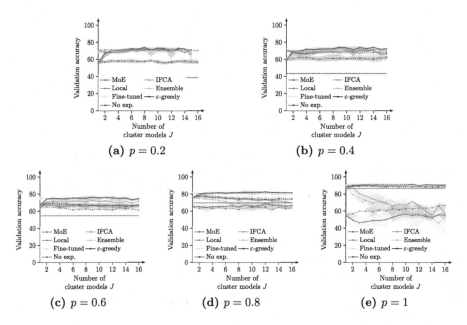

Fig. 4. Results for CIFAR-10. Comparison between no exploration (colored dashed lines) and the ε-greedy exploration method (colored solid lines). Our proposed MoE solution with the ε-greedy exploration outperforms all other solutions, including the baseline from IFCA [11]. It performs better the greater the non-IIDness, here seen by varying the majority class fraction p. Furthermore, our solution is robust to changes in the number of cluster models J.

For the rotated CIFAR-10 case in Table 4 and 7b we see that IFCA manages to assign each client to the correct clusters at $J = 2$, and in this *Same label, different features* case our exploration method requires a larger J to achieve the same performance. We also note the very high $\varepsilon = 0.82$. More work is needed on better exploration methods for this case.

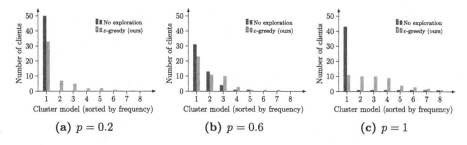

(a) $p = 0.2$ **(b)** $p = 0.6$ **(c)** $p = 1$

Fig. 5. Results for CIFAR-10. The number of clients in each cluster for the different exploration methods. Clusters are sorted—the lowest index corresponds to the most picked cluster. Our ε-greedy exploration method picks the cluster models more evenly.

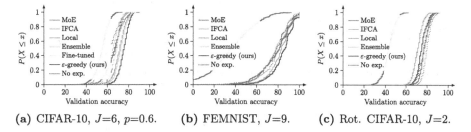

(a) CIFAR-10, $J=6$, $p=0.6$.   **(b)** FEMNIST, $J=9$.   **(c)** Rot. CIFAR-10, $J=2$.

Fig. 6. CDF of client accuracy. Comparison between no exploration (colored dashed lines) and the ε-greedy exploration method (colored solid lines). Our proposed MoE solution with ε-greedy exploration improves accuracy and fairness for two of the datasets.

The FEMNIST dataset represents a more difficult scenario since there are many non-IID aspects in this dataset. We find from Table 5 and Fig. 7a that for FEMNIST the best performance is achieved when $J = 9$ and in Fig. 6b we show the distribution of accuracy for the clients for the different models.

5 Related Work

The FEDAVG algorithm [27] is the most prevalent algorithm for learning a global model in FL. This algorithm has demonstrated that an average over model parameters is an efficient way to aggregate local models into a global model. However, when data is non-IID, FEDAVG converges slowly or not at all. This has given rise to personalization methods for FL [14,18]. Research on how to handle non-IID data among clients is ample and expanding. Solutions include fine-tuning locally [33], meta-learning [9,17], MAB [30], multi-task learning [22], model heterogeneous methods [7,13], data extension [32], distillation-based methods [16,21] and Prototypical Contrastive FL [28].

Mixing local and global models has been explored by [6], where a scalar α is optimized to combine global and local models. In [29] the authors propose to use MoE [15] and learn a gating function that weighs a local and global expert to

Table 4. Results for Rotated CIFAR-10. Mean μ and standard deviation σ with varying number of cluster models J, for our exploration method ε-greedy and for the baseline exploration method from IFCA. At $J=2$ all clients have picked the correct cluster model.

J	Exp. strategy	# trials	MoE μ	σ	IFCA μ	σ	Ensemble μ	σ	Local μ	σ
1	ε-greedy (ours)	7	70.20	1.35	72.63	2.01	67.89	1.23	42.79	1.10
	No exploration	10	70.70	0.95	73.08	0.87	68.14	1.15	43.27	0.92
3	ε-greedy (ours)	7	75.45	2.44	77.91	1.90	71.45	1.97	42.76	1.15
	No exploration	10	76.94	1.14	79.95	0.92	71.51	1.13	42.94	1.65
6	ε-greedy (ours)	3	75.59	1.20	78.59	0.92	71.26	1.55	43.70	0.84
	No exploration	4	76.49	0.86	79.30	0.51	70.78	0.82	43.09	1.12
9	ε-greedy (ours)	1	77.58		**80.33**		72.65		40.55	
	No exploration	6	76.96	0.96	79.6	1.27	71.38	1.46	42.53	1.90

Table 5. Results for FEMNIST. Mean μ and standard deviation σ with varying number of cluster models J for our exploration method ε-greedy and for the baseline exploration method from IFCA.

J	Exp. strategy	# trials	MoE μ	σ	IFCA μ	σ	Ensemble μ	σ	Local μ	σ
1	ε-greedy (ours)	3	75.99	3.03	77.80	3.88	75.14	3.20	36.27	0.76
	No exploration	3	78.15	0.79	80.48	0.77	77.53	0.57	36.35	0.39
3	ε-greedy (ours)	3	**82.07**	0.22	78.35	0.74	80.49	1.28	36.12	0.78
	No exploration	3	77.59	0.60	78.21	3.63	76.52	1.95	36.15	0.43
6	ε-greedy (ours)	3	**82.72**	0.81	77.11	1.03	80.48	1.57	36.90	0.88
	No exploration	3	78.26	0.71	79.04	1.58	77.42	0.89	36.13	1.04
9	ε-greedy (ours)	3	**84.37**	1.01	78.05	0.84	81.82	1.62	36.72	0.85
	No exploration	3	77.06	1.88	78.73	1.35	76.49	1.45	36.52	0.76

enhance user privacy. This work is developed further in [24], where the authors use a gating function with larger capacity to learn a personalized model when client data is non-IID. We differ in using cluster models as expert models, and by evaluating our method on datasets with different non-IID characteristics. Recent work has studied clustering in FL settings for non-IID data [3,11,19,26]. In [11] the authors implement a clustering algorithm for handling non-IID data in form of covariate shift. Their proposed algorithm learns one global model per cluster with a central parameter server, using the training loss of global models on local data of clients to perform cluster assignment. In their work, they only perform clustering in the last layer and aggregate the rest into a single model. If a global model cluster is unused for some communication rounds, the global cluster model

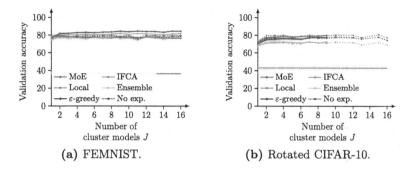

Fig. 7. Results for FEMNIST and rotated CIFAR-10. Comparison between no exploration (colored dashed lines) and the ε-greedy exploration method (colored solid lines). Our proposed MoE solution is superior in the FEMNIST case, but need more cluster models to achieve similar performance to the baseline in the rotated CIFAR-10 case.

is removed from the list to reduce communication overhead. However, this means that a client cannot use other global cluster models to increase performance.

6 Discussion

We adapted the inspiring work by [11] to work better in our setting and efficiently learned expert models for non-IID client data. Sending all cluster models in each iteration introduces more communication overhead. We addressed this by removing converged cluster models from the set of selectable cluster models in Algorithm 1, although this is not used in our main results. This only affects the result to a minor degree, but has a larger effect on training time due to wasting client updates on already converged models. Another improvement is the reduces complexity in the cluster assignment step. A notable difference between our work and IFCA is that we share *all* weights, as opposed to only the last layer in [11]. These differences increase the communication overhead further, but this has not been our priority and we leave this for future work.

7 Conclusion

In this chapter, we have investigated personalization in a distributed and decentralized ML setting where the data generated on the clients is heterogeneous with non-IID characteristics. We noted that neither FEDAVG nor state-of-the-art solutions achieve high performance in this setting. To address this problem, we proposed a practical framework of MoE using cluster models and local models as expert models and improved the adaptiveness of the expert models by balancing exploration and exploitation. Specifically, we used a MoE [24] to make better use of the cluster models available in the clients and added a local model. We showed that IFCA [11] does not work well in our setting, and inspired by the MAB field, added an ε-greedy exploration [31] method to improve the adaptiveness of the cluster models which increased their usefulness in the MoE. We evaluated our method on three datasets representing different non-IID settings, and found that our approach achieve superior performance in two of the datasets, and is robust in the third. Even though we tune our algorithm and hyperparameters in the IID setting, it generalizes well in non-IID settings or with varying number of cluster models—a testament to its robustness. For example, for CIFAR-10 we see an average accuracy improvement of 29.78% compared to IFCA and 4.38% compared to a local model in the pathological non-IID setting. Furthermore, our approach improved the inter-client accuracy variance with 60.39% compared to IFCA, which indicates improved fairness, but 60.98% worse than a local model.

In real-world scenarios data is distributed and often displays non-IID characteristics, and we consider personalization to be a very important direction of research. Finding clusters of similar clients to make learning more efficient is still an open problem. We believe there is potential to improve the convergence of the cluster models further, and that privacy, security and system aspects provide interesting directions for future work.

Acknowledgment. This work was partially supported by the Wallenberg AI, Autonomous Systems and Software Program (WASP) funded by the Knut and Alice Wallenberg Foundation.

The computations were enabled by the supercomputing resource Berzelius provided by National Supercomputer Centre at Linköping University and the Knut and Alice Wallenberg foundation.

We thank all reviewers who made suggestions to help improve and clarify this manuscript, especially Dr. A. Alam, F. Cornell, Dr. R. Gaigalas, T. Kvernvik, C. Svahn, F. Vannella, Dr. H. Shokri Ghadikolaei, D. Sandberg and Prof. S. Haridi.

References

1. Bonawitz, K., Eichner, H., et al.: Towards federated learning at scale: system design. In: Proceedings of Machine Learning and Systems (MLSys), Stanford, CA, USA (2019). https://proceedings.mlsys.org/book/271.pdf
2. Bottou, L., Curtis, F.E., Nocedal, J.: Optimization methods for large-scale machine learning. SIAM Rev. **60**(2), 223–311 (2018). https://doi.org/10.1137/16M1080173, https://epubs.siam.org/doi/10.1137/16M1080173
3. Briggs, C., Fan, Z., Andras, P.: Federated learning with hierarchical clustering of local updates to improve training on non-IID data. In: International Joint Conference on Neural Networks (IJCNN), Glasgow, United Kingdom. IEEE (2020). https://doi.org/10.1109/IJCNN48605.2020.9207469
4. Caldas, S., et al.: LEAF: a benchmark for federated settings. CoRR abs/1812.01097 (2018). http://arxiv.org/abs/1812.01097
5. Cohen, G., Afshar, S., Jonathan, T., van Schaik, A.: EMNIST: extending MNIST to handwritten letters. In: International Joint Conference on Neural Networks (IJCNN), Anchorage, AK, USA. IEEE (2017). https://doi.org/10.1109/IJCNN.2017.7966217
6. Deng, Y., Kamani, M.M., Mahdavi, M.: Adaptive personalized federated learning. CoRR abs/2003.13461 (2020). https://arxiv.org/abs/2003.13461

7. Diao, E., Ding, J., Tarokh, V.: HeteroFL: Computation and Communication Efficient Federated Learning for Heterogeneous Clients. In: 9th International Conference on Learning Representations (ICLR), Austria (2021). https://openreview. net/forum?id=TNkPBBYFkXg

8. Berggren, V., Inam, R., Mokrushin, L., Hata, A., Jeong, J., Mohalik, S.K., Forgeat, J., Sorrentino, S.: Artificial intelligence and machine learning in next-generation systems. Technical report, Ericsson Research, Ericsson AB (2018). https://www. ericsson.com/en/white-papers/machine-intelligence

9. Finn, C., Abbeel, P., Levine, S.: Model-agnostic meta-learning for fast adaptation of deep networks. In: Proceedings of the 34th International Conference on Machine Learning (ICML), Sydney, NSW, Australia. PMLR (2017). https://doi. org/10.5555/3305381.3305498, http://proceedings.mlr.press/v70/finn17a.html

10. GDPR: Regulation (EU) 2016/679 on the protection of natural persons with regard to the processing of personal data and the free movement of such data (2016). https://eur-lex.europa.eu/legal-content/EN/TXT/? uri=CELEX:02016R0679-20160504

11. Ghosh, A., Chung, J., Yin, D., Ramchandran, K.: An efficient framework for clustered federated learning. In: Advances in Neural Information Processing Systems (NeurIPS) (2020). https://proceedings.neurips.cc/paper/2020/file/ e32cc80bf07915058ce90722ee17bb71-Paper.pdf

12. Hanzely, F., Richtárik, P.: Federated learning of a mixture of global and local models. CoRR abs/2002.05516 (2020). https://arxiv.org/abs/2002.05516

13. He, C., Annavaram, M., Avestimehr, S.: FedNAS: federated deep learning via neural architecture search. CoRR abs/2004.08546 (2020). https://arxiv.org/abs/2004. 08546

14. Hsieh, K., Phanishayee, A., Mutlu, O., Gibbons, P.B.: The non-IID data quagmire of decentralized machine learning. In: Proceedings of the 37th International Conference on Machine Learning (ICML). PMLR (2020). http://proceedings.mlr. press/v119/hsieh20a.html

15. Jacobs, R.A., Jordan, M.I., Nowlan, S.J., Hinton, G.E.: Adaptive mixtures of local experts. Neural Comput. 3(1), 79–87 (1991). https://doi.org/10.1162/neco.1991.3. 1.79, https://ieeexplore.ieee.org/document/6797059

16. Jeong, E., Oh, S., Kim, H., Park, J., Bennis, M., Kim, S.L.: Communication-efficient on-device machine learning: federated distillation and augmentation under non-IID private data. CoRR abs/1811.11479 (2018). http://arxiv.org/abs/1811. 11479

17. Jiang, Y., Konečný, J., Rush, K., Kannan, S.: Improving federated learning personalization via model agnostic meta learning. CoRR abs/1909.12488 (2019). http:// arxiv.org/abs/1909.12488

18. Kairouz, P., McMahan, H.B., et al., B.A.: Advances and open problems in federated learning, vol. 14, pp. 1–210 (2021). https://doi.org/10.1561/2200000083

19. Kim, Y., Hakim, E.A., Haraldson, J., Eriksson, H., da Silva Jr., J.M.B., Fischione, C.: Dynamic clustering in federated learning. In: International Conference on Communications (ICC), Montreal, QC, Canada, pp. 1–6. IEEE (2021). https://doi.org/ 10.1109/ICC42927.2021.9500877

20. Krizhevsky, A.: Learning multiple layers of features from tiny images (2009). https://www.cs.toronto.edu/~kriz/learning-features-2009-TR.pdf

21. Li, D., Wang, J.: FedMD: heterogenous federated learning via model distillation. CoRR abs/1910.03581 (2019). http://arxiv.org/abs/1910.03581

22. Li, T., Hu, S., Beirami, A., Smith, V.: Ditto: fair and robust federated learning through personalization. In: Proceedings of the 38th International Conference on Machine Learning (ICML). PMLR (2021). http://proceedings.mlr.press/v139/li21h.html

23. Liaw, R., Liang, E., Nishihara, R., Moritz, P., Gonzalez, J.E., Stoica, I.: Tune: a research platform for distributed model selection and training. CoRR abs/1807.05118 (2018). http://arxiv.org/abs/1807.05118

24. Listo Zec, E., Mogren, O., Martinsson, J., Sütfeld, L.R., Gillblad, D.: Federated learning using a mixture of experts. CoRR abs/2010.02056 (2020). https://arxiv.org/abs/2010.02056

25. Loshchilov, I., Hutter, F.: Decoupled weight decay regularization. In: 7th International Conference on Learning Representations (ICLR), New Orleans, LA, USA (2019). https://openreview.net/forum?id=Bkg6RiCqY7

26. Mansour, Y., Mohri, M., Ro, J., Suresh, A.T.: Three approaches for personalization with applications to federated learning. CoRR abs/2002.10619 (2020). https://arxiv.org/abs/2002.10619

27. McMahan, B., Moore, E., Ramage, D., Hampson, S., y Arcas, B.A.: Communication-efficient learning of deep networks from decentralized data. In: Proceedings of the 20th International Conference on Artificial Intelligence and Statistics (AISTATS), Fort Lauderdale, FL, USA. PMLR (2017). http://proceedings.mlr.press/v54/mcmahan17a.html

28. Mu, X., et al.: FedProc: prototypical contrastive federated learning on non-IID data. CoRR abs/2109.12273 (2021). https://arxiv.org/abs/2109.12273

29. Peterson, D.W., Kanani, P., Marathe, V.J.: Private federated learning with domain adaptation. CoRR abs/1912.06733 (2019). http://arxiv.org/abs/1912.06733

30. Shi, C., Shen, C., Yang, J.: Federated multi-armed bandits with personalization. In: The 24th International Conference on Artificial Intelligence and Statistics (AISTATS) (2021). http://proceedings.mlr.press/v130/shi21c.html

31. Sutton, R.S.: Generalization in reinforcement learning: successful examples using sparse coarse coding. In: Advances in Neural Information Processing Systems (NeurIPS). MIT Press (1995). https://proceedings.neurips.cc/paper/1995/file/8f1d43620bc6bb580df6e80b0dc05c48-Paper.pdf

32. Tijani, S.A., Ma, X., Zhang, R., Jiang, F., Doss, R.: Federated learning with extreme label skew: a data extension approach. In: International Joint Conference on Neural Networks (IJCNN), Shenzhen, China. IEEE (2021). https://doi.org/10.1109/IJCNN52387.2021.9533879

33. Wang, K., Mathews, R., Kiddon, C., Eichner, H., Beaufays, F., Ramage, D.: Federated evaluation of on-device personalization. CoRR abs/1910.10252 (2019). http://arxiv.org/abs/1910.10252

34. Wu, S., et al.: Motley: benchmarking heterogeneity and personalization in federated learning. CoRR abs/2206.09262 (2022). https://doi.org/10.48550/arXiv.2206.09262

Federated Learning with GAN-Based Data Synthesis for Non-IID Clients

Zijian Li[1]([✉])[iD], Jiawei Shao[1][iD], Yuyi Mao[2][iD], Jessie Hui Wang[3][iD], and Jun Zhang[1][iD]

[1] The Hong Kong University of Science and Technology, Hong Kong, China
zijian.li@connect.ust.hk
[2] The Hong Kong Polytechnic University, Hong Kong, China
[3] Tsinghua University, Beijing, China

Abstract. Federated learning (FL) has recently emerged as a popular privacy-preserving collaborative learning paradigm. However, it suffers from the non-independent and identically distributed (non-IID) data among clients. In this chapter, we propose a novel framework, named *Synthetic Data Aided Federated Learning* (SDA-FL), to resolve this non-IID challenge by sharing synthetic data. Specifically, each client pretrains a local generative adversarial network (GAN) to generate differentially private synthetic data, which are uploaded to the parameter server (PS) to construct a global shared synthetic dataset. To generate confident pseudo labels for the synthetic dataset, we also propose an iterative pseudo labeling mechanism performed by the PS. The assistance of the synthetic dataset with confident pseudo labels significantly alleviates the data heterogeneity among clients, which improves the consistency among local updates and benefits the global aggregation. Extensive experiments evidence that the proposed framework outperforms the baseline methods by a large margin in several benchmark datasets under both the supervised and semi-supervised settings.

Keywords: Federated Learning · Non-Independent and Identically Distributed (non-IID) Problem · Generative Adversarial Network (GAN)

1 Instruction

The recent development of deep learning technologies has led to major breakthroughs in various domains. This results in a tremendous amount of valuable data that can facilitate the training of deep learning models for intelligent applications. A traditional approach to exploit these distributed data samples is to upload them to a centralized server for model training. However, directly offloading data raises severe privacy concerns as data collected from mobile clients may contain sensitive information.

By decoupling model training from the need of transferring private data to the cloud, federated learning (FL) offers a promising approach to collaboratively learn a global model without directly sharing the local data [46]. Particularly, [23] introduced the Federated Averaging (FedAvg) algorithm where the clients train the local models based on the private local data and upload the model updates to the parameter server (PS) for aggregation.

R. Goebel et al. (Eds.): FL 2022, LNAI 13448, pp. 17–32, 2023.
https://doi.org/10.1007/978-3-031-28996-5_2

Despite its success in the independent and identically distributed (IID) scenarios, FL still suffers from significant performance degradation when the data distribution among clients becomes skewed. In particular, different clients learn from different data distributions in the non-IID scenarios, which leads to high inconsistency among the local updates and thus degrades the effectiveness of global model aggregation [34].

Many works have been proposed to alleviate the non-IID issue by regularizing the local models with the knowledge of the global model and local models from other clients [1,13,18,34]. These methods, however, aim to reduce the local model bias and cannot achieve a significant improvement in scenarios with extreme non-IIDness [17]. Recent studies have also attempted to tackle the non-IID problem with data augmentation techniques [46]. Specifically, [27,32,39] proposed to generate synthetic samples by mixing the real samples. Nevertheless, without implementing a privacy-protection mechanism, these methods are susceptible to data leakage. In addition, another recent work attempts to overcome the non-IID issue via secrete data sharing [28], but it confronts with additional communication costs and implementation challenges.

Observing the data heterogeneity problem and the privacy leakage of the existing data augmentation methods for FL, we propose a novel framework, named *Synthetic Data Aided Federated Learning* (SDA-FL), which resolves the non-IID issue by sharing the differentially private synthetic data. In this framework, each client pretrains a local differentially private generative adversarial network (GAN) [8] to generate synthetic data, thus avoiding sharing the raw data. These synthetic data are then collected by the PS to construct a global synthetic dataset. To generate confident pseudo labels for the synthetic data, we propose an iterative pseudo label update mechanism, in which the PS utilizes the received local models to update the pseudo labels in each training round. As the local models are progressively improved over the FL process, the confidence of pseudo labels is thus enhanced, which is beneficial for the server updates and local updates in future rounds and in turn results in a well-performed global model. It is worth noting that the SDA-FL framework is compatible with many existing FL methods and can be applied in both supervised and semi-supervised settings without requiring labels of the real data, which will be validated in the experiments. Ablation studies are also conducted to illustrate the impact of the privacy budget and the effectiveness of the key procedures in SDA-FL.

2 Related Works

Non-IID Challenges in Federated Learning. The non-IID data distribution has been a fundamental obstacle for FL [46]. This is because the highly skewed data distribution significantly amplifies the local model divergence and thus deteriorates the performance of the aggregated model [20,44]. To mitigate the client drift caused by the non-IID data, many works proposed to modify the local objective function with the additional knowledge from the global model and local models of other clients [1,13,18,34]. Such methods, however, cannot achieve satisfactory performance in many non-IID scenarios [17]. In addition to training the same model structure at clients, some studies proposed to combat the negative impact of non-IID data by keeping the specific local model structures individually, including local batch normalization layers [19], local extractors [2,21], and local classifiers [47]. Moreover, some prior researches addressed the data heterogeneity problem by optimizing the operations at the PS, such as model aggregation [34], client selection [33,43], client clustering [7,14], classifier calibration [20,22,45], and domain adaptation [31,36].

Data Augmentation and Privacy Preserving. Recently, FL methods based on some form of data sharing have received increasing attention for their prominent performance [44,46]. A popular approach is to leverage the Mixup technique [41] for data augmentation, so that the clients can share the blended local data and collaboratively construct a new global dataset to tackle the non-IID issue [27,29,39]. However, simply combination of the real samples may be vulnerable to privacy attacks. Alternatively, GAN-based data augmentation [11,40,44] was shown to be effective in reducing the degree of local data imbalance in FL. The general idea is to train a good generative model at the server based on a few seed data samples uploaded by the clients. Then this well-trained generator is downloaded by all clients for local model updating. Nevertheless, since sending local data samples to the server violates the data privacy requirement, FedDPGAN [42] suggested all the clients collaboratively train a global generative model based on the FL framework to supplement the scarce local data. Unfortunately, the GAN training process also requires frequent generative models exchanges, leading to extremely high communication costs and risks of adversarial attacks [4]. In addition, existing GAN-based methods require the fully labeled data at clients to train the supervised GANs to generate the synthetic samples with labels, which is impractical in Internet of Things (IoT) and healthcare systems. Instead, our proposed algorithm allow clients to train the unsupervised GANs locally without requiring the labeled data and it is able to provide confident pseudo labels for the synthetic samples.

3 Preliminary

Federated Learning. Federated learning aims to train a promising global model w without disclosing any local data samples of clients. In each training round $t = 0, 1, \ldots, T - 1$, FedAvg [23] tries to minimize the global objective function $F(w_t)$ as follows:

$$\min_{w_t} F(w_t) \triangleq \sum_{k \in \mathcal{S}_t} p_k F_k(w_t), \quad p_k = \frac{|\mathcal{D}_k|}{\sum_{i \in \mathcal{S}_t} |\mathcal{D}_i|}, \tag{1}$$

where $\mathcal{S}_t$ is the subset of clients activated in round t, p_k is the aggregation weight for client k that is normally chosen according to the size of its local dataset $\mathcal{D}_k$, and $F_k(w_t)$ is the local objective function of client k in round t defined as follows:

$$F_k(w_t) \triangleq \mathbb{E}_{(x,y) \sim \mathcal{D}_k} \ell(w_{t-1}^k; x, y), \tag{2}$$

where $\ell(\cdot)$ is the cross-entropy loss and w_{t-1}^k is the global model downloaded from the PS. Specifically, in each local training step $e = 0, 1, \ldots, E - 1$, every client in set $\mathcal{S}_t$ updates the local model with the real batch samples $(\mathbf{X}_{t,e}^k, \mathbf{Y}_{t,e}^k)$ via stochastic gradient descent (SGD), i.e., $w_{t,e+1}^k \leftarrow w_{t,e}^k - \eta_t \nabla F_k(w_{t,e}^k; \mathbf{X}_{t,e}^k, \mathbf{Y}_{t,e}^k)$, $w_t^k \leftarrow w_{t,E-1}^k$. The updated local models w_t^k are then sent back to the PS for weighted aggregation. These procedures repeat until all the T training rounds are exhausted.

With the iterative local training and global aggregation procedures, the PS is expected to obtain a well-performed global model even without access to any local data. However, the highly skewed data distribution among clients easily leads to severe local model divergence and consequently degrades the global model performance [17]. To resolve this issue and avoid sharing the real data, we exploit the generative adversarial network (GAN) to generate high-quality synthetic data that can be shared among clients, which are used to update the local and global models.

Differentially Private Generative Adversarial Network. To avoid the gradient vanishing and mode collapse problems encountered by conventional GAN models [3], the Wasserstein GAN with gradient penalty (WGAN-GP) [9], which penalizes the gradient norm of the critic to stabilize the training process of the generator G and discriminator D, is adopted. With the real data distribution $p_r(x)$ and input noise distribution of the generator $p_z(z)$, the objective function of the WGAN-GP is expressed as follows:

$$\min_{G} \max_{D} \mathbb{E}_{x \sim p_r(x)}\left[D(x)\right] - \mathbb{E}_{z \sim p_z(z)}\left[D\left(G(z)\right)\right] + \gamma \left\|\nabla_{\hat{x}} D(\hat{x}) - 1\right\|_2^2, \quad (3)$$

where $\hat{x}$ is a mixture of the real sample x and the fake sample $G(z)$, and γ is a hyperparameter. To provide differential privacy protection for the synthetic data, we inject Gaussian noise into the GAN training process. The definition of differential privacy (DP) is given as follows:

Definition 1. *(Differential privacy [6]): A random mechanism $\mathcal{A}_p$ satisfies (ϵ, δ)-differential privacy if for any output's subset (S) and any two adjacent datasets $\mathcal{M}$, $\mathcal{M}'$, the following probability inequality holds:*

$$\mathbb{P}\left(\mathcal{A}_p(\mathcal{M}) \in \mathcal{S}\right) \leq e^{\epsilon} \cdot \mathbb{P}\left(\mathcal{A}_p\left(\mathcal{M}'\right) \in \mathcal{S}\right) + \delta, \quad (4)$$

where $\delta > 0$ and ϵ is the privacy budget indicating the privacy level, i.e., a smaller value of ϵ implies stronger privacy protection.

To satisfy the (ϵ, δ)-DP, we follow [38] and add Gaussian noise to the updated gradients at each discriminator training iteration. The relationship between the noise variance and differential privacy is shown below:

$$\sigma_n = \frac{2q}{\epsilon} \sqrt{n_d \log\left(\frac{1}{\delta}\right)}, \quad (5)$$

where q and n_d denote the sample probability for each instance and the total batch number of the local dataset, respectively. Besides, according to the post-processing property of DP [6], any mapping from the differentially private output also satisfies the same level of DP. In other words, the gradients of the generator, which are obtained via the backpropagation from the noisy discriminator output, also meet the (ϵ, δ)-DP condition.

Based on the training algorithm of WGAN-GP, it is desirable to train the generators with the label information, e.g., Auxiliary Classifier Generative Adversarial Network (ACGAN) [25,26], so that the synthetic data can be generated with labels. However, considering the label scarcity problem in the federated semi-supervised settings, this form of the conditional generative model cannot be trained at clients. Therefore, we resort to a more general paradigm that trains an unsupervised generator, and propose a pseudo labeling procedure within the FL process to generate high-confidence pseudo labels.

Pseudo Labeling. To generate confident pseudo labels, following [30], only the class with an extremely high prediction probability is regarded as the pseudo label. Specifically, with a predefined threshold τ, class c is deemed as the label of sample x if the output prediction probability $f_c(\boldsymbol{w}; x)$ is the largest among all the classes and also larger than the threshold τ. Hence, the pseudo labeling function can be expressed as follows:

$$\hat{y} = \begin{cases} c & \text{if } \max_c f_c(\boldsymbol{w}; x) > \tau, \\ \text{None} & \text{otherwise.} \end{cases} \tag{6}$$

With such a pseudo labeling procedure, only the high-quality synthetic data can output a high prediction probability by model $\boldsymbol{w}$ and obtain their pseudo labels. As such, the unqualified synthetic samples are filtered, leaving only the qualified ones to update the local models.

In our proposed FL framework, the local models are used to predict the pseudo labels for the synthetic data generated by the corresponding local generators, and the pseudo labels are continuously updated with the improved local models during the FL process, as will be discussed in the next section.

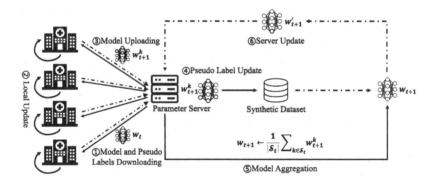

Fig. 1. Overview of the proposed SDA-FL framework. Before the FL process starts, the synthetic data from all clients are sent to the PS to construct a global synthetic dataset. In each training round, every client first downloads the global model and updates the pseudo labels of the synthetic data for local training. The local models are then uploaded to the PS for pseudo label updating and model aggregation. Lastly, the PS updates the global model $\boldsymbol{w}_{t+1}$ with the updated synthetic dataset.

4   Synthetic Data Aided Federated Learning (SDA-FL)

We now introduce the SDA-FL framework that adopts GAN-based data augmentation to alleviate the negative effect of the non-IID data. The overview of the SDA-FL framework is shown in Fig. 1, and key algorithmic innovations built upon the classic FL framework are elaborated below.

Global Synthetic Dataset Construction. At the start of the FL process, we propose to train the generative model based on the local samples and then utilize it to generate synthetic samples to tackle the non-IID problem. Although there are some recent works suggest to collaboratively train the global generator based on the FL framework [25,42], such a cooperative training strategy for GANs requires significant communication bandwidth and incurs additional privacy leakage due to frequent exchanges of the generators and discriminators.

To avoid these problems, we resort to local training strategies for the generative models. In particular, each client pretrains a local GAN model to generate synthetic samples based on its local data. Then, the synthetic samples are sent to the PS to construct a global shared synthetic dataset. To effectively leverage the synthetic dataset for FL, we perform pseudo labeling for these samples, which is critical to the effectiveness of the SDA-FL framework.

Synthetic Samples Annotation. Unlike the prior work in [12] where each client leverages the local models from other clients to annotate the unlabeled data that encounters a bottleneck with highly skewed data distribution, we only utilize the local models to perform pseudo labeling for the corresponding unlabeled synthetic data. This is because the local model and the corresponding synthetic data are trained with the same local data at each client, and only the high-quality synthetic samples can obtain a high prediction probability with this local model. In addition, the confidence of the pseudo labels heavily relies on the local model quality, but the under-trained local models at the beginning of the FL process fail to accomplish this task. Therefore, we update the pseudo labels for the global shared synthetic dataset with the improved local models in each FL round. Specifically, after receiving the local model w_t^k in round t, the PS assigns a pseudo label for each unlabeled synthetic instance x according to (6), i.e., its maximum class probability $f_c(w_t^k; x)$ is higher than the predefined threshold τ. In this way, we can gradually generate high-quality pseudo labels for the synthetic data samples.

Synthetic Data Aided Model Training. Augmented by the samples $\hat{\mathbf{X}}$ and confident pseudo labels $\hat{\mathbf{Y}}_t$ from the shared synthetic dataset, the data available for local training at different clients are approximately homogeneously distributed. To make good use of the synthetic data, we leverage the Mixup method proposed in [41], which utilizes a linear interpolation between the real batch samples $(\mathbf{X}_{t,e}^k, \mathbf{Y}_{t,e}^k)$ and the synthetic batch samples $(\hat{\mathbf{X}}_e, \hat{\mathbf{Y}}_{t,e})$, to augment the real data for client k at the local training step e of round t:

$$\bar{\mathbf{X}}_{t,e}^k = \lambda_1 \hat{\mathbf{X}}_e + (1 - \lambda_1)\mathbf{X}_{t,e}^k,$$
$$\bar{\mathbf{Y}}_{t,e}^k = \lambda_1 \hat{\mathbf{Y}}_{t,e} + (1 - \lambda_1)\mathbf{Y}_{t,e}^k, \tag{7}$$

where λ_1 follows the Beta distribution for each batch, i.e., $\text{Beta}(\alpha, \alpha)$ with $\alpha \in [0, 1]$. By combining the cross-entropy loss $\ell(\cdot)$, the mixup loss for the local model update becomes:

$$\ell_1 = \lambda_1 \ell\big(f(\bar{\mathbf{X}}_{t,e}^k; \boldsymbol{w}_{t,e}^k), \hat{\mathbf{Y}}_{t,e}\big) + (1 - \lambda_1)\ell\big(f(\bar{\mathbf{X}}_{t,e}^k; \boldsymbol{w}_{t,e}^k), \mathbf{Y}_{t,e}^k\big). \qquad (8)$$

In addition, since the loss in (8) is fragile at the beginning of the FL process caused by the unconfident pseudo labels, another cross-entropy loss term is introduced for the real batch samples $(\mathbf{X}_{t,e}^k, \mathbf{Y}_{t,e}^k)$ to stabilize the training process:

$$\ell_2 = \ell\big(f(\mathbf{X}_{t,e}^k; \boldsymbol{w}_{t,e}^k), \mathbf{Y}_{t,e}^k\big). \qquad (9)$$

Then, SGD is applied to update the local model as follows:

$$\boldsymbol{w}_{t,e+1}^k \leftarrow \boldsymbol{w}_{t,e}^k - \eta_t \nabla(\ell_1 + \lambda_2 \ell_2), \qquad (10)$$

where λ_2 is a hyper-parameter to control the retention of the local data.

In contrast to traditional FL where the PS does not have access to any data to update the global model, the PS in our framework keeps the entire global synthetic dataset $\hat{\mathcal{D}}_s$ and uses it to train the global model. Particularly, since there is no real data in the PS, two batches of synthetic samples are used to update the global model with (10) at each iteration.

Interplay Between Model Training and Synthetic Dataset Updating. In each FL round, the aid of synthetic data improves the generalization of local models. Since the updated local models are used for pseudo labeling and the global synthetic dataset construction at the PS, the confidence of the pseudo label is thus boosted. With the enhanced synthetic dataset, the PS can refine the global model and all the clients can improve their local models subsequently at the next round. Therefore, the interplay between model training and synthetic dataset updating at every training round is critical to achieving a well-performed global model.

SDA-FL vs. Traditional FL. Compared with traditional FL, the proposed SDA-FL framework introduces additional operations at both the clients and PS. These innovations contribute to the performance improvement of FL with non-IID data. Specifically, in traditional FL algorithms [13, 18], clients update their models based only on the local data, which easily leads to performance degradation when data are heterogeneous among clients. In our framework, the local datasets are augmented by the GAN-based synthetic samples to alleviate the non-IID problem. Furthermore, the PS in traditional FL algorithms only performs simple model aggregation. In contrast, the PS in the SDA-FL updates the global model with the high-confidence synthetic data, which further improves the global model performance. Overall, with a shared synthetic dataset and an iterative pseudo labeling mechanism, SDA-FL overcomes the issue of heterogeneous data distributions among clients and enhances the global model at the PS. We envision that this framework can be extended to develop other data augmentation-based methods for both federated supervised learning and federated semi-supervised learning.

5 Experiments

In this section, we evaluate the proposed SDA-FL framework in the presence of non-IID data for both federated supervised learning and federated semi-supervised learning. The experimental results on different benchmark datasets demonstrate the superiority of the proposed framework over the baseline methods. Ablation studies are also conducted to discuss the effectiveness of key procedures and hyper-parameters in SDA-FL.

5.1 Experiment Setup

Datasets. Following [17], we use four benchmark datasets, including MNIST [16], FashionMNIST [37], CIFAR-10 [15], and SVHN [24], to evaluate the proposed method. In all the experiments, we equally divide the training samples and assign them to the clients. Specifically, given the number of classes per client as C and total K clients, the whole training dataset is split into $K \times C$ subsets, and each subset only has a single class. Then all the subsets of data are randomly shuffled and distributed to the clients. Besides, a Dirichlet-based label imbalance distribution is also used to validate all the methods, for which we sample $p_c \sim Dir_K(0.1)$ and allocate a proportion $p_{c,k}$ of samples of class c to client k. We assume two classes of FashionMNIST data at each client in the ablation studies.

To guarantee the effectiveness of SDA-FL, we set the hyper-parameters γ, λ_2, and threshold τ to be 10.0, 1.0, and 0.95, respectively. We deploy ten clients in the experiments, and all of them are selected in each round. To generate high-quality synthetic data, we pretrain the generator and discriminator with 36,000 iterations for CIFAR-10 and 18,000 for the other datasets in both the federated supervised learning experiments and federated semi-supervised learning experiments. Each client uploads 4,000 synthetic samples to the PS to construct the global synthetic dataset. There are 200 rounds for all the methods. In each round of SDA-FL, the PS utilizes the synthetic dataset to update the global model with 10 iterations for CIFAR-10 and 50 iterations for the other datasets. Besides, we set the local training step size $E = 90$ in the federated supervised learning experiments and $E = 40$ in the federated semi-supervised learning experiments, and select the SGD with learning rate $\alpha = 0.03$ as the optimizer. In each iteration, the clients update the local models with batch size $B = 64$ for the federated supervised learning experiments and $B = 80$, including 16 labeled samples and 64 unlabeled samples, for the federated semi-supervised learning experiments.

Moreover, to evaluate the proposed SDA-FL in practical applications, we also test all the methods on a realistic COVID-19 dataset [35]. Because of the scarcity of Pneumonia samples, we only assume six clients in this experiment, each of which has two classes of data as shown in Table 1. We train the GAN models locally with 4,500 iterations, and update the local models with 30 iterations and the global model with 10 iterations.

Table 1. Data distribution of the COVID-19 dataset.

Hospital	0	1	2	3	4	5
Data	Normal 2,000	COVID-19 750	Pneumonia 250	Normal 2,000	COVID-19 750	Pneumonia 250
	COVID-19 750	Pneumonia 250	Normal 2,000	COVID-19 750	Pneumonia 250	Normal 2,000

Table 2. Test accuracy (%) of different methods on various datasets. $\#C$ represents the number of sample classes at each client.

Datasets	Data distribution	FedAvg	FedProx	SCAFFOLD	Naivemix	FedMix	SDA-FL
MNIST	$p_k \sim Dir(0.1)$	96.71	96.78	96.72	96.03	96.55	**98.20**
	$\#C = 1$	83.44	84.17	25.39	84.35	90.96	**98.19**
	$\#C = 2$	97.61	97.55	94.17	84.35	90.96	**98.26**
	$\#C = 3$	98.42	98.38	96.89	98.11	98.46	**98.50**
FashionMNIST	$p_k \sim Dir(0.1)$	79.76	80.02	80.10	78.68	79.02	**91.20**
	$\#C = 1$	16.50	57.14	56.80	66.62	72.11	**85.70**
	$\#C = 2$	73.50	75.76	70.82	79.54	82.41	**86.87**
	$\#C = 3$	82.47	83.43	77.68	82.09	84.65	**87.06**
CIFAR-10	$p_k \sim Dir(0.1)$	78.20	77.71	77.57	75.92	77.92	**82.57**
	$\#C = 1$	18.36	11.24	12.81	14.39	13.57	**37.70**
	$\#C = 2$	61.28	63.16	60.78	64.39	65.76	**67.89**
	$\#C = 3$	79.33	79.54	79.35	78.92	79.49	**84.56**
SVHN	$p_k \sim Dir(0.1)$	90.22	90.32	90.01	90.05	91.24	**92.41**
	$\#C = 1$	14.05	17.53	11.64	14.35	16.78	**88.46**
	$\#C = 2$	81.11	86.28	73.34	84.64	86.61	**90.70**
	$\#C = 3$	84.18	92.15	80.13	92.30	92.61	**93.16**

Baselines. For the federated supervised learning experiments, we compare the SDA-FL framework with FedAvg [23], FedProx [18], SCAFFOLD [13], Naivemix, and FedMix [39] on the MNIST, FashionMNIST, CIFAR-10, SVHN, and COVID-19 datasets. For the COVID-19 dataset, we also adopt FedDPGAN [42] for comparisons, which trains a global GAN to resolve the non-IID issue for medical applications. We report the best results by tuning the hyperparameter μ of the regularization term for FedProx and the mixup ratio λ for FedMix. Besides, we extend our framework to the semi-supervised learning setting on the MNIST, FashionMNIST, and CIFAR-10 datasets by performing pseudo labeling for the unlabeled local data. We compare the SDA-FL framework with Semi-FL [5], Local Fixmatch [30], and Local Mixup [41] to show its effectiveness.

Models. We adopt a simple CNN model that consists of two convolutional layers and two fully-connected layers for the MNIST and FashionMNIST classification tasks. Meanwhile, ResNet18 [10] is used for classifying the CIFAR-10, SVHN, and COVID-19 datasets. To generate qualified synthetic samples, we use a generator with four deconvolution layers and a discriminator with four convolutional layers followed by a fully-connected layer.

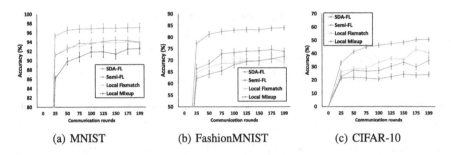

(a) MNIST   (b) FashionMNIST   (c) CIFAR-10

Fig. 2. Test accuracy of different methods for federated semi-supervised learning on the MNIST, FashionMNIST, and CIFAR-10 datasets.

5.2   Evaluation Results

Performance in Federated Supervised Learning. With varying numbers of classes per client, the experimental results in Table 2 show that our framework outperforms the baselines by a significant margin, which attributes to the GAN-based data augmentation that mitigates the detrimental effects of the data heterogeneity on FL. Under the severe non-IID scenario (i.e., each client only has one class of data), our SDA-FL method maintains an accuracy of 88.46% in the SVHN classification task, while other baselines suffer from great performance degradation. In the CIFAR-10 experiments, our framework is superior to the Naivemix and FedMix algorithms at least by 5.0% with three classes of data at each client, which verifies the competence of the GAN-based data compared with the mixing data.

In the COVID-19 experiments, besides the better performance over the aforementioned baselines, SDA-FL also surpasses FedDPGAN by 1.68% in accuracy. This demonstrates that the individually trained GANs generate synthetic data of higher quality than the global GAN trained based on the FL framework. Furthermore, in addition to resolving the non-IID issue, we find that SDA-FL even outperforms FedAvg (IID) by 1.14% in accuracy, which shows its advantages in supplementing more valuable training samples for the local training and thus improving the generalizability of the global model (Table 3).

Table 3. Test accuracy (%) on the COVID-19 dataset. FedAvg (IID) represents the scenario where the training samples are uniformly distributed to all clients to achieve the IID distribution.

Algorithm	FedAvg	FedProx	SCAFFOLD	Naivemix	FedMix	FedDPGAN	FedAvg (IID)	SDA-FL
Accuracy	94.05	95.03	94.30	94.14	94.28	94.57	95.19	**96.25**

Performance in Federated Semi-Supervised Learning. The results in Fig. 2 show that the SDA-FL framework achieves faster convergence and better performance than other algorithms in the federated semi-supervised learning setting, indicating its robustness and generalizability. Particularly, compared with Semi-FL, our method improves

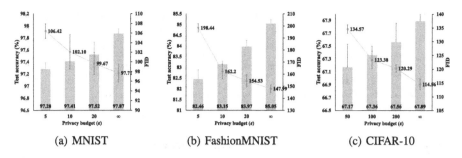

(a) MNIST   (b) FashionMNIST   (c) CIFAR-10

Fig. 3. Test accuracy and FID score with respect to the privacy budget. We run three trails and report the mean and the standard deviation of the test accuracy. The FID scores of the real samples on MNIST, FashionMNIST, and CIFAR-10 are 10.54, 23.17, and 42.70, respectively, which are much larger than those of the synthetic data.

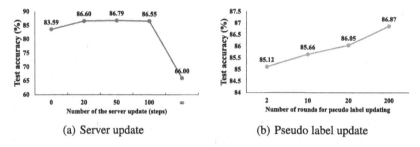

(a) Server update   (b) Pseudo label update

Fig. 4. Test accuracy on FashionMNIST with varying step sizes for server updating and rounds for pseudo label updating. The "∞ steps" in (a) means that the model is only trained with the synthetic data, and the "10 rounds" in (b) represents that the PS only updates the pseudo labels in the first 10 rounds.

the accuracy by almost 10% on the FashionMNIST classification task. In the CIFAR-10 dataset, the baseline methods are not able to train a usable global model (i.e., with a test accuracy below 40%), while the proposed framework converges in this challenging scenario and improves the test accuracy significantly. This is because the proposed pseudo labeling mechanism can provide high-quality labels for the synthetic and unlabeled samples, which are beneficial to the FL process.

Tradeoff Between the Privacy Budgets and Model Performance. To investigate the impact of the privacy budgets, we evaluate the model performance of the SDA-FL framework under different values of ϵ. The Fréchet inception distance (FID) is used to measure the quality of the generated samples, where a smaller FID score indicates better image quality. As illustrated in Fig. 3, a strict privacy budget of $\epsilon = 5$ increases the FID score compared with that in the protection-free scenario, which implies quality degradation of the generated samples. This negative impact on the synthetic samples also leads to around 0.61% and 2.59% accuracy drop on the MNIST and FashionMNIST datasets, respectively. The CIFAR-10 classification task follows a similar trajectory. Please note that although the proposed SDA-FL framework is trained under strict privacy requirements, compared with the results in Table 2, it still maintains supreme performance.

Table 4. Test accuracy and FID comparison with WGAN-GP/AC-WGAN-GP on various datasets.

Datasets	FashionMNIST		CIFAR-10 (2class/client)		CIFAR-10 (3class/client)	
Algorithms	WGAN-GP	AC-WGAN-GP	WGAN-GP	AC-WGAN-GP	WGAN-GP	AC-WGAN-GP
FID	**217.81**	220.39	**114.56**	154.27	**129.25**	162.16
Accuracy (%)	**83.76**	82.03	**67.89**	67.22	**84.56**	83.53

Effectiveness of Server Update and Pseudo Label Update. In comparison to the traditional FL, our framework updates the global model with the synthetic data at the PS, which has the potential to further improve the performance. The results in Fig. 4(a) show that the model performance on FashionMNIST reduces by nearly 3% without any server updates. Nevertheless, updating the global model too much by the PS may degrade the performance because of the excessive involvement of synthetic data. Empirical results show that the model trained solely with the synthetic data (i.e., the server updates the global model for ∞ steps) can only obtain an accuracy of 66.0%, which highlights the necessity of judicious utilization of the synthetic and local data for model training.

Besides, keeping updating pseudo labels in each round adopted by the SDA-FL framework for the synthetic data improves the model performance. As illustrated in Fig. 4(b), the accuracy increases with the number of rounds for pseudo label updating, which demonstrates that the SDA-FL framework can improve the confidence level of the pseudo labels over the training process. Note that since our framework only transmits the pseudo labels instead of the synthetic samples, the extra communication overhead is negligible.

Performance Comparison with Auxiliary Classifier WGAN-GP (AC-WGAN-GP). We can also include the label information in the GAN training to generate synthetic data with labels in the federated supervised learning experiments. As such, we compare the performance of SDA-FL with WGAN-GP and AC-WGAN-GP [26] on the Fashion-MNIST and CIFAR-10 datasets. As shown in Table 4, with the same number of training iterations for the generators, WGAN-GP achieves higher synthetic data quality as implied by the higher FID scores. Although AC-WGAN-GP can generate labeled synthetic data, WGAN-GP still performs better in accuracy performance with the higher-quality synthetic data. This is because our proposed pseudo labeling mechanism provides confident pseudo labels for the synthetic data.

Ablation Studies on the Computational Cost and Number of Samples for Training the Generators. We present the results in Fig. 5 and Fig. 6, which show that insufficient training rounds and training samples for generators result in low-quality synthetic data and degraded performance. The generator only gets an FID score of 217.81 (23.17 for real data) and an accuracy of 83.76% when training the generators with 30 rounds. In addition, as shown in Fig. 6, under the fixed 30-round computational cost, using fewer samples for training the generators reduces the quality of the synthetic data and thus affects the performance. Nonetheless, despite the low computational cost (30 rounds) and the small number of samples (1000 samples) used to train the generators individually, our framework still outperforms other baselines (82.41% in Fedmix), demonstrating the robustness of the proposed method.

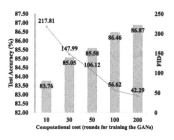

Fig. 5. Test accuracy and FID on Fashion-MNIST, under varying training rounds (i.e., computational cost) for the GANs.

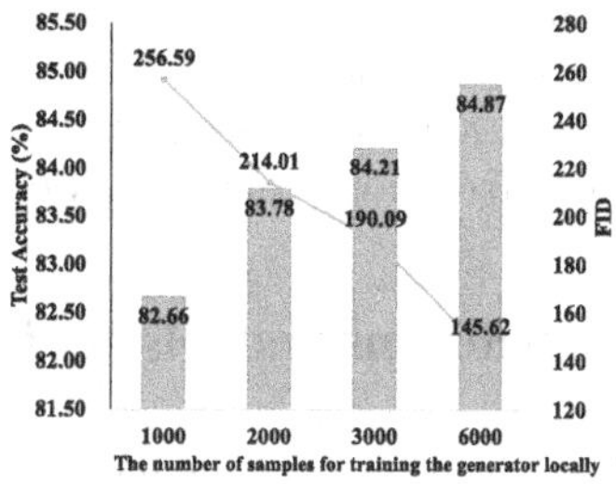

Fig. 6. Test accuracy and FID on FashionM-NIST, under varying samples for training the GANs locally.

Ablation Study on the Size of the Synthetic Dataset. Before the federated learning process, all clients construct the synthetic dataset together. Larger synthetic datasets can typically provide more qualified data to clients and PS to improve the performance, but they require larger storage space for clients. The results in Fig. 7 show that, although the test accuracy on FashionMNIST decreases as the size of the synthetic dataset declines, our framework achieves 85.44% test accuracy with each client only uploading 200 samples, which is acceptable in exchange for less storage space requirement.

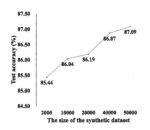 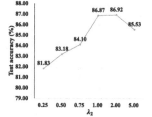 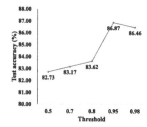

Fig. 7. Test accuracy on FashionMNIST, under varying sizes of the synthetic dataset.

Fig. 8. Test accuracy on FashionMNIST, under varying values of λ_2 in the local update.

Fig. 9. Test accuracy on FashionMNIST, under varying threshold values.

Ablation Study on the Hyper-parameter λ_2. λ_2 is the parameter to control the use of the local real data. The results in Fig. 8 show that compared with other values of λ_2, the test accuracy on FashionMNIST drops by nearly 5.0% with $\lambda_2 = 0.25$, indicating that the training of the models is heavily reliant on the real data. Besides, an excessive value of λ_2 also degrades the performance since it eliminates the benefits of the synthetic data and cannot mitigate the non-IID problem as much as possible. In comparison, a moderate value of λ_2 is capable of combining the real data and the synthetic data intelligently and thus enhancing the models and solving the non-IID issue in FL.

Ablation Study on the Threshold τ**.** The threshold τ sets the criterion for selecting the high-confidence pseudo labels. The results on FashionMNIST are shown in Fig. 9, which indicates that a small threshold impairs the performance because some synthetic data with low-confidence pseudo labels are still considered qualified and used to train the models. A too large threshold value, on the other hand, filters out a lot of qualified data, which affects performance. In our experiment setup, $\tau = 0.95$ is a reasonable value to strike a good balance between quality and the quantity of the pseudo labels.

6   Conclusions and Discussions

We proposed a new data augmentation method to resolve the heterogeneous data distribution problem in federated learning by sharing the differentially private GAN-based synthetic data. To effectively utilize the synthetic data, a novel framework, named Synthetic Data Aided Federated Learning (SDA-FL), was developed, which generates and updates confident pseudo labels for the synthetic data samples. Experiment results showed that SDA-FL outperforms many existing baselines by remarkable margins in both supervised learning and semi-supervised learning under strict differential privacy protection. In this study, we limit our attention to the WGAN-GP and AC-WGAN-GP in SDA-FL. Despite their performance improvements compared with the baselines, it is interesting to investigate other GAN structures. In addition, WGAN-GP requires significant computational resources at clients. Therefore, to improve the applicability of SDA-FL, it is important to develop a computation-efficient GAN-based structure for clients in future research.

References

1. Acar, D.A.E., Zhao, Y., Matas, R., Mattina, M., Whatmough, P., Saligrama, V.: Federated learning based on dynamic regularization. In: International Conference on Learning Representations (2020)
2. Arivazhagan, M.G., Aggarwal, V., Singh, A.K., Choudhary, S.: Federated learning with personalization layers. arXiv preprint arXiv:1912.00818 (2019)
3. Arjovsky, M., Chintala, S., Bottou, L.: Wasserstein GAN (2017)
4. Chen, D., Yu, N., Zhang, Y., Fritz, M.: GAN-leaks: a taxonomy of membership inference attacks against generative models. In: Proceedings of the 2020 ACM SIGSAC Conference on Computer and Communications Security, pp. 343–362 (2020)
5. Diao, E., Ding, J., Tarokh, V.: Semifl: Communication efficient semi-supervised federated learning with unlabeled clients. arXiv e-prints, p. arXiv-2106 (2021)
6. Dwork, C., Roth, A., et al.: The algorithmic foundations of differential privacy. Found. Trends Theor. Comput. Sci. **9**(3–4), 211–407 (2014)
7. Ghosh, A., Chung, J., Yin, D., Ramchandran, K.: An efficient framework for clustered federated learning. In: Conference on Neural Information Processing Systems (NIPS) (2020)
8. Goodfellow, I., et al.: Generative adversarial nets. Adv. Neural Inf. Process. Syst. **27** (2014)
9. Gulrajani, I., Ahmed, F., Arjovsky, M., Dumoulin, V., Courville, A.C.: Improved training of Wasserstein GANs. In: NIPS (2017)
10. He, K., Zhang, X., Ren, S., Sun, J.: Deep residual learning for image recognition. In: Conference on Conference on Computer Vision and Pattern Recognition (CVPR) (2016)

11. Jeong, E., Oh, S., Kim, H., Park, J., Bennis, M., Kim, S.L.: Communication-efficient on-device machine learning: federated distillation and augmentation under non-IID private data. arXiv preprint arXiv:1811.11479 (2018)
12. Jeong, W., Yoon, J., Yang, E., Hwang, S.J.: Federated semi-supervised learning with inter-client consistency & disjoint learning. In: International Conference on Learning Representations (2020)
13. Karimireddy, S.P., Kale, S., Mohri, M., Reddi, S.J., Stich, S.U., Suresh, A.T.: SCAFFOLD: stochastic controlled averaging for federated learning. In: ICML (2020)
14. Kopparapu, K., Lin, E., Zhao, J.: FedCD: improving performance in non-IID federated learning. arXiv preprint arXiv:2006.09637 (2020)
15. Krizhevsky, A.: Learning multiple layers of features from tiny images. Master's thesis, University of Tront (2009)
16. LeCun, Y., Bottou, L., Bengio, Y., Haffner, P.: Gradient-based learning applied to document recognition. Proc. IEEE 86(11), 2278–2324 (1998)
17. Li, Q., Diao, Y., Chen, Q., He, B.: Federated learning on non-IID data silos: an experimental study (2021). https://doi.org/10.48550/ARXIV.2102.02079, https://arxiv.org/abs/2102.02079
18. Li, T., Sahu, A.K., Zaheer, M., Sanjabi, M., Talwalkar, A., Smith, V.: Federated optimization in heterogeneous networks. In: Proceedings of Machine Learning and Systems (MLSys) (2020)
19. Li, X., JIANG, M., Zhang, X., Kamp, M., Dou, Q.: FedBN: federated learning on non-IID features via local batch normalization. In: International Conference on Learning Representations (2020)
20. Li, X.C., Zhan, D.C.: FedRS: federated learning with restricted softmax for label distribution non-IID data. In: Proceedings of the 27th ACM SIGKDD Conference on Knowledge Discovery & Data Mining, pp. 995–1005 (2021)
21. Liang, P.P., et al.: Think locally, act globally: federated learning with local and global representations. arXiv preprint arXiv:2001.01523 (2020)
22. Luo, M., Chen, F., Hu, D., Zhang, Y., Liang, J., Feng, J.: No fear of heterogeneity: classifier calibration for federated learning with non-IID data. Adv. Neural Inf. Process. Syst. 34 (2021)
23. McMahan, H.B., Moore, E., Ramage, D., Hampson, S., Agüera y Arcas, B.: Communication-efficient learning of deep networks from decentralized data. In: International Conference on Artificial Intelligence and Statistics (AISTATS) (2017)
24. Netzer, Y., Wang, T., Coates, A., Bissacco, A., Wu, B., Ng, A.Y.: Reading digits in natural images with unsupervised feature learning (2011)
25. Nguyen, D.C., Ding, M., Pathirana, P.N., Seneviratne, A., Zomaya, A.Y.: Federated learning for COVID-19 detection with generative adversarial networks in edge cloud computing. IEEE Internet Things J. 9, 0257–10271 (2021)
26. Odena, A., Olah, C., Shlens, J.: Conditional image synthesis with auxiliary classifier GANs. In: International Conference on Machine Learning, pp. 2642–2651. PMLR (2017)
27. Oh, S., Park, J., Jeong, E., Kim, H., Bennis, M., Kim, S.L.: Mix2fld: downlink federated learning after uplink federated distillation with two-way mixup. IEEE Commun. Lett. 24, 2211–2215 (2020)
28. Shao, J., Sun, Y., Li, S., Zhang, J.: DReS-FL: dropout-resilient secure federated learning for non-IID clients via secret data sharing (2022)
29. Shin, M., Hwang, C., Kim, J., Park, J., Bennis, M., Kim, S.L.: XOR mixup: privacy-preserving data augmentation for one-shot federated learning. In: International Workshop on Federated Learning for User Privacy and Data Confidentiality in Conjunction with ICML 2020 (FL-ICML 2020) (2020)

30. Sohn, K., et al.: FixMatch: simplifying semi-supervised learning with consistency and confidence. Adv. Neural Inf. Process. Syst. **33**, 596–608 (2020)
31. Tang, Z., Zhang, Y., Shi, S., He, X., Han, B., Chu, X.: Virtual homogeneity learning: defending against data heterogeneity in federated learning. arXiv preprint arXiv:2206.02465 (2022)
32. Wang, H., Muñoz-González, L., Eklund, D., Raza, S.: Non-IID data re-balancing at IoT edge with peer-to-peer federated learning for anomaly detection. In: Proceedings of the 14th ACM Conference on Security and Privacy in Wireless and Mobile Networks, pp. 153–163 (2021)
33. Wang, H., Kaplan, Z., Niu, D., Li, B.: Optimizing federated learning on non-IID data with reinforcement learning. In: IEEE INFOCOM 2020-IEEE Conference on Computer Communications, pp. 1698–1707. IEEE (2020)
34. Wang, J., Liu, Q., Liang, H., Joshi, G., Poor, H.V.: Tackling the objective inconsistency problem in heterogeneous federated optimization. Adv. Neural Inf. Process. Syst. **33**, 7611–7623 (2020)
35. Wang, L., Lin, Z.Q., Wong, A.: COVID-net: a tailored deep convolutional neural network design for detection of COVID-19 cases from chest X-ray images. Sci. Rep. **10**(1), 19549 (2020). https://doi.org/10.1038/s41598-020-76550-z
36. Wicaksana, J., Yan, Z., Yang, X., Liu, Y., Fan, L., Cheng, K.T.: Customized federated learning for multi-source decentralized medical image classification. IEEE J. Biomed. Health Inform. **26**, 5596–5607 (2022)
37. Xiao, H., Rasul, K., Vollgraf, R.: Fashion-MNIST: a novel image dataset for benchmarking machine learning algorithms. arXiv preprint arXiv:1708.07747 (2017)
38. Xie, L., Lin, K., Wang, S., Wang, F., Zhou, J.: Differentially private generative adversarial network. arXiv preprint arXiv:1802.06739 (2018)
39. Yoon, T., Shin, S., Hwang, S.J., Yang, E.: FedMix: approximation of mixup under mean augmented federated learning. In: International Conference on Learning Representations (2020)
40. Yoshida, N., Nishio, T., Morikura, M., Yamamoto, K., Yonetani, R.: Hybrid-FL for wireless networks: Cooperative learning mechanism using non-IID data. In: ICC 2020–2020 IEEE International Conference on Communications (ICC), pp. 1–7. IEEE (2020)
41. Zhang, H., Cisse, M., Dauphin, Y.N., Lopez-Paz, D.: Mixup: beyond empirical risk minimization. International Conference on Learning Representations (ICLR) (2018)
42. Zhang, L., Shen, B., Barnawi, A., Xi, S., Kumar, N., Wu, Y.: FedDPGAN: federated differentially private generative adversarial networks framework for the detection of COVID-19 pneumonia. Inf. Syst. Front. **23**, 1–13 (2021)
43. Zhang, W., Wang, X., Zhou, P., Wu, W., Zhang, X.: Client selection for federated learning with non-IID data in mobile edge computing. IEEE Access **9**, 24462–24474 (2021)
44. Zhao, Y., Li, M., Lai, L., Suda, N., Civin, D., Chandra, V.: Federated learning with non-IID data. arXiv preprint arXiv:1806.00582 (2018)
45. Zhou, T., Zhang, J., Tsang, D.: FedFA: federated learning with feature anchors to align feature and classifier for heterogeneous data. arXiv preprint arXiv:2211.09299 (2022)
46. Zhu, H., Xu, J., Liu, S., Jin, Y.: Federated learning on non-IID data: a survey. Neurocomputing **465**, 371–390 (2021)
47. Zhu, Z., Hong, J., Zhou, J.: Data-free knowledge distillation for heterogeneous federated learning. In: International Conference on Machine Learning, pp. 12878–12889. PMLR (2021)

Practical and Secure Federated Recommendation with Personalized Mask

Liu Yang[1,2]([✉]) [iD], Junxue Zhang[1,2] [iD], Di Chai[1,2] [iD], Leye Wang[3] [iD], Kun Guo[4] [iD], Kai Chen[1] [iD], and Qiang Yang[1] [iD]

[1] Hong Kong University of Science and Technology, Hong Kong, China
{lyangau,jzhangcs,dchai,kaichen,qyang}@cse.ust.hk
[2] Clustar, Shenzhen, China
[3] Peking University, Beijing, China
leyewang@pku.edu.cn
[4] Fuzhou University, Fuzhou, China
gukn@fzu.edu.cn

Abstract. Federated recommendation addresses the data silo and privacy problems altogether for recommender systems. Current federated recommender systems mainly utilize cryptographic or obfuscation methods to protect the original ratings from leakage. However, the former comes with extra communication and computation costs, and the latter damages model accuracy. Neither of them could simultaneously satisfy the real-time feedback and accurate personalization requirements of recommender systems. In this work, we proposed federated masked matrix factorization (FedMMF) to protect the data privacy in federated recommender systems without sacrificing efficiency and effectiveness. In more details, we introduce the new idea of personalized mask generated only from local data and apply it in FedMMF. On the one hand, personalized mask offers protection for participants' private data without effectiveness loss. On the other hand, combined with the adaptive secure aggregation protocol, personalized mask could further improve efficiency. Theoretically, we provide security analysis for personalized mask. Empirically, we also show the superiority of the designed model on different real-world data sets.

Keywords: Federated learning · Recommender system · Personalized mask

1 Introduction

Federated recommender system (FedRec) is an essential application of federated learning in the recommendation scenario [19]. In recent years, federated learning has been a fast-growing research field, which keeps private data locally at multiple parties and trains models collaboratively in a secure and privacy-preserving way [13,14,20]. For example, [2] proposed a federated matrix factorization algorithm, which distributes the training process at each local party and aggregates the computed gradients on the central server. Privacy-preserving is one of the major challenges in federated learning. Data decentralization does alleviate privacy risks compared with the conventional data-center

R. Goebel et al. (Eds.): FL 2022, LNAI 13448, pp. 33–45, 2023.
https://doi.org/10.1007/978-3-031-28996-5_3

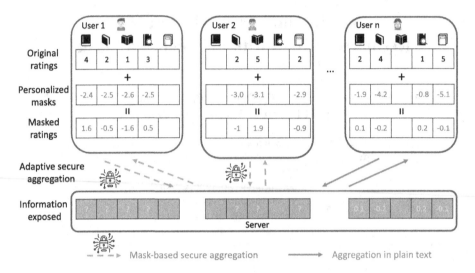

Fig. 1. Illustration of the proposed FedMMF method. First, each party generates personalized masks via training a local model. Second, masked ratings are constructed via a combination of original ratings and personalized masks. Then, federated matrix factorization is performed on the masked ratings of all parties. An adaptive secure aggregation method is adopted. The parties with well-protected original data could share model updates via vanilla aggregation in plain-text format. And the other parties carry out a mask-based secure aggregation protocol. Finally, only the masked ratings with limited information are exposed to the server, leaking no data privacy.

training scheme. However, the gradients transmitted among different parties could still leak user privacy [3, 23].

To address the privacy problem, current FedRec methods can be broadly divided into two categories. The first-kind solutions are based on cryptographic techniques such as homomorphic encryption (HE) [8] or secure multi-party computation (SMC) [21]. For example, HE-based FedRec [6] utilizes HE to protect the transmitted gradients. These methods could lead to lossless model performance. However, they produce extra computation and communication costs since federated learning needs a large amount of calculation and intermediate results exchange. The second-kind solutions utilize the obfuscation methods such as differential privacy (DP) [7]. For instance, DP-based FedRec [10] has been designed to provide a recommendation service without leaking the data privacy of multiple sources. Although DP-based federated algorithms are efficient, they damage the accuracy of models. Therefore, the above solutions all have difficulties when applying to practical problems. They cannot satisfy both the two requirements of recommender system (RecSys), i.e., personalization and real-time.

In this work, we propose federated masked matrix factorization (FedMMF) as a novel FedRec method. The designed FedMMF method could protect the data privacy of FedRec without sacrificing efficiency and effectiveness. Shown in Fig. 1, instead of using cryptographic or obfuscation methods, we introduce a new idea of protecting private data from leakage in FedRec, which is called personalized mask. Personalized mask is a locally generated mask that adds on the original data for preserving privacy without effectiveness loss. Gradients computed on the masked ratings of one participant could be secure enough to directly share with other parties. Moreover, combined with the adaptive secure aggregation protocol, personalized mask also further relieves the efficiency problem of FedRec. Theoretically and empirically, we show the superiority of FedMMF.

The paper is organized as follows, in Sect. 2, we first introduce the basic models and the privacy leakage problem; in Sect. 3, we explain the FedMMF algorithm, the training process, and the privacy guarantee; in Sect. 4, we show the performance of FedMMF in three real-world datasets.

2   Preliminaries

In this section, we first introduce the traditional matrix factorization for recommendation. Then, based on the current challenges of RecSys, we explain federated matrix factorization (FedMF). Although FedMF alleviates the privacy problem of FedRec, there still exists leakage in the training process. Finally, we talk about the current solutions of secure FedMF.

2.1   Matrix Factorization

Given a rating matrix $R \in \mathbb{R}^{n \times m}$, the recommender system aims to fill in the missing values of the matrix. Matrix factorization (MF) is regarded as one of the most classic recommendation algorithm [11]. It decouples the original matrix R into two low-rank matrices. The rating r_{ui} that user u gives to the item i can be approximated as:

$$\hat{r}_{ui} = q_i^T p_u, \tag{1}$$

where $q_i \in \mathbb{R}^{k \times 1}$ represents the latent factors of item i, $p_u \in \mathbb{R}^{k \times 1}$ represents the latent factors of user u, and the latent dimension k can be regarded as the item's implicit characteristics. We could optimize the latent factors via minimizing the loss given below using the existing ratings:

$$\min_{q_i^*, p_u^*} \frac{1}{2} \sum_{(u,i) \in \mathcal{K}} (r_{ui} - q_i^T p_u)^2 + \lambda(\|q_i\|_2^2 + \|p_u\|_2^2), \tag{2}$$

where $\mathcal{K}$ stands for the set of user-item pairs whose rating r_{ui} is already known and λ is the regularization coefficient. Stochastic gradient descent is utilized to update each parameter:

$$q_i \leftarrow q_i - \gamma \cdot (\lambda \cdot q_i - e_{ui} \cdot p_u), \tag{3}$$

$$p_u \leftarrow p_u - \gamma \cdot (\lambda \cdot p_u - e_{ui} \cdot q_i), \tag{4}$$

where $e_{ui} = r_{ui} - q_i^T p_u$ and γ is the learning rate. Conventional recommender systems centrally collect users' private data and train MF algorithm on the server, which leads to immense privacy risks.

2.2   Federated Matrix Factorization

With the development of federated learning, federated recommender system (FedRec) was proposed to address the privacy and data silo problems in the recommendation scenarios [19]. In this work, we focus on the horizontal FedRec, where each party only contains the rating information of one individual user and the user's private data is not allowed to leave the local device. Federated matrix factorization (FedMF) was designed to train recommendation models in such a naturally distributed situation. In the vanilla FedMF algorithm [2], all the item latent factors $\{q_i\}_{i \in \mathcal{I}}$ are maintained on the central server, while each user's latent factors p_u is kept on the local party. The training process is as follows and loops until the convergence of model parameters: 1) party u downloads item i's latent factors q_i from the server; 2) party u updates user's latent factors p_u using private local data r_u; 3) party u computes the gradients of each item's latent factors $\eta_{ui} = \lambda \cdot q_i - e_{ui} \cdot p_u$ with r_u and the updated p_u; 4) party u sends η_{ui} to server; 5) server aggregates the gradients $\sum_{u \in \mathcal{U}} \eta_{ui}$ and updates q_i.

Privacy Leakage from Gradients in FedMF. Vanilla FedMF makes sure that users' private data never leaves the local parties. However, the transmitted gradients could also lead to privacy leakage [6]. From user u, the server continuously receives the gradients of the item i's latent vector at step $t - 1$ and step t:

$$\eta_{ui}^{t-1} = \lambda \cdot q_i^{t-1} - e_{ui}^{t-1} \cdot p_u^{t-1}, \tag{5}$$

$$\eta_{ui}^t = \lambda \cdot q_i^t - e_{ui}^t \cdot p_u^t, \tag{6}$$

where $e_{ui}^{t-1} = r_{ui} - q_i^{t-1^T} p_u^{t-1}$ and $e_{ui}^t = r_{ui} - q_i^{t^T} p_u^t$. Besides, the server also knows the update rule of the latent vector of user u:

$$p_u^t = p_u^{t-1} + \gamma \cdot \sum_{i \in \mathcal{K}_u} (\lambda \cdot p_u^{t-1} - e_{ui}^t \cdot q_i^t), \tag{7}$$

where $\mathcal{K}_u$ stands for the set of items that user u has rated. Obviously, only p_u^{t-1}, p_u^t and r_{ui} are unknown to the server. Combining Eqs. 5, 6, and 7, the server could solve the unknown variables [12]. In this way, private raw ratings of each user are revealed.

Secure FedMF. To address the gradient leakage problem of vanilla FedMF, a few secure FedMF algorithms have been proposed. For example, HE-based FedMF [6] and DP-based FedMF [10], respectively, utilize HE and DP to further preserve privacy. HE-based FedMF encrypts gradients of item latent factors with HE before transmitting them to the server. Then, the server performs secure aggregation on the encrypted gradients, updates item latent factors in ciphertext state, and distributes the new encrypted item latent factors to each user. In a similar way, DP-based FedMF adds noises to gradients before aggregation. However, the former one causes extra costs and the latter one results in accuracy losses.

3   Federated Masked Matrix Factorization

In this section, we explain the proposed FedMMF method. First, FedMMF adopts a new idea of the personalized mask and we analyze its security. Then, FedMMF applies an adaptive secure aggregation protocol according to different protection situations provided by personalized masks on various users.

3.1   Personalized Mask

We generate the personalized masks via private well-trained model separately at each party. As shown in Fig. 1, FedMMF applies the idea of personalized mask in the previous FedMF architecture. The whole training process is as follows. Firstly, before the federated training of latent factors, each local party u trains a private local model using only the user's own data. The corresponding loss function is shown below:

$$L_u = \frac{1}{|\mathcal{K}_u|} \sum_{i \in \mathcal{K}_u} (r_{ui} - f_u^{mask}(i))^2 \tag{8}$$

Without loss of generality, we define the private model of user u as f_u^{mask}. Then, the model is used to give prediction $f_u^{mask}(i)$ on each user-item pair u, i, where $i \in \mathcal{K}_u$. The opposite of the prediction is regarded as the personalized mask. Finally, all parties collaboratively train a matrix factorization model on the masked rating:

$$r_{u,i}^{masked} = r_{u,i} - f_u^{mask}(i). \tag{9}$$

The prediction of FedMMF algorithm for one specific user-item pair (u, i) is:

$$\hat{r}_{ui} = q_i^T p_u + f_u^{mask}(i). \tag{10}$$

The private model f_u^{mask} could be an arbitrary model which only trains on the local data. The well-behaved private model at each local party could protect the privacy of original ratings. Thus, parties with well-behaved private models are able to directly share their gradients computed on the masked ratings. Theorem 1 provides us with how much privacy could be protected by personalized masks.

Security Analysis. The private model f_u^{mask} aims to hide the information of $r_{ui} \in \mathcal{R}$, which is the rating that each user $u \in \mathcal{U}$ gives to item $i \in \mathcal{I}$. For user u, the training data of f_u^{mask} is denoted by $\mathcal{Z}^l = \{(i, r_{ui})\}_{i \in \{1,...,l\}}$. The training data is sampled from a joint distribution $P_{\mathcal{I}\mathcal{R}}$. We assume $\mathcal{R} \in [0, 1]$.

Definition 1 (Privacy indicator of personalized mask). *We define the private information exposed by one specific user u after applying personalized masks as:*

$$J(f_u^{mask}, P_{\mathcal{I}\mathcal{R}}) = E_{(\mathcal{I},\mathcal{R}) \sim P_{\mathcal{I}\mathcal{R}}}[\|\mathcal{R} - f_u^{mask}(\mathcal{I})\|^2]. \tag{11}$$

With a smaller value of privacy indicator J, personalized mask could provide a better protection. If the local private model predicts more accurately, personalized masks will cover more information of the original ratings.

Theorem 1. *Personalized mask is* $(\epsilon, \delta) - private$ *for user* u *if there exists a function* $n_{\mathcal{F}_u} : (0,1) \times (0,1) \to \mathbb{N}$. *For any* $\epsilon, \delta \in (0,1)$ *and any distribution* $P_{\mathcal{IR}}$, *if* $n > n_{\mathcal{F}}$, *then*

$$Pr_{\mathcal{Z}^n \sim P_{\mathcal{IR}}} (J(f_u^{mask}, P_{\mathcal{IR}}) \leq \min_{f_u \in \mathcal{F}_u} J(f_u, P_{\mathcal{IR}}) + \epsilon)$$

$$\geq 1 - \delta. \tag{12}$$

Proof. For any $f_u \in \mathcal{F}_u$, the privacy indicator of user u calculated on the training sample $\mathcal{Z}^n$ is:

$$J(f_u, P_{\mathcal{IR}}^n) = \frac{1}{n} \sum_{j=1}^n \|\mathcal{R}_j - f_u(\mathcal{I}_j)\|^2. \tag{13}$$

Each $\|\mathcal{R}_j - f_u(\mathcal{I}_j)\|^2$ is an independent random variable with mean $J(f_u, P_{\mathcal{IR}})$. We further assume that $\|\mathcal{R}_j - f_u(\mathcal{I}_j)\|^2 \in [0,1]$. According to Hoeffding's inequality[1], we obtain:

$$Pr_{\mathcal{Z}^n \sim P_{\mathcal{IR}}} (|(f_u, P_{\mathcal{IR}}^n) - J(f_u, P_{\mathcal{IR}})| \geq \epsilon) \leq 2e^{-2n\epsilon^2}, \tag{14}$$

then we could get:

$$Pr_{\mathcal{Z}^n \sim P_{\mathcal{IR}}} (\exists f_u \in \mathcal{F}_u, s.t. |(f_u, P_{\mathcal{IR}}^n) - J(f_u, P_{\mathcal{IR}})|$$

$$\geq \epsilon) \leq 2|\mathcal{F}_u| e^{-2n\epsilon^2}. \tag{15}$$

This shows that if

$$n \geq \frac{\log(2|\mathcal{F}_u|/\delta)}{2\epsilon^2}, \tag{16}$$

then

$$Pr_{\mathcal{Z}^n \sim P_{\mathcal{IR}}} (|(f_u, P_{\mathcal{IR}}^n) - J(f_u, P_{\mathcal{IR}})| \leq \epsilon,$$

$$\forall f_u \in \mathcal{F}_u) \geq 1 - \delta, \tag{17}$$

which is equivalent to:

$$Pr_{\mathcal{Z}^n \sim P_{\mathcal{IR}}} (J(f_u^{mask}, P_{\mathcal{IR}}) \leq \min_{f_u \in \mathcal{F}} J(f_u, P_{\mathcal{IR}}) + 2\epsilon)$$

$$\geq 1 - \delta. \tag{18}$$

The reason is that, given

$$\forall f_u \in \mathcal{F}_u, |(f_u, P_{\mathcal{IR}}^n) - J(f_u, P_{\mathcal{IR}})| \leq \epsilon, \tag{19}$$

---

[1] https://en.wikipedia.org/wiki/Hoeffding's_inequality.

we could obtain step by step:

$$
\begin{aligned}
J(f_u^{mask}, P_{\mathcal{IR}}) &\leq J(f_u^{mask}, P_{\mathcal{IR}}^n) + \epsilon \\
&\leq \min_{f_u \in \mathcal{F}} J(f_u, P_{\mathcal{IR}}^n) + \epsilon \\
&\leq \min_{f_u \in \mathcal{F}} J(f_u, P_{\mathcal{IR}}) + \epsilon + \epsilon \\
&= \min_{f_u \in \mathcal{F}} J(f_u, P_{\mathcal{IR}}) + 2\epsilon.
\end{aligned}
\tag{20}
$$

Let $\epsilon = \frac{\epsilon}{2}$, we finally get

$$
n_{\mathcal{F}_u}(\epsilon, \delta) \leq \frac{2\log(2|\mathcal{F}_u|/\delta)}{2\epsilon^2}.
\tag{21}
$$

The function $n_{\mathcal{F}_u}$ determines the sample complexity of user u for training a Fed-MMF algorithm. It stands for how many samples at least are required by personalized masks to guarantee the privacy of user u. Besides, we assume the hypothesis class $\mathcal{F}_u$ of local private model is finite. However, it is not a necessary condition, and Theorem 1 can be further generalized. From Theorem 1, we know that the privacy-preserving ability of personalized mask decides on the quality of local training data. The users with good enough local data could generate secure enough personalized masks, which successfully limit the exposed information from the masked ratings. The privacy indicator J can be used to judge if the personalized masks are secure enough. In addition, we should also try to find the most suitable hypothesis class $\mathcal{F}_u$ on various data sets.

3.2 Adaptive Secure Aggregation

The data quality of different users varies in the real world. Therefore, not all users can generate perfect personalized masks for protection. We propose an adaptive secure aggregation protocol to address this problem. For a given privacy indicator threshold th_J, we could divide the users into two groups, i.e., secure masked group $\mathcal{U}_{secure}$ and insecure masked group $\mathcal{U}_{insecure}$. The privacy indicator J of user in $\mathcal{U}_{secure}$ is larger than th_J, while the privacy indicator J of user in $\mathcal{U}_{insecure}$ is smaller than th_J.

For user $u \in \mathcal{U}_{secure}$ with secure enough personalized masks, the gradients η_{ui} could be directly shared with the central server for aggregation. And the server could get $\sum_{u \in \mathcal{U}_{secure}} \eta_{ui}$. However, for user $u \in \mathcal{U}_{insecure}$ with insecure personalized masks, sharing plain-text gradients will disclose the privacy of local rating data. Therefore, we adopt a mask-based secure aggregation method designed by [4]. For an arbitrary pair of users $u, v \in \mathcal{U}_{insecure}$ and $u < v$, they decide a random mask $s_{u,v} \in \mathbb{R}^{k \times 1}$ together. User u adds this random mask $s_{u,v}$ to its gradients, while user v substracts $s_{u,v}$ from its gradients. Then, each user u could calculate:

$$
\tilde{\eta}_{ui} = \eta_{ui} + \sum_{u<v} s_{u,v} - \sum_{u>v} s_{v,u} \quad \mod l,
\tag{22}
$$

where l is a large prime number. Next, each user $u \in \mathcal{U}_{insecure}$ sends the computed $\tilde{\eta}_{ui}$ to the server. The server will calculate:

Algorithm 1. Federated Masked Matrix Factorization

1: **Input:** $r_{u\in\{1,...,n\}}, th_J$
2: **Output:** $q_{i\in\{1,...,m\}}, p_{u\in\{1,...,n\}}, f^{mask}_{u\in\{1,...,n\}}$
3: Server initializes $q^0_{i\in\{1,...,m\}}$, each party u initializes $p^0_{u\in\{1,...,n\}}$ and $f^{mask}_{u\in\{1,...,n\}}(\theta_u)$.

4: **for** each party $u \in \{1,...,n\}$ in parallel **do**
5:     // run on each party u
6:     Train private model $f^{mask}_u(\theta_u)$ on local data r_u;
7:     Compute personalized masked rating $r^{masked}_{u,i}$ according to Eq. 9 for each $i \in \mathcal{K}_u$;
8:     Grouped to $\mathcal{U}_{secure}$ or $\mathcal{U}_{insecure}$ with th_J;
9: **end for**

10: // run on the server
11: **for** each $t = 1, 2, ..., T$ **do**
12:     **for** each party $u \in \mathcal{U}_{secure}$ in parallel **do**
13:         Get gradients $\eta^t_{ui\in\mathcal{K}_u} = \mathbf{MaskedUpdate}(q^{t-1}_{i\in\mathcal{K}_u})$;
14:     **end for**
15:     **for** each party $u \in \mathcal{U}_{insecure}$ in parallel **do**
16:         Get gradients $\tilde{\eta}^t_{ui\in\mathcal{K}_u} = \mathbf{MaskedUpdate}(q^{t-1}_{i\in\mathcal{K}_u})$;
17:     **end for**
18:     Get the aggregated gradients $\sum_{u\in\mathcal{U}} \eta^t_{i\in\mathcal{I}}$ according to Eq. 24;
19:     Update item factors $q^t_i = q^{t-1}_i - \gamma \cdot \sum_{u\in\mathcal{U}} \eta^t_i$ for each $i \in \mathcal{I}$;
20: **end for**

21: // run on each party u
22: **MaksedUpdate:**
23: Compute $e^t_{ui} = r^{masked}_{ui} - q^{t^T}_i p^t_u$ for each $i \in \mathcal{K}_u$;
24: Update user factors p^t_u according to Eq. 7;
25: Compute gradient η^t_{ui} according to Eq. 6 for each $i \in \mathcal{K}_u$;
26: **Return** $\eta^t_{ui\in\mathcal{K}_u}$ or $\tilde{\eta}^t_{ui\in\mathcal{K}_u}$ to the server with adaptive secure aggregation protocol.

$$\sum_{u\in\mathcal{U}_{insecure}} \tilde{\eta}_{ui} = \sum_{u\in\mathcal{U}_{insecure}} \left(\eta_{ui} + \sum_{u<v} s_{u,v} - \sum_{u>v} s_{v,u}\right)$$
$$= \sum_{u\in\mathcal{U}_{insecure}} \eta_{ui} \mod l. \tag{23}$$

The aggregated gradients could be obtained, and the gradients of one specific user are protected by the designed random masks. Furthermore, secret sharing [18] is utilized to solve the dynamic user problem. With the adaptive secure aggregation protocol, the server could obtain

$$\sum_{u\in\mathcal{U}} \eta_{ui} = \sum_{u\in\mathcal{U}_{secure}} \eta_{ui} + \sum_{u\in\mathcal{U}_{insecure}} \tilde{\eta}_{ui} \tag{24}$$

The details of FedMMF are shown in Algorithm 1. Compared with only applying the original aggregation in [4], FedMMF utilizes the adaptive secure aggregation to further improve efficiency.

4 Experiments

In this section, we show that FedMMF could improve efficiency without the loss of privacy and model effectiveness. Firstly, we explain the data sets, baseline models, and other settings in the experiments. Then, we show the improvements of FedMMF on model efficiency. With the help of adaptive secure aggregation protocol based on personalized masks, FedMMF accelerates the training process. At last, we discuss the model effectiveness of FedMMF with different kinds of personalized masks, compared to the baseline model.

4.1 Settings

We verify FedMMF on three real-world data sets. Two of them are MovieLens data sets [9], *i.e.*, MovieLens 100K and MovieLens 10M. The other one is the LastFM data set [5]. In our experiment, each user is regarded as a participant in the collaborative training process. Therefore, the user's own ratings are kept on the local party. Besides, we utilize the side information (*i.e.*, user profiles and item attributes) to train the local private model. To construct features from tags in the data set, we utilize TFIDF [17] and PCA [1] techniques. Besides, we set bins for the listening counts of music of the LastFM data set and convert them into ratings scaling from 1 to 5. In addition, the evaluation metrics of model efficacy are root mean square error (RMSE) and mean absolute error (MAE). They are averaged by each user-item pair but not each user, which is an alignment with most current works. Besides, we run each experiment ten times to obtain the mean and standard deviation values.

The compared models are: 1) **FedMF**: parties collaboratively train matrix factorization models via sharing the latent factors of common users, where neither HE nor DP is utilized; 2) **One-order FedMMF**: each party locally learns linear personalized masks to hide private rating information via a linear regression model [15]. Then, all parties collaboratively train FedMF on the one-order masked ratings; 3) **Two-order FedMMF**: similarly, each party constructs two-order masks to protect private ratings via locally learning a factorization machine model [16]; 4) **High-order FedMMF**: each party captures high-order and nonlinear feature interactions through a neural network model [22]. We do not compare FedMMF with DP-based FedMF, because DP causes effectiveness loss while FedMMF does not. Besides, we also show the performance of various local context models and federated context models for reference.

4.2 Efficiency Promotion and Privacy Discussion

Compared with HE-based FedMF [6], FedMMF with all users in the insecure user group could largely speed up the training process [4]. Then, the personalized mask technique could further improve the efficiency of the secure aggregation process via sharing plain-text gradients of parties with well-protected ratings. We provide two attack methods, i.e., recovery attack and ranking attack, for analyzing how much the personalized mask technique could further promote model efficiency. Taking two-order FedMMF on MovieLens 10M data set as an example, we conduct the attack experiments. The rating range of the MovieLens 10M data set is from 0.5 to 5.0. And the rating interval is 0.5.

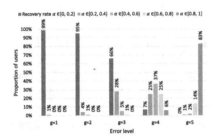

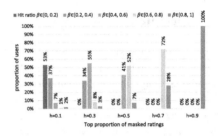

(a) The results of recovery attack under different error levels. On the one hand, when error level g is small, the recovery attack could hardly reveal the original rating information. On the other hand, when error level g grows, the recovery attack becomes more accurate. However, the utility of recovered ratings also decreases.

(b) The results of ranking attack under different top proportions. With the masked ratings of each party, the adversary wants to choose the actual high-rated items. When the adversary utilizes a small top proportion h, the attacks performs on most parties achieve a poor hit ratio, which is less than 0.5. Although the hit ratio grows as h increases, a large h results in a useless ranking attack.

Fig. 2. Experiments results on recovery and ranking attacks.

Recovery Attack. Against the masked ratings, an adversary could conduct an intuitive attack to recover the original ratings. However, the attack could be difficult if only the masked ratings are exposed. Therefore, for each party, we assume that the adversary knows the minimum and maximum values of the original ratings. Then, the adversary could scale the masked ratings to the range of original ratings for recovery. We define g as the error level. If the difference between one recovered value and the corresponding original rating is less than α, the recovery is considered successful. Thus, there exists a recovery rate α for each party's masked rating. In Fig. 2a, we show the proportion of parties whose recovery rate is in a certain range under different error levels. As we can see, when the error level is small, *e.g.*, $g = 1$ and $g = 2$, the adversary could nearly reveal no party's privacy with a recovery rate larger than 0.5. And as the error level increases, the recovery rate begins to grow. However, a higher error level means a more inaccurate recovery, and the utility of the recovered ratings is poorer.

Ranking Attack. Since the intuitive recovery attack seems not successful enough, we introduce another method named ranking attack. Instead of recovering the original concrete ratings, ranking attack tries to find the high-rating items from their masked ratings. First, for each party, the adversary ranks the rated items according to their masked ratings. Then, items in the top h proportion of masked ratings are selected as the high-rating items. Similarly, given h, we also sort these items with regard to their original ratings as the true high-rating item set. Thus, we could evaluate the ranking attack with hit ratio β, which is calculated as the ratio that items selected using masked ratings are in the true high-rating item set. Figure 2b shows that, under different top proportion h, the ranking attack could reveal the rating ranking privacy of parties. If the selected top proportion is small, *e.g.*, $h = 1$ and $h = 2$, the attacks performed on most parties' masked

Table 1. Performance of FedMMF compared with baseline models on different data sets. Fed-MMF models with different personalized masks have no effectiveness loss compared with FedMF in all data sets. Besides the comparison between FedMMF and FedMF, we also show that Fed-MMF outperforms local context models and federated context models.

Models	MovienLens 100K		MovienLens 10M		LastFM	
	RMSE	MAE	RMSE	MAE	RMSE	MAE
FedMF	0.9491 ± 0.0040	0.7412 ± 0.0027	0.7753 ± 0.0034	0.5827 ± 0.0015	1.2235 ± 0.0068	0.8780 ± 0.0047
LocalLR	1.0107 ± 0.0025	0.8040 ± 0.0022	0.8818 ± 0.0023	0.6766 ± 0.0011	1.1081 ± 0.0099	0.8163 ± 0.0085
FedLR	1.0796 ± 0.0081	0.8844 ± 0.0058	0.9703 ± 0.0020	0.7497 ± 0.0012	1.5448 ± 0.0110	1.3538 ± 0.0137
One-order FedMMF	0.9340 ± 0.0043	0.7340 ± 0.0035	0.7695 ± 0.0013	0.5808 ± 0.0008	1.0886 ± 0.0109	0.8066 ± 0.0092
LocalFM	1.0083 ± 0.0019	0.8054 ± 0.0019	0.8938 ± 0.0023	0.6862 ± 0.0012	1.0845 ± 0.0130	0.7988 ± 0.0035
FedFM	1.0628 ± 0.0070	0.8644 ± 0.0053	0.9639 ± 0.0022	0.7445 ± 0.0015	1.5301 ± 0.0133	1.3369 ± 0.0117
Two-order FedMMF	0.9218 ± 0.0037	0.7250 ± 0.0030	0.7720 ± 0.0013	0.5827 ± 0.0007	1.0842 ± 0.0090	0.7964 ± 0.0031
LocalNN	1.0114 ± 0.0021	0.8087 ± 0.0017	0.8819 ± 0.0020	0.6816 ± 0.0009	1.1007 ± 0.0068	0.8007 ± 0.0123
FedNN	1.0945 ± 0.0074	0.9176 ± 0.0060	0.9756 ± 0.0024	0.7689 ± 0.0028	1.5461 ± 0.0060	1.3598 ± 0.0075
High-order FedMMF	0.9319 ± 0.0025	0.7317 ± 0.0018	0.7648 ± 0.0016	0.5772 ± 0.0008	1.0860 ± 0.0055	0.7933 ± 0.0070

ratings obtain a hit ratio less than 0.5. It means that more than half of the selected items do not have high ratings. When the adversary tunes h larger, the attack becomes more effective. However, a large h is relatively meaningless because the adversary does not want to choose all items to be high-rating in reality.

According to the experiment results of the above two attack methods, we find that a considerable number of users get their rating privacy well-protected with the help of personalized masks. These users can be put in the secure group and transfer their gradients in plain text. Therefore, the personalized mask could further accelerate the training process of federated recommendation. Besides federated learning, the person-alized masked ratings of users in the secure group could also be centrally collected and used for training without privacy leakage. This operation is able to reduce the commu-nication and computation costs once again.

4.3   Discussion on Model Effectiveness

In this section, we verify the effectiveness of FedMMF on three real-world data sets. We implement three private models to construct personalized masks with different prop-erties: the one-order mask, two-order mask, and high-order mask. The performances of FedMMF with these three masks are shown in Table 1. RMSE and MAE are both regression evaluation metrics. Smaller value stands for better model efficacy. As we can see, FedMMF models with different personalized masks have no effectiveness loss compared with FedMF in all data sets.

Moreover, FedMMF even outperforms FedMF. The effectiveness improvements could be divided into two parts. The first part benefits from the ensemble training scheme of FedMMF. The incorporation of personalized masks utilizes the idea of ensemble learning to combine weak learners for a better generalization ability. The second part takes advantage of the side information utilized in the private model of Fed-MMF. In the recommendation scenario, feature interactions are important information to capture. Another observation is that, on all three data sets, two-order FedMMF and high-order FedMMF dominate alternatively. It means we should utilize cross features to construct personalized masks in the recommendation scenarios. We also compare Fed-MMF models with corresponding local context and federated context models, shown in Table 1. Comparing FedMMF with different local context models and federated context models, we could see that FedMMF also outperforms both of them. This observation verifies the main contribution to the effectiveness improvement is the incorporation of ensemble learning. On the other hand of the shield, FedMMF can also be regarded as an excellent way to combine collaborative information and feature information.

5   Conclusion

In this work, we provide a new idea of personalized masks to protect data privacy in federated learning, which neither slows the training process down nor damages model performance. Taking the recommendation scenario as an example, we apply it in the FedMMF algorithm. Combining with the adaptive secure aggregation protocol, Fed-MMF shows superiority theoretically and empirically. In our future work, we would like to extend personalized masks to more general federated learning tasks besides recommender systems and try to combine personalized masks with differential privacy theory.

References

1. Abdi, H., Williams, L.J.: Principal component analysis. Wiley Interdisc. Rev. Comput. Stat. **2**(4), 433–459 (2010)
2. Ammad-Ud-Din, M., et al.: Federated collaborative filtering for privacy-preserving personalized recommendation system. arXiv preprint arXiv:1901.09888 (2019)
3. Aono, Y., Hayashi, T., Wang, L., Moriai, S., et al.: Privacy-preserving deep learning via additively homomorphic encryption. IEEE Trans. Inf. Forensics Secur. **13**(5), 1333–1345 (2017)
4. Bonawitz, K., et al.: Practical secure aggregation for privacy-preserving machine learning. In: Proceedings of the 2017 ACM SIGSAC Conference on Computer and Communications Security, pp. 1175–1191 (2017)
5. Cantador, I., Brusilovsky, P., Kuflik, T.: 2nd workshop on information heterogeneity and fusion in recommender systems (HETREC 2011). In: Proceedings of the 5th ACM Conference on Recommender Systems, RecSys 2011. ACM, New York (2011)
6. Chai, D., Wang, L., Chen, K., Yang, Q.: Secure federated matrix factorization. IEEE Intell. Syst. **36**, 11–20 (2020)
7. Dwork, C., Roth, A., et al.: The algorithmic foundations of differential privacy. Found. Trends Theor. Comput. Sci. **9**(3–4), 211–407 (2014)
8. Gentry, C.: Fully homomorphic encryption using ideal lattices. In: Proceedings of the Forty-First Annual ACM Symposium on Theory of Computing, pp. 169–178 (2009)
9. Harper, F.M., Konstan, J.A.: The movielens datasets: history and context. ACM Trans Interact. Intell. Syst. (TiiS) **5**(4), 1–19 (2015)
10. Hua, J., Xia, C., Zhong, S.: Differentially private matrix factorization. In: Proceedings of the Twenty-Fourth International Joint Conference on Artificial Intelligence, pp. 1763–1770. AAAI Press (2015)

11. Koren, Y., Bell, R., Volinsky, C.: Matrix factorization techniques for recommender systems. Computer **42**(8), 30–37 (2009)
12. Lazard, D.: Thirty years of polynomial system solving, and now? J. Symb. Comput. **44**(3), 222–231 (2009)
13. McMahan, B., Moore, E., Ramage, D., Hampson, S., Arcas, B.A.: Communication-efficient learning of deep networks from decentralized data. In: Artificial Intelligence and Statistics, pp. 1273–1282. PMLR (2017)
14. McMahan, H.B., et al.: Advances and open problems in federated learning. Found. Trends® Mach. Learn. **14**(1) (2021)
15. Montgomery, D.C., Peck, E.A., Vining, G.G.: Introduction to Linear Regression Analysis, vol. 821. Wiley, Hoboken (2012)
16. Rendle, S.: Factorization machines. In: 2010 IEEE International Conference on Data Mining, pp. 995–1000. IEEE (2010)
17. Robertson, S.: Understanding inverse document frequency: on theoretical arguments for IDF. J. Documentation (2004)
18. Shamir, A.: How to share a secret. Commun. ACM **22**(11), 612–613 (1979)
19. Yang, L., Tan, B., Zheng, V.W., Chen, K., Yang, Q.: Federated recommendation systems. In: Yang, Q., Fan, L., Yu, H. (eds.) Federated Learning. LNCS (LNAI), vol. 12500, pp. 225–239. Springer, Cham (2020). https://doi.org/10.1007/978-3-030-63076-8_16
20. Yang, Q., Liu, Y., Chen, T., Tong, Y.: Federated machine learning: concept and applications. ACM Trans. Intell. Syst. Technol. (TIST) **10**(2), 1–19 (2019)
21. Yao, A.C.: Protocols for secure computations. In: 23rd Annual Symposium on Foundations of Computer Science (SFCS 1982), pp. 160–164. IEEE (1982)
22. Yegnanarayana, B.: Artificial Neural Networks. PHI Learning Pvt., Ltd. (2009)
23. Zhu, L., Liu, Z., Han, S.: Deep leakage from gradients. In: Advances in Neural Information Processing Systems, pp. 14774–14784 (2019)

A General Theory for Client Sampling in Federated Learning

Yann Fraboni[1,2(✉)], Richard Vidal[2], Laetitia Kameni[2], and Marco Lorenzi[1]

[1] Université Côte d'Azur, Inria Sophia Antipolis, Epione Research Group,
Sophia Antipolis, France
{yann.fraboni,marco.lorenzi}@inria.fr
[2] Accenture Labs, Sophia Antipolis, France

Abstract. While client sampling is a central operation of current state-of-the-art federated learning (FL) approaches, the impact of this procedure on the convergence and speed of FL remains under-investigated. In this work, we provide a general theoretical framework to quantify the impact of a client sampling scheme and of the clients heterogeneity on the federated optimization. First, we provide a unified theoretical ground for previously reported sampling schemes experimental results on the relationship between FL convergence and the variance of the aggregation weights. Second, we prove for the first time that the quality of FL convergence is also impacted by the resulting *covariance* between aggregation weights. Our theory is general, and is here applied to Multinomial Distribution (MD) and Uniform sampling, two default unbiased client sampling schemes of FL, and demonstrated through a series of experiments in non-iid and unbalanced scenarios. Our results suggest that MD sampling should be used as default sampling scheme, due to the resilience to the changes in data ratio during the learning process, while Uniform sampling is superior only in the special case when clients have the same amount of data.

1 Introduction

Federated Learning (FL) has gained popularity in the last years as it enables different clients to jointly learn a global model without sharing their respective data. Among the different FL approaches, federated averaging (FEDAVG) has emerged as the most popular optimization scheme (McMahan *et al.* 2017). An optimization round of FEDAVG requires data owners, also called clients, to receive from the server the current global model which they update on a fixed amount of Stochastic Gradient Descent (SGD) steps before sending it back to the server. The new global model is then created as the weighted average of the client updates, according to their data ratio. FL specializes the classical problem of distributed learning (DL), to account for the private nature of clients information (i.e. data and surrogate features), and for the potential data and hardware heterogeneity across clients, which is generally unknown to the server.

In FL optimization, FEDAVG was first proven to converge experimentally (McMahan *et al.* 2017), before theoretical guarantees were provided for any non-iid federated dataset (Wang *et al.* 2020a; Karimireddy *et al.* 2020; Haddadpour and Mahdavi 2019; Khaled *et al.* 2020). A drawback of naive implementations of FEDAVG consists

R. Goebel et al. (Eds.): FL 2022, LNAI 13448, pp. 46–58, 2023.
https://doi.org/10.1007/978-3-031-28996-5_4

in requiring the participation of all the clients to every optimization round. As a consequence, the efficiency of the optimization is limited by the communication speed of the slowest client, as well as by the server communication capabilities. To mitigate this issue, the original FEDAVG algorithm already contemplated the possibility of considering a random subset of m clients at each FL round. It has been subsequently shown that, to ensure the convergence of FL to its optimum, clients must be sampled such that in expectation the resulting global model is identical to the one obtained when considering all the clients (Wang *et al.* 2020a; Cho *et al.* 2020). Clients sampling schemes compliant with this requirement are thus called *unbiased*. Due to its simplicity and flexibility, the current default unbiased sampling scheme consists in sampling m clients according to a Multinomial Distribution (MD), where the sampling probability depends on the respective data ratio (Li *et al.* 2020a; Wang *et al.* 2020a; Li *et al.* 2020c; Haddad-pour and Mahdavi 2019; Li *et al.* 2020b; Wang and Joshi 2018; Fraboni *et al.* 2021a). Nevertheless, when clients have identical amount of data, clients can also be sampled uniformly without replacement (Li *et al.* 2020c; Karimireddy *et al.* 2020; Reddi *et al.* 2021; Rizk *et al.* 2020). In this case, Uniform sampling has been experimentally shown to yield better results than MD sampling (Li *et al.* 2020c).

Previous works proposed unbiased sampling strategies alternative to MD and Uniform sampling with the aim of improving FL convergence. In Fraboni *et al.* (2021a), MD sampling was extended to account for clusters of clients with similar data characteristics, while in Chen *et al.* (2020), clients sampling probabilities are defined depending on the Euclidean norm of the clients local work. While these works are based on the definition and analysis of specific sampling procedures, aimed at satisfying a given FL criterion, there is currently a need for a general theoretical framework to elucidate the impact of client sampling on FL convergence.

The main contribution of this work consists in deriving a general theoretical framework for FL optimization allowing to clearly quantify the impact of client sampling on the global model update at any FL round. This contribution has important theoretical and practical implications. First, we demonstrate the dependence of FL convergence on the variance of the aggregation weights. Second, we prove for the first time that the convergence speed is also impacted through sampling by the resulting *covariance* between aggregation weights. From a practical point of view, we establish both theoretically and experimentally that client sampling schemes based on aggregation weights with sum different than 1 are less efficient. We also prove that MD sampling is outperformed by Uniform sampling only when clients have identical data ratio. Finally, we show that the comparison between different client sampling schemes is appropriate only when considering a small number of clients. Our theory ultimately shows that MD sampling should be used as default sampling scheme, due to the favorable statistical properties and to the resilience to FL applications with varying data ratio and heterogeneity.

Our work is structured as follows. In Sect. 2, we provide formal definitions for FL, unbiased client sampling, and for the server aggregation scheme. In Sect. 3, we introduce our convergence guarantees (Theorem 1) relating the convergence of FL to the aggregation weight variance of the client sampling scheme. Consistently with our theory, in Sect. 4, we experimentally demonstrate the importance of the clients aggregation weights variance and covariance on the convergence speed, and conclude by recommending Uniform sampling for FL applications with identical client ratio, and MD sampling otherwise.

2 Background

Before investigating in Sect. 3 the impact of client sampling on FL convergence, we recapitulate in Sect. 2 the current theory behind FL aggregation schemes for clients local updates. We then introduce a formalization for *unbiased* client sampling.

2.1 Aggregating Clients Local Updates

In FL, we consider a set I of n clients each respectively owning a dataset $\mathcal{D}_i$ composed of n_i samples. FL aims at optimizing the average of each clients local loss function weighted by p_i such that $\sum_{i=1}^{n} p_i = 1$, i.e.

$$\mathcal{L}(\theta) = \sum_{i=1}^{n} p_i \mathcal{L}_i(\theta), \tag{1}$$

where θ represents the model parameters. The weight p_i can be interpreted as the importance given by the server to client i in the federated optimization problem. While any combination of $\{p_i\}$ is possible, we note that in practice, either (a) every device has equal importance, i.e. $p_i = 1/n$, or (b) every data point is equally important, i.e. $p_i = n_i/M$ with $M = \sum_{i=1}^{n} n_i$. Unless stated otherwise, in the rest of this work, we consider to be in case (b), i.e. $\exists i, \; p_i \neq 1/n$.

In this setting, to estimate a global model across clients, FEDAVG (McMahan *et al.* 2017) is an iterative training strategy based on the aggregation of local model parameters. At each iteration step t, the server sends the current global model parameters θ^t to the clients. Each client updates the respective model by minimizing the local cost function $\mathcal{L}_i(\theta)$ through a fixed amount K of SGD steps initialized with θ^t. Subsequently each client returns the updated local parameters θ_i^{t+1} to the server. The global model parameters θ^{t+1} at the iteration step $t + 1$ are then estimated as a weighted average:

$$\theta^{t+1} = \sum_{i=1}^{n} p_i \theta_i^{t+1}. \tag{2}$$

To alleviate the clients workload and reduce the amount of overall communications, the server often considers $m \leq n$ clients at every iteration. In heterogeneous datasets containing many workers, the percentage of sampled clients m/n can be small, and thus induce important variability in the new global model, as each FL optimization step necessarily leads to an improvement on the m sampled clients to the detriment of the non-sampled ones. To solve this issue, Reddi *et al.* (2021); Karimireddy *et al.* (2020); Wang *et al.* (2020b) propose considering an additional learning rate η_g to better account for the clients update at a given iteration. We denote by $\omega_i(S_t)$ the stochastic aggregation weight of client i given the subset of sampled clients S_t at iteration t. The server aggregation scheme can be written as:

$$\theta^{t+1} = \theta^t + \eta_g \sum_{i=1}^{n} \omega_i(S_t)(\theta_i^{t+1} - \theta^t). \tag{3}$$

Table 1. Synthesis of statistical properties of different sampling schemes.

SAMPLING	$\mathrm{Var}\left[\omega_i(S_t)\right]$	α	$\mathrm{Var}\left[\sum_{i=1}^n \omega_i(S_t)\right]$
FULL PARTICIPATION	$= 0$	$= 0$	$= 0$
MD	$= -\frac{1}{m}p_i^2 + \frac{1}{m}p_i$	$= 1/m$	$= 0$
UNIFORM	$= \left(\frac{n}{m} - 1\right)p_i^2$	$= \frac{n-m}{m(n-1)}$	$= \frac{n-m}{m(n-1)}[n\sum_{i=1}^n p_i^2 - 1]$

2.2 Unbiased Data Agnostic Client Samplings

While FEDAVG was originally based on the uniform sampling of clients (McMahan *et al.* 2017), this scheme has been proven to be biased and converge to a suboptimal minima of problem (1) (Wang *et al.* 2020a; Cho *et al.* 2020; Li *et al.* 2020c). This was the motivation for Li *et al.* (2020c) to introduce the notion of *unbiasedness*, where clients are considered in expectation subject to their importance p_i, according to Definition 1 below. Unbiased sampling guarantees the optimization of the original FL cost function, while minimizing the number of active clients per FL round. We note that unbiased sampling is not necessarily related to the clients distribution, as this would require to know beforehand the specificity of the clients' datasets.

Unbiased sampling methods (Li et al. 2020a,c; Fraboni *et al.* 2021a) are currently among the standard approaches to FL, as opposed to *biased* approaches, known to over- or under-represent clients and lead to suboptimal convergence properties (McMahan *et al.* 2017; Nishio and Yonetani 2019; Jeon *et al.* 2020; Cho *et al.* 2020), or to methods requiring additional computation work from clients (Chen *et al.* 2020).

Definition 1 (Unbiased Sampling). *A client sampling scheme is said unbiased if the expected value of the client aggregation is equal to the global deterministic aggregation obtained when considering all the clients, i.e.*

$$\mathbb{E}_{S_t}\left[\sum_{i=1}^n w_i(S_t)\theta_i^t\right] := \sum_{i=1}^n p_i\theta_i^t, \tag{4}$$

where $w_j(S_t)$ is the aggregation weight of client j for subset of clients S_t.

The sampling distribution uniquely defines the statistical properties of stochastic weights. In this setting, unbiased sampling guarantees the equivalence between deterministic and stochastic weights in expectation. Unbiased schemes of primary importance in FL are MD and Uniform sampling, for which we can derive a close form formula for the aggregation weights:

MD Sampling. This scheme considers $l_1, ..., l_m$ to be the m iid sampled clients from a Multinomial Distribution with support on $\{1, ..., m\}$ satisfying $\mathbb{P}(l_k = i) = p_i$ (Wang *et al.* 2020a; Li et al. 2020a,c; Haddadpour and Mahdavi 2019; Li *et al.* 2020b; Wang and Joshi 2018; Fraboni *et al.* 2021a). By definition, we have $\sum_{i=1}^n p_i = 1$, and the clients aggregation weights take the form:

$$\omega_i(S_t) = \frac{1}{m}\sum_{k=1}^m \mathbb{I}(l_k = i). \tag{5}$$

Uniform Sampling. This scheme samples m clients uniformly without replacement. Since in this case a client is sampled with probability $p(\{i \in S_t\}) = m/n$, the requirement of Definition 1 implies:

$$\omega_i(S_t) = \mathbb{I}(i \in S_t)\frac{n}{m}p_i. \tag{6}$$

We note that this formulation for Uniform sampling is a generalization of the scheme previously used for FL applications with identical client importance, i.e. $p_i = 1/n$ (Karimireddy *et al.* 2020; Li *et al.* 2020c; Reddi *et al.* 2021; Rizk *et al.* 2020). We note that Var$[\sum_{i=1}^{n} \omega_i(S_t)] = 0$ if and only if $p_i = 1/n$ for all the clients as, indeed, $\sum_{i=1}^{n} \omega_i(S_t) = m\frac{n}{m}\frac{1}{n} = 1$.

With reference to Eq. (3), we note that by setting $\eta_g = 1$, and by imposing the condition $\forall S_t$, $\sum_{i=1}^{n} \omega_i(S_t) = 1$, we retrieve Eq. (2). This condition is satisfied for example by MD sampling and Uniform sampling for identical clients importance.

We finally note that the covariance of the aggregation weights for both MD and Uniform sampling satisfies Assumption 1.

Assumption 1 (Client Sampling Covariance). *There exists a constant α such that the client sampling covariance satisfies $\forall i \neq j$,* Cov$[\omega_i(S_t), \omega_j(S_t)] = -\alpha p_i p_j$.

We provide in Table 1 the derivation of α and the resulting covariance for these two schemes with calculus detailed in (Fraboni *et al.* 2021b, Appendix A). Furthermore, this property is common to a variety of sampling schemes, for example based on Binomial or Poisson Binomial distributions (detailed derivations can be found in (Fraboni et al. 2021b, Appendix A)). Following this consideration, in addition to Definition 1, in the rest of this work we assume the additional requirement for a client sampling scheme to satisfy Assumption 1.

2.3   Advanced Client Sampling Techniques

Importance sampling for centralized SGD Zhao and Zhang (2015); Csiba and Richtárik (2018) has been developed to reduce the variance of the gradient estimator in the centralized setting and provide faster convergence. According to this framework, each data point is sampled according to a probability based on a parameter of its loss function (e.g. its Lipschitz constant), in opposition to classical sampling where clients are sampled with same probability. These works cannot be seamlessly applied in FL, since in general no information on the clients loss function should be disclosed to the server. Therefore, the operation of client sampling in FL cannot be seen as an extension of importance sampling. Regarding advanced FL client sampling, Fraboni *et al.* (2021a) extended MD sampling to account for collections of sampling distributions with varying client sampling probability. From a theoretical perspective, this approach was proven to have identical convergence guarantees of MD sampling, with albeit experimental improvement justified by lower variance of the clients' aggregation weights. In Chen *et al.* (2020), clients probability are set based on the euclidean norm of the clients local work. We show in (Fraboni *et al.* 2021b, Appendix A) that these advanced client sampling strategies also satisfy our covariance Assumption 1, and are thus encompassed by the general theory developed in Sect. 3.

3 Convergence Guarantees

Based on the assumptions introduced in Sect. 2, in what follows we elaborate a new theory relating the convergence of FL to the statistical properties of client sampling schemes. In particular, Theorem 1 quantifies the asymptotic relationship between client sampling and FL convergence.

3.1 Asymptotic FL Convergence with Respect to Client Sampling

To prove FL convergence with client sampling, our work relies on the following three assumptions (Wang *et al.* 2020a; Li *et al.* 2020a; Karimireddy *et al.* 2020; Haddadpour and Mahdavi 2019; Wang et al. 2019a,b):

Assumption 2 (Smoothness). *The clients local objective function is L-Lipschitz smooth, that is,* $\forall i \in \{1, ..., n\}$, $\|\nabla \mathcal{L}_i(x) - \nabla \mathcal{L}_i(y)\| \le L \|x - y\|$.

Assumption 3 (Bounded Dissimilarity). *There exist constants* $\beta^2 \ge 1$ *and* $\kappa^2 \ge 0$ *such that for every combination of positive weights* $\{w_i\}$ *such that* $\sum_{i=1}^n w_i = 1$, *we have* $\sum_{i=1}^n w_i \|\nabla \mathcal{L}_i(x)\|^2 \le \beta^2 \|\nabla \mathcal{L}(x)\|^2 + \kappa^2$. *If all the local loss functions are identical, then we have* $\beta^2 = 1$ *and* $\kappa^2 = 0$.

Assumption 4 (Unbiased Gradient and Bounded Variance). *Every client stochastic gradient* $g_i(x|B)$ *of a model* x *evaluated on batch* B *is an unbiased estimator of the local gradient. We thus have* $\mathbb{E}_B [\xi_i(B)] = 0$ *and* $0 \le \mathbb{E}_B \left[\|\xi_i(B)\|^2 \right] \le \sigma^2$, *with* $\xi_i(B) = g_i(x|B) - \nabla \mathcal{L}_i(x)$.

We formalize in the following theorem the relationship between the statistical properties of the client sampling scheme and the asymptotic convergence of FL (proof in (Fraboni *et al.* 2021b, Appendix C)).

Theorem 1 (FL convergence). *Let us consider a client sampling scheme satisfying Definition 1 and Assumption 1. Under Assumptions 2, 3, and 4, and with sufficiently small local step size* η_l, *the following convergence bound holds:*

$$\frac{1}{T} \sum_{t=0}^{T-1} \mathbb{E} \left[\|\nabla \mathcal{L}(\theta^t)\|^2 \right] \le \mathcal{O} \left(\frac{1}{\tilde{\eta} KT} \right)$$

$$+ \mathcal{O} \left(\eta_l^2 (K-1) \sigma^2 \right) + \mathcal{O} \left(\tilde{\eta} \left[\Sigma + \sum_{i=1}^n p_i^2 \right] \sigma^2 \right) \qquad (7)$$

$$+ \mathcal{O} \left(\eta_l^2 K(K-1) \kappa^2 \right) + \mathcal{O} \left(\tilde{\eta} \gamma \left[(K-1) \sigma^2 + K \kappa^2 \right] \right),$$

where $\tilde{\eta} = \eta_g \eta_l$, K *is the number of local SGD,*

$$\Sigma = \sum_{i=1}^n \mathrm{Var} \left[\omega_i(S_t) \right] \qquad (8)$$

and

$$\gamma = \sum_{i=1}^n \mathrm{Var} \left[\omega_i(S_t) \right] + \alpha \sum_{i=1}^n p_i^2. \qquad (9)$$

We first observe that any client sampling scheme satisfying the assumptions of Theorem 1 converges to its optimum. Through Σ and γ, Eq. (7) shows that our bound is proportional to the clients aggregation weights through the quantities $\text{Var}\left[\omega_i(S_t)\right]$ and α, which thus should be minimized. These terms are non-negative and are minimized and equal to zero only with full participation of the clients to every optimization round. Theorem 1 does not require the sum of the weights $\omega_i(S_t)$ to be equal to 1. Yet, for client sampling satisfying $\text{Var}\left[\sum_{i=1}^{n}\omega_i(S_t)\right] = 0$, we get $\alpha \propto \Sigma$. Hence, choosing an optimal client sampling scheme amounts at choosing the client sampling with the smallest Σ. This aspect has been already suggested in Fraboni *et al.* (2021a).

The convergence guarantee proposed in Theorem 1 extends the work of Wang *et al.* (2020a) where, in addition of considering FEDAVG with clients performing K vanilla SGD, we include a server learning rate η_g and integrate client sampling (Eq. (3)). With full client participation ($\Sigma = \gamma = 0$) and $\eta_g = 1$, we retrieve the convergence guarantees of Wang *et al.* (2020a). Furthermore, our theoretical framework can be applied to any client sampling satisfying the conditions of Theorem 1. In turn, Theorem 1 holds for full client participation, MD sampling, Uniform sampling, as well as for the other client sampling schemes detailed in (Fraboni *et al.* 2021b, Appendix A). Finally, the proof of Theorem 1 is general enough to account for FL regularization methods (Li et al. 2019, 2020a; Acar *et al.* 2021), other SGD solvers (Kingma and Ba 2015; Ward *et al.* 2019; Li and Orabona 2019), and/or gradient compression/quantization (Reisizadeh *et al.* 2020; Basu *et al.* 2019; Wang *et al.* 2018). For all these applications, the conclusions drawn for client samplings satisfying the assumptions of Theorem 1 still hold.

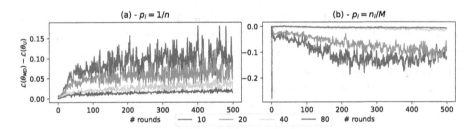

Fig. 1. Difference between the convergence of the global losses resulting from MD and Uniform sampling when considering $n \in \{10, 20, 40, 80\}$ clients and sampling $m = n/2$ of them. In (a), clients have identical importance, i.e. $p_i = 1/n$. In (b), clients importance is proportional to their amount of data, i.e. $p_i = n_i/M$. Differences in global losses are averaged across 30 FL experiments with different model initialization (global losses are provided in Fig. 2).

3.2   Application to Current Client Sampling Schemes

MD Sampling. When using Table 1 to compute Σ and γ close-form we obtain:

$$\Sigma_{MD} = \frac{1}{m}\left[1 - \sum_{i=1}^{n} p_i^2\right] \text{ and } \gamma_{MD} = \frac{1}{m}, \qquad (10)$$

where we notice that $\Sigma_{MD} \leq \frac{1}{m} = \gamma_{MD}$. Therefore, one can obtain looser convergence guarantees than the ones of Theorem 1, independently from the amount of participating clients n and set of clients importance $\{p_i\}$, while being inversely proportional to the amount of sampled clients m. The resulting bound shows that FL with MD sampling converges to its optimum for any FL application.

Uniform Sampling. Contrarily to MD sampling, the stochastic aggregation weights of Uniform sampling do not sum to 1. As a result, we can provide FL scenarios diverging when coupled with Uniform sampling. Indeed, using Table 1 to compute Σ and γ close-form we obtain

$$\Sigma_U = \left[\frac{n}{m} - 1\right] \sum_{i=1}^{n} p_i^2, \tag{11}$$

and

$$\gamma_U = \left[1 + \frac{1}{n-1}\right] \left[\frac{n}{m} - 1\right] \sum_{i=1}^{n} p_i^2, \tag{12}$$

where we notice that $\gamma_U = \left[1 + \frac{1}{n-1}\right] \Sigma_U$. Considering that $\sum_{i=1}^{n} p_i^2 \leq 1$, we have $\Sigma_U \leq \frac{n}{m} - 1$, which goes to infinity for large cohorts of clients and thus prevents FL with Uniform sampling to converge to its optimum. Indeed, the condition $\sum_{i=1}^{n} p_i^2 \leq 1$ accounts for every possible scenario of client importance $\{p_i\}$, including the very heterogeneous ones. In the special case where $p_i = 1/n$, we have $\sum_{i=1}^{n} p_i^2 = 1/n$, such that Σ_U is inversely proportional to both n and m. Such FL applications converge to the optimum of Eq. (1) for any configuration of n, $\{p_i\}$ and m.

Moreover, the comparison between the quantities Σ and γ for MD and Uniform sampling shows that Uniform sampling outperforms MD sampling when $p_i = 1/n$. More generally, Corollary 1 provides sufficient conditions with Theorem 1 for Uniform sampling to have better convergence guarantees than MD sampling (proof in (Fraboni et al. 2021b, Appendix C)).

Corollary 1. *Uniform sampling has better convergence guarantees than MD sampling when $\Sigma_U \leq \Sigma_{MD}$, and $\gamma_U \leq \gamma_{MD}$ which is equivalent to*

$$\sum_{i=1}^{n} p_i^2 \leq \frac{1}{n - m + 1}. \tag{13}$$

Corollary 1 can be related to $\text{Var}\left[\sum_{i=1}^{n} \omega_i(S_t)\right]$, the variance for the sum of the aggregation weights, which is always null for MD sampling, and different of 0 for Uniform sampling except when $p_i = 1/n$ for all the clients.

A last point of interest for the comparison between MD and Uniform sampling concerns the respective time complexity for selecting clients. Sampling with a Multinomial Distribution has time complexity $\mathcal{O}(n + m \log(n))$, where $\mathcal{O}(n)$ comes from building the probability density function to sample clients indices (Tang 2019). This makes MD sampling difficult to compute or even intractable for large cohorts of clients. On the contrary sampling m elements without replacement from n states is a reservoir sampling problem and takes time complexity $\mathcal{O}(m(1 + \log(n/m)))$ (Li 1994). In practice, clients either receive identical importance ($p_i = 1/n$) or an importance proportional to their data ratio, for which we may assume computation $p_i = \mathcal{O}(1/n)$. As a result, for important amount n of participating clients, Uniform sampling should be used as the default client sampling due to its lower time complexity. However, for small amount of clients and heterogeneous client importance, MD sampling should be used by default.

Due to space constraints, we only consider in this manuscript applying Theorem 1 to Uniform and MD sampling, which can also be applied to Binomial and Poisson Binomial sampling (Fraboni *et al.* 2021b, Appendix A), and satisfying our covariance assumption. To the best of our knowledge, we could only find *Clustered sampling* introduced in Fraboni *et al.* (2021a) not satisfying this assumption. Still, with minor changes, we provide for this sampling scheme a similar bound to the one of Theorem 1 (Fraboni *et al.* 2021b, Appendix C), ultimately proving that clustered sampling improves MD sampling.

4 Experiments on Real Data

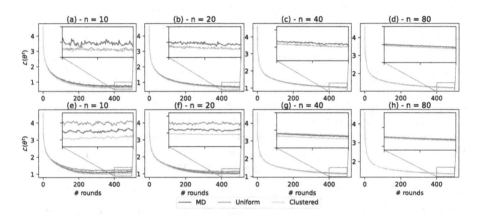

Fig. 2. Convergence of the global losses for MD, Uniform, and Clustered sampling when considering $n \in \{10, 20, 40, 80\}$ clients and sampling $m = n/2$ of them. In (a-d), clients have identical importance, i.e. $p_i = 1/n$. In (e-h), clients importance is proportional to their amount of data, i.e. $p_i = n_i/M$. Zoom of the global losses over the last 100 server aggregations and a variation of 0.5 in the global loss.

In this section, we provide an experimental demonstration of the convergence properties identified in Theorem 1. We study a LSTM model for next character prediction on the dataset of *The complete Works of William Shakespeare* (McMahan *et al.* 2017; Caldas *et al.* 2018). We use a two-layer LSTM classifier containing 100 hidden units with an 8 dimensional embedding layer. The model takes as an input a sequence of 80 characters, embeds each of the characters into a learned 8-dimensional space and outputs one character per training sample after 2 LSTM layers and a fully connected one.

When selected, a client performs $K = 50$ SGD steps on batches of size $B = 64$ with local learning rate $\eta_l = 1.5$. The server considers the clients local work with

$\eta_g = 1$. We consider $n \in \{10, 20, 40, 80\}$ clients, and sample half of them at each FL optimization step. While for sake of interpretability we do not apply a decay to local and global learning rates, we note that our theory remains unchanged even in presence of a learning rate decay. In practice, for dataset with important heterogeneity, considering $\eta_g < 1$ can speed-up FL with a more stable convergence.

We compare the impact of MD, Uniform, and Clustered sampling, on the convergence speed of FEDAVG. With Clustered sampling, the server selects m clients from m different clusters of clients created based on the clients importance (Fraboni *et al.* 2021a, Algorithm 1). MD sampling is a special case of Clustered sampling, where every cluster is identical.

Clients Have Identical Importance $[p_i = 1/n]$**.** We note that Uniform sampling consistently outperforms MD sampling due to the lower covariance parameter, while the improvement between the resulting convergence speed is inversely proportional to the number of participating clients n (Fig. 1a and Fig. 2a–d). This result confirms the derivations of Sect. 3. Also, with Clustered sampling and identical client importance, every client only belongs to one cluster. Hence, Clustered sampling reduces to Uniform sampling and we retrieve identical convergence for both samplings (Fig. 2a–d). This point was not raised in Fraboni *et al.* (2021a).

Clients Importance Depends on the Respective Data Ratio $[p_i = n_i/M]$**.** In this experimental scenario the aggregation weights for Uniform sampling do not always sum to 1, thus leading to the slow-down of FL convergence. Hence, we see in Fig. 1b that MD always outperforms Uniform sampling. This experiment shows that the impact on FL convergence of the variance of the sum of the stochastic aggregation weights is more relevant than the one due to the covariance parameter α. We also retrieve in Fig. 2e–h that Clustered sampling always outperform MD sampling, which confirms that for two client samplings with a null variance of the sum of the stochastic aggregation weights, the one with the lowest covariance parameter α converges faster. We also note that the slow-down induced by the variance is reduced when more clients do participate. This is explained by the fact that the standard deviation of the clients data ratio is reduced with larger clients participation, e.g. $p_i = 1/10 \pm 0.13$ for $n = 10$ and $p_i = 1/80 \pm 0.017$ for $n = 80$. We thus conclude that the difference between the effects of MD, Uniform, and Clustered sampling is mitigated with a large number of participating clients (Fig. 1b and Fig. 2e–h).

Additional experiments on Shakespeare are provided in (Fraboni *et al.* 2021b, Appendix E). We show the influence of the amount of sampled clients m and amount of local work K on the convergence speed of MD and Uniform sampling.

Finally, additional experiments on CIFAR10 (Krizhevsky 2009) are provided in (Fraboni *et al.* 2021b, Appendix E), where we replicate the experimental scenario previously proposed in Fraboni *et al.* (2021a). In these applications, 100 clients are partitioned using a Dirichlet distribution which provides federated scenarios with different level of heterogeneity. For all the experimental scenarios considered, both results and conclusions are in agreement with those here derived for the Shakespeare dataset.

5   Conclusion

In this work, we highlight the asymptotic impact of client sampling on FL with Theorem 1, and shows that the convergence speed is inversely proportional to both the sum of the variance of the stochastic aggregation weights, and to their covariance parameter α. Moreover, to the best of our knowledge, this work is the first one accounting for schemes where the sum of the weights is different from 1.

Thanks to our theory, we investigated MD and Uniform sampling from both theoretical and experimental standpoints. We established that when clients have approximately identical importance, i.e. $p_i = 1/n$, Uniform outperforms MD sampling, due to the larger impact of the covariance term for the latter scheme. On the contrary, Uniform sampling is outperformed by MD sampling in more general cases, due to the slowdown induced by its stochastic aggregation weights not always summing to 1. Yet, in practical scenario with very large number of clients, MD sampling may be unpractical, and Uniform sampling could be preferred due to the more advantageous time complexity.

In this work, we also showed that our theory encompasses advanced FL sampling schemes, such as the one recently proposed in Fraboni *et al.* (2021a), and Chen *et al.* (2020). Finally, while the contribution of this work is in the study of the impact of a client sampling on the global optimization objective, further extensions may focus on the analysis of the impact of clients selection method on individual users' performance, especially in presence of heterogeneity.

Acknowledgements. This work has been supported by the French government, through the 3IA Côte d'Azur Investments in the Future project managed by the National Research Agency (ANR) with the reference number ANR-19-P3IA-0002, and by the ANR JCJC project Fed-BioMed 19-CE45-0006-01. The project was also supported by Accenture. The authors are grateful to the OPAL infrastructure from Université Côte d'Azur for providing resources and support.

References

Acar, D.A.E., Zhao, Y., Matas, R., Mattina, M., Whatmough, P., Saligrama, V.: Federated learning based on dynamic regularization. In: International Conference on Learning Representations (2021)

Basu, D., Data, D., Karakus, C., Diggavi, S.: Qsparse-local-SGD: distributed SGD with quantization, sparsification and local computations. In: Wallach, H., Larochelle, H., Beygelzimer, A., d'Alché-Buc, F., Fox, E., Garnett, R. (eds.) Advances in Neural Information Processing Systems, vol. 32. Curran Associates Inc. (2019)

Caldas, S., et al.: LEAF: a benchmark for federated settings. In: NeurIPS, pp. 1–9 (2018)

Chen, W., Horvath, S., Richtarik, P.: Optimal client sampling for federated learning. In: Workshop in NeurIPS: Privacy Preserving Machine Learning (2020)

Cho, Y.J., Wang, J., Joshi, G.: Client selection in federated learning: convergence analysis and power-of-choice selection strategies (2020)

Csiba, D., Richtárik, P.: Importance sampling for minibatches. J. Mach. Learn. Res. **19**(27), 1–21 (2018)

Fraboni, Y., Vidal, R., Kameni, L., Lorenzi, M.: Clustered sampling: low-variance and improved representativity for clients selection in federated learning. In: Meila, M., Zhang, T. (eds.) Proceedings of the 38th International Conference on Machine Learning. Proceedings of Machine Learning Research, vol. 139, pp. 3407–3416. PMLR (2021a)

Fraboni, Y., Vidal, R., Kameni, L., Lorenzi, M.: On the impact of client sampling on federated learning convergence. CoRR, abs/2107.12211 (2021b)

Haddadpour, F., Mahdavi, M.: On the convergence of local descent methods in federated learning (2019)

Jeon, J., Park, S., Choi, M., Kim, J., Kwon, Y.-B., Cho, S.: Optimal user selection for high-performance and stabilized energy-efficient federated learning platforms. Electronics **9**(9) (2020)

Karimireddy, S.P., Kale, S., Mohri, M., Reddi, S., Stich, S., Suresh, A.T.: SCAFFOLD: stochastic controlled averaging for federated learning. In: Daumé, H., III., Singh, A. (eds.) Proceedings of the 37th International Conference on Machine Learning. Proceedings of Machine Learning Research, vol. 119, pp. 5132–5143. PMLR (2020)

Khaled, A., Mishchenko, K., Richtarik, P.: Tighter theory for local SGD on identical and heterogeneous data. In: Chiappa, S., Calandra, R. (eds.) Proceedings of the Twenty Third International Conference on Artificial Intelligence and Statistics. Proceedings of Machine Learning Research, vol. 108, pp. 4519–4529. PMLR (2020)

Kingma, D.P., Ba, J.: Adam: a method for stochastic optimization. In: ICLR (Poster) (2015)

Krizhevsky, A.: Learning multiple layers of features from tiny images (2009)

Li, X., Orabona, F.: On the convergence of stochastic gradient descent with adaptive stepsizes. In: Chaudhuri, K., Sugiyama, M. (eds.) Proceedings of the Twenty-Second International Conference on Artificial Intelligence and Statistics. Proceedings of Machine Learning Research, vol. 89, pp. 983–992. PMLR (2019)

Li, T., Sahu, A.K., Zaheer, M., Sanjabi, M., Talwalkar, A., Smithy, V.: FedDANE: a federated newton-type method. In: 2019 53rd Asilomar Conference on Signals, Systems, and Computers, pp. 1227–1231 (2019)

Li, T., Sahu, A.K., Zaheer, M., Sanjabi, M., Talwalkar, A., Smith, V.: Federated optimization in heterogeneous networks. In: Dhillon, I., Papailiopoulos, D., Sze, V. (eds.) Proceedings of Machine Learning and Systems, vol. 2, pp. 429–450 (2020a)

Li, T., Sanjabi, M., Beirami, A., Smith, V.: Fair resource allocation in federated learning. In: International Conference on Learning Representations (2020b)

Li, X., Huang, K., Yang, W., Wang, S., Zhang, Z.: On the convergence of FedAvg on non-IID data. In: International Conference on Learning Representations (2020c)

Li, K.-H.: Reservoir-sampling algorithms of time complexity o(n(1 + log(n/n))). ACM Trans. Math. Softw. **20**(4), 481–493 (1994)

McMahan, B., Moore, E., Ramage, D., Hampson, S., Arcas, B.A.: Communication-efficient learning of deep networks from decentralized data. In: Singh, A., Zhu, J. (eds.) Proceedings of the 20th International Conference on Artificial Intelligence and Statistics. Proceedings of Machine Learning Research, vol. 54, pp. 1273–1282. PMLR (2017)

Nishio, T., Yonetani, R.: Client selection for federated learning with heterogeneous resources in mobile edge. In: 2019 IEEE International Conference on Communications (ICC), ICC 2019, pp. 1–7 (2019)

Reddi, S.J., et al.: Adaptive federated optimization. In: International Conference on Learning Representations (2021)

Reisizadeh, A., Mokhtari, A., Hassani, H., Jadbabaie, A., Pedarsani, R.: FedPAQ: a communication-efficient federated learning method with periodic averaging and quantization. In: Chiappa, S., Calandra, R. (eds.) Proceedings of the Twenty Third International Conference on Artificial Intelligence and Statistics. Proceedings of Machine Learning Research, vol. 108, pp. 2021–2031. PMLR (2020)

Rizk, E., Vlaski, S., Sayed, A.H.: Dynamic federated learning. In: 2020 IEEE 21st International Workshop on Signal Processing Advances in Wireless Communications (SPAWC), pp. 1–5 (2020)

Tang, D.: Efficient algorithms for modifying and sampling from a categorical distribution. CoRR, abs/1906.11700 (2019)

Wang, J., Joshi, G.: Cooperative SGD: a unified framework for the design and analysis of communication-efficient SGD algorithms (2018)

Wang, H., Sievert, S., Liu, S., Charles, Z., Papailiopoulos, D., Wright, S.: Atomo: communication-efficient learning via atomic sparsification. In: Bengio, S., Wallach, H., Larochelle, H., Grauman, K., Cesa-Bianchi, N., Garnett, R. (eds.) Advances in Neural Information Processing Systems, vol. 31. Curran Associates Inc. (2018)

Wang, J., Sahu, A.K., Yang, Z., Joshi, G., Kar, S.: MATCHA: speeding up decentralized SGD via matching decomposition sampling. In: 2019 Sixth Indian Control Conference (ICC), pp. 299–300 (2019a)

Wang, S., et al.: Adaptive federated learning in resource constrained edge computing systems. IEEE J. Sel. Areas Commun. 37(6), 1205–1221 (2019b)

Wang, J., Liu, Q., Liang, H., Joshi, G., Vincent Poor, H.: Tackling the objective inconsistency problem in heterogeneous federated optimization. In: Larochelle, H., Ranzato, M., Hadsell, R., Balcan, M.-F., Lin, H.-T. (eds.) Advances in Neural Information Processing Systems 33: Annual Conference on Neural Information Processing Systems 2020, NeurIPS 2020, 6–12 December 2020, Virtual (2020a)

Wang, J., Tantia, V., Ballas, N., Rabbat, M.: SlowMo: improving communication-efficient distributed SGD with slow momentum. In: International Conference on Learning Representations (2020b)

Ward, R., Wu, X., Bottou, L.: AdaGrad stepsizes: sharp convergence over nonconvex landscapes. In: Chaudhuri, K., Salakhutdinov, R. (eds.) Proceedings of the 36th International Conference on Machine Learning. Proceedings of Machine Learning Research, vol. 97, pp. 6677–6686. PMLR (2019)

Zhao, P., Zhang, T.: Stochastic optimization with importance sampling for regularized loss minimization. In: Bach, F., Blei, D. (eds.) Proceedings of the 32nd International Conference on Machine Learning. Proceedings of Machine Learning Research, Lille, France, 07–09 July 2015, vol. 37, pp. 1–9. PMLR (2015)

Decentralized Adaptive Clustering of Deep Nets is Beneficial for Client Collaboration

Edvin Listo Zec[1,2(✉)], Ebba Ekblom[1], Martin Willbo[1], Olof Mogren[1], and Sarunas Girdzijauskas[1,2]

[1] RISE Research Institutes of Sweden, Gothenburg, Sweden
edvin.listo.zec@ri.se
[2] KTH Royal Institute of Technology, Gothenburg, Sweden

Abstract. We study the problem of training personalized deep learning models in a decentralized peer-to-peer setting, focusing on the setting where data distributions differ between the clients and where different clients have different local learning tasks. We study both covariate and label shift, and our contribution is an algorithm which for each client finds beneficial collaborations based on a similarity estimate for the local task. Our method does not rely on hyperparameters which are hard to estimate, such as the number of client clusters, but rather continuously adapts to the network topology using soft cluster assignment based on a novel adaptive gossip algorithm. We test the proposed method in various settings where data is not independent and identically distributed among the clients. The experimental evaluation shows that the proposed method performs better than previous state-of-the-art algorithms for this problem setting, and handles situations well where previous methods fail.

Keywords: decentralized learning · federated learning · deep learning

1 Introduction

The study of machine learning on decentralized data has been of interest for a long time and has received much attention in the last decades. With the spread of smartphones and other mobile devices, an immense increase of data collected has highlighted the need for responsible mining. Modern mobile devices are equipped with sensors that can collect a multitude of data streams related to people's everyday lives, providing a promising source of training data for smart services. However, such data requires special care not only due to increasing privacy concerns among users but also due to regulatory privacy laws. Decentralized machine learning is relevant in many related research communities, such as data mining and telecommunication. The overarching goal is to efficiently learn from and analyze data distributed among several clients, without the data leaving the clients. The aforementioned developments have given rise to a need for algorithms that can efficiently leverage large volumes of data residing on the collecting devices without compromising privacy.

Distributed data collection unlocks the potential of data that would otherwise be difficult or impossible to obtain, but may also lead to heterogeneity between the different

© The Author(s), under exclusive license to Springer Nature Switzerland AG 2023
R. Goebel et al. (Eds.): FL 2022, LNAI 13448, pp. 59–71, 2023.
https://doi.org/10.1007/978-3-031-28996-5_5

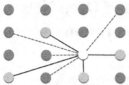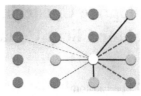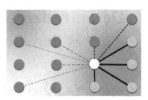

(a) Communication round zero. The client has a uniform probability distribution over all other clients in the network. At this point in time the communication strategy is equivalent to random communication.

(b) After a couple of communication rounds the client's probability distribution over all other clients has been updated based on the similarity measure. A client topology is taking form.

(c) The client's probability distribution over all other clients has converged. The communication strategy is now similar to an oracle sampling only within the cluster identity of the client.

Fig. 1. Visualization of three consecutive points in time (communication rounds) for DAC. The client in focus (white) selects other clients (green) to communicate with, indicated by solid edges. The probability to do so is indicated by edge thickness. Note that there is a non-zero probability assigned to all other clients in the network, indicated by dashed lines, again with thickness proportional to the probability. For visual clarity only some of these have been explicitly drawn out. The background color indicates the convergence to a network topology from the perspective of client similarity, see Eq. (2). (Color figure online)

datasets. Different clients often have different types of biases and their data may not always be independently and identically distributed (iid). This results in differing client data distributions (the non-iid data paradigm), which hinders efficient training of deep learning models [5].

In *decentralized learning*, no central server exists and the clients communicate through a peer-to-peer network. The central server in a centralized setup such as federated learning [8] is a potential point of weakness: it could fail or be maliciously attacked, leading to failure for the distributed learning. A decentralized system is inherently robust to this. In such a framework, the clients follow a communication protocol in order to leverage each other's data privately. A commonly used protocol is the gossip framework [6], where clients communicate and aggregate their models randomly. Gossip based learning between clients works well for the emergence of a single (global) model at each participating node. However, in a non-iid setting, such convergence to a one-size-fits-all solution might be sub-optimal, and even detrimental for some clients.

How to train a deep learning model in a non-iid data setting is an active area of research in the federated learning literature. However, this is a relatively understudied problem in the decentralized setting [5]. In this work, we propose a solution to the decentralized distributed learning problem where each client adaptively detects which peers to collaborate with during every communication round. The solution is based on a similarity score defined as the inverse of the training loss of one client's model on another client's data. This promotes initiating collaborations which are the most beneficial to the learning of each client. We name this solution *Decentralized adaptive clustering (DAC)* and demonstrate with a thorough experimental investigation that DAC effectively identifies clusters in the network topology and thus achieves strong results in all settings examined. In some experiments, we even outperform the oracle solution which is given complete and perfect information about which peers have the same data distribution.

2   Related Work

Learning personalized models when data is heterogeneously distributed over the clients is a problem setting studied in both federated learning and decentralized learning.

Gossip learning is a peer-to-peer communication protocol which has been studied in many different machine learning settings [2,6,10]. Most work on Gossip learning has focused on convex optimization rather than the non-convex optimization associated with training deep neural networks. The first decentralized work on gossip-based optimization for non-convex deep learning studied convolutional neural networks (CNNs) [1]. The authors showed experimentally that high accuracies with low communication costs are achievable with a decentralized and asynchronous framework. Gossip learning however is not suitable for non-iid settings where several distinct learning objectives may be present as the protocol does not take into consideration which peers may be beneficial for communication during training.

In previous work on federated learning, [4] showed that having several global models in a federated setup improves performance over a single global model when client data is not identically distributed. The goal was to have clients with similar learning objectives assigned to their own cluster, then aggregate parameters internally and create one global model for each cluster. The algorithm thus alternates between client cluster assignment and loss minimization. Cluster identity is estimated by empirical loss given current global models evaluated on client data. However, a drawback of this method is that it relies on hyperparameters such as the number of clusters (i.e. the number of global models to learn). Additionally, the experiments are limited to hard cluster assignment, and cannot handle soft clustering. Further, the client data heterogeneity is limited to covariate-shift.

In previous work on decentralized learning, [9] developed an algorithm based on training loss which identifies similar clients. While their experimental results are strong, they also limit themselves to uniform cluster sizes and only study covariate-shift. Further, their method is based on two steps: 1) a cluster identification step, and 2) random communication within the identified clusters. The approach requires a hyperparameter search for the length of the search for similar clients, and the hard cluster assignment has no way of handling varying degrees of similarity between local training datasets. It is also not obvious that the optimal strategy is to only communicate within your own cluster - especially if you belong to a cluster with few members. In this work, we also explore the robustness of different algorithms in such cases.

The approach proposed in this work is a decentralized learning algorithm that continuously adapts the client communication topology every communication round based on a client similarity metric. Compared to previous work on clustered federated learning this approach does not rely on specifying the number of clusters a priori. Similarly, our method eliminates the need for a cluster identification step as used in [9]. We show that a soft cluster assignment based on a client similarity measure instead of just finding and communicating with clients with the same learning objective makes it possible to beat an all-knowing oracle which only communicates within pre-defined clusters. This is especially the case in situations where clusters consist of only a few clients.

3 Method

We assume a decentralized learning setting with K clients which are able to communicate in a communication network for T number of rounds. Each client i has a *private* training data distribution $\mathcal{D}_i(x, y)$ over input features x and labels y. Each client also has a deep neural network f_i with model parameters $w_i \in \mathbb{R}^d$. Let $\ell(f_i(w_i; x), y) : \mathbb{R}^d \to \mathbb{R}$ be the loss as a function of the model parameters w_i and data (x, y) for client i. The principal problem of this work is then to define a decentralized learning algorithm which leverages the client's own data and models of other clients over the T communication rounds in such a way that the resulting w_i are a solution to the optimization problem described in (1) below, which corresponds to each client i learning its local task:

$$\min_{w_i \in \mathbb{R}^d} \mathcal{L}(f_i(w_i)) := \min_{w_i \in \mathbb{R}^d} \mathbb{E}_{x_i \sim \mathcal{D}_i}[\ell(f(x_i; w_i); y_i)], \tag{1}$$

for all $i = 1, \dots, K$. We tackle the problem using empirical risk minimization (ERM) [11], as commonly done in statistical learning setups, and in particular, we study vision classifications tasks in this work. Meanwhile, our proposed framework is general enough to tackle any problem that fits into ERM as long as a loss function is defined.

3.1 Non-IID Data

In this work, we study the problem when data is non-iid between the clients, specifically in the context of *covariate-shift* and *prior probability shift*. The client datasets are assumed to be private and cannot be shared, instead, the clients are allowed to communicate model parameters. In our experiments we define label shift to mean different label skews for the client data distributions, whereas covariate shift is defined as different degrees of rotation of the input images. For K clients we define $N \le K$ different data distributions $D^n(x, y)$, and divide the clients into N groups defined by the N distributions. Note that when $N = K$ each group is made up of a single client, resulting in all clients having different distributions of data. On the contrary, a group can also contain multiple clients and we will refer to this as a cluster. Furthermore, inter-cluster data similarity may not be uniform and some pairs of clusters may have a higher similarity than others. The client data distributions $\mathcal{D}_i^n$ are however assumed to be *unknown for all clients* i, and each client can only see its own local data.

Despite keeping the data private, training can be enhanced by allowing communication between the clients in the network. The training procedure, therefore, consists of each client i training on the local data for E local epochs and then communicating the trained model to other clients in the network. The receiving client merges its model with the received models using federated averaging and then starts a new training round of E local epochs. In this work, we propose *Decentralized Adaptive Clustering (DAC)* and show how this approach can find beneficial collaborations between clients in the network to better solve the local learning task.

3.2 DAC: Decentralized Adaptive Clustering

The intuition behind DAC is that it is beneficial for clients with similar local data distributions to communicate more frequently. For each client i, we use a similarity measure to compute a vector of probabilities, which is used each communication round in a weighted sampling to determine which clients $j \neq i$ to collaborate with. We use training loss as a proxy for similarity, as was previously done in [4] and [9]. This similarity score is updated as the training progresses, see Fig. 1 for a visualization of the algorithm. Throughout the training, we also store a history of sampled clients up until the current communication round t. This set is defined as $\bar{M}_i^t = \cup_{t'=0}^t M_i^{t'}$, where M_i^t is the set of sampled clients for client i at communication round t.

For each communication round t, the following steps are performed for all clients $i \in 1, ...K$.

1. Sample $m \leq K$ clients $M_i^t = \{c_1, c_2, \ldots, c_m\}$ without replacement with probability $p_i^t = [p_{i1}^t, p_{i2}^t, \ldots, p_{iK}^t]$, where p_{ik}^t is the similarity-based probability between clients i and k at time t. At $t = 0$, the sampling probability is uniform, i.e. $p_{ij}^0 = \frac{1}{K}$ for all i, j.

2. Update $p_{ik} \ \forall k \in M_i^t$. This is done by computing a similarity score between client i and k. The model of client i is sent to client k, where the loss is computed training data of client k. We define the similarity between client i and k at round t as the inverse of the training loss:

$$s_{ik}^t = \frac{1}{\ell(w_i^t; z_k)}, \tag{2}$$

   with $s_i = [s_{i1}, s_{i2}, \ldots, s_{iK}]$. This vector is transformed into a probability vector for all k using a softmax function

$$p_i(s_i) = \frac{e^{\tau s_i}}{\sum_{k=1}^K e^{\tau s_{ik}}}. \tag{3}$$

3. In large peer-to-peer networks, it is unlikely that clients will sample all other clients in finite time. Thus, there are likely some clients that never get to calculate similarities between each other. For this reason, we define an approximated similarity score $\hat{s}_{ij}^t$ for clients j that have not been sampled by i, but that have been sampled by clients that i has sampled. In other words, we use two-hop neighbors from i to estimate the approximation similarity, and it is defined as $\hat{s}_{ij}^t = s_{k*j}^t$, where k^* is the client in $\bar{M}_i^t$ that is most similar to client i and that has communicated with j. Formally, $k^* = \arg\min_k s_i^t$ for all k that have communicated with i and j. This will make the estimation of similarities across the network more efficient as information will propagate much faster.

4. Merge the model of client i with the models of the sampled clients M_i^t using federated averaging.

5. Train the merged model locally for E local epochs. Repeat starting from step 1.

3.3   Variable DAC

The τ parameter in Eq. (3) of DAC regulates the relative differences between the sampling probabilities. A higher τ results in a larger difference between the large and small probabilities, and in the extreme when $\tau \to \infty$ it becomes an argmax function. It is not given that a fixed τ is optimal, and we therefore also perform experiments where we let τ grow during every communication round. We start close to a random algorithm in the beginning of training, and later on, converge to more exploitation when τ increases. We name this method *DAC-var*, and we increase τ every round using a sigmoid function starting at 1 when $t = 0$ and ending at a maximum value of τ_{max}.

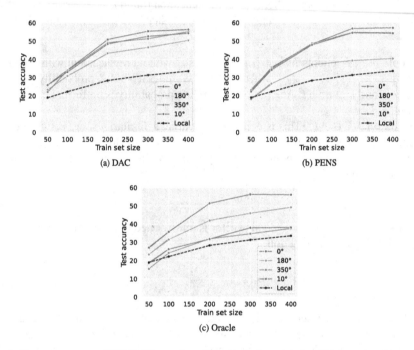

Fig. 2. Test accuracy on **CIFAR-10** as a function of train set size for different algorithms. The number of clients is fixed to 100, and the validation set is fixed to 100 samples.

4   Experimental Setup

We consider two main problems for decentralized learning: covariate shift and label shift. Similar to previous work, we assume that all clients can communicate with all other clients in the peer-to-peer network. For reasons of reproducibility, our code is made available on github.[1]

---

[1] https://github.com/edvinli/DAC.

Baselines. We compare our proposed method DAC to three baselines and an oracle. The baselines are random communication, PENS [9] and local training (without communication) on each client. The oracle has perfect cluster information and only communicates within the clusters.

Model. For all experiments presented in this section, we train and evaluate a 2-layer CNN with ReLU activations and max-pooling. This model is not state-of-the-art for the datasets used in our experiments, but it has sufficient capacity to solve the classification tasks in such a way that meaningful comparisons between the algorithms are possible. It is also suited for the limited amount of data available to each client in our experiments. We experiment on the CIFAR-10 [7] and Fashion-MNIST [12] datasets and we use cross-entropy as our loss function.

Evaluation. All models are evaluated on a test set drawn from the same distribution as the training set for each client in the network, that is the test set has the same (label or covariate) shift as the training set. This is since the goal is to solve the local learning task for each client as well as possible. We consider $K = 100$ clients, and unless otherwise stated we distribute the number of data points uniformly over the clients. For CIFAR-10, this means 400 training samples and 100 validation samples for each client. For Fashion-MNIST it means 500 training samples and 100 validation samples. We use early stopping locally on each client, and save the model that achieved the lowest validation loss which is later used to calculate a test accuracy after T communication rounds.

Hyperparameters. We use a fixed batch size of 8. The Adam optimizer is used locally on each client, and learning rates are locally tuned for each dataset. For the covariate shift experiments, this results in learning rates of $\eta = 3 \cdot 10^{-4}$ and $\eta = 1 \cdot 10^{-5}$ for all clients on CIFAR-10 and Fashion-MNIST respectively. For the label shift experiment, a learning rate of $\eta = 3 \cdot 10^{-5}$ is used. The number of local epochs is fixed to $E = 3$ for all experiments, and we run $T = 200$ communication rounds for the covariate shift experiments and $T = 600$ rounds for the label shift experiments. For PENS we use the first 10% rounds for the neighbour selection step and then use remaining 90% for cluster communication. For all algorithms each client samples and aggregates models from five clients in every communication round. For DAC, we set $\tau = 30$ and for DAC-var we set $\tau_{max} = 30$ for all experiments except where we analyze the effect of τ. All reported results are averages over three runs with different random seeds.

We simulate a decentralized peer-to-peer network in a computer, and all models are trained using either an NVIDIA GeForce RTX 3090 Ti or an NVIDIA Tesla V100 GPU.

5 Results on Covariate Shift

Here we summarize our findings on experiments on *covariate-shift* with $K = 100$ clients on both CIFAR-10 and Fashion-MNIST with equal number of data points per client. We create a setup where each client belongs to a cluster defined by rotating the input images r degrees and we consider two different settings: $r \in \{0°, 90°, 180°, 270°\}$ and $r \in \{0°, 180°, 10°, 350°\}$. In the first case, we have four well-separated clusters and we assign equally many (25) clients to each cluster. This setting was explored in [9]. In the other setting, we create three similar clusters and one that differs more from the rest ($r = 180°$). Here, we assign 70, 20, 5 and 5 clients to each cluster respectively, which also makes the problem heterogeneous with respect to the cluster sizes. This setting has not been investigated in previous works.

Local Baseline. All methods implemented in this work are also compared to local training (without any decentralized learning). For CIFAR-10, a local model trained on 400 training samples and 100 validation samples achieves on average a 33.57% test accuracy, and for Fashion-MNIST a model trained on 500 training samples with 100 validation samples achieves on average a test accuracy of 73.1%.

The results for the first setup of rotations $\{0°, 90°, 180°, 270°\}$ are summarized in Table 1, and we note that our proposed method outperforms all baselines except the oracle. In Table 2, we present the results for the second setting of heterogeneous cluster sizes for both CIFAR-10 and Fashion-MNIST. The oracle is not effective in this setup, since if we only communicate inside our own (hard) cluster we will not get any benefit from other clusters which might be similar to ourselves. This is shown in our results, where the oracle only achieves around 39–40% accuracy for the two small clusters. Further, we note that PENS is deteriorating in this setting, especially for the 180° cluster. This most likely is a result of the hard cluster assignment that PENS performs in its first neighbour selection step. This is further visualised in Fig. 2 which shows test accuracy as a function of training samples on each client for DAC, PENS and an oracle.

Observing Fig. 2c, we see that an oracle fails to perform for the two small clusters (10° and 350°) since there are not enough clients to communicate with to learn meaningful representations, even when the number of training samples reaches 400. Here, our proposed method beats all baselines and more importantly achieves high accuracy for cluster 1 ($r = 180°$). Further, as seen in Fig. 2, the performance of all algorithms increases faster than that of local training since they benefit from the decentralized training, while DAC sees the largest increase in test accuracy for all clusters.

Moreover, we note in Table 2 that the random baseline performs quite well in this setting, achieving a mean accuracy of 54.17% over all clusters. This result stems from the fact that the largest cluster $r = 0°$ is dominating with 70 clients in the peer-to-peer network. Also, since cluster $r = 0°$ is very similar to $r = 350°$ and $r = 10°$, the random baseline performs well also on these. However, we see that it under-performs with a test accuracy of 46.50% on the $r = 180°$ cluster, which is relatively different from the other clusters. Meanwhile, our proposed method achieves stable accuracies over all clusters and most notably achieves a high accuracy of 49.63% for the 180° cluster. Observing the results for Fashion-MNIST, the same conclusions can be drawn, but we observe an even larger difference between our proposed method and the baselines for the $r = 180°$ cluster.

Ablation. An ablation experiment was performed on CIFAR-10, where we investigated the effect of the approximation similarities $\hat{s}_{ij}$ on test accuracy. This is presented as DAC - $\hat{s}_{ij}$ in Table 2, and we note that we get a higher standard deviation between the clusters without them due to lower achieved accuracy in the 180° cluster. This is most likely due to the algorithm having a hard time identifying the clusters since it only calculates the similarity between clients that communicate with each other. We thus conclude that the approximation similarity helps in cluster identification and strengthens the performance of the algorithm.

Effect of τ. Experiments were also carried out to investigate how τ in Eq. (3) affects the performance of DAC. For this, we ran DAC on the 0-180-10-350 cluster setup while varying τ. The results are summarized in Fig. 3. We note that for all values of τ, the similar clusters are robust with respect to test accuracy. Meanwhile, for small values of τ, the 'different' cluster of $r = 180°$ achieves a relatively poor test accuracy (around 44 to 46%), similar to that of the random baseline. This is expected, as low τ means that the differences between the similarity scores between clusters are small. However, as τ increases, the differences become larger and DAC is able to distinguish between clusters more efficiently which results in higher accuracy for the 180° cluster. Moreover, we note that we do not see a decrease in performance for large values of τ for any cluster.

Table 1. Test accuracies for covariate shift on **CIFAR-10**. 25 clients in each cluster. The last column presents means over the clusters. Best mean score in bold.

Method	0°	90°	180°	270°	Mean
DAC	**50.27**	**49.47**	**51.36**	**47.79**	**49.72**
Random	43.49	43.58	43.73	44.32	43.77
PENS	48.30	49.30	47.69	47.52	48.20
Oracle	52.19	52.72	50.32	52.02	51.81

Table 2. Test accuracies for covariate shift on CIFAR-10 and Fashion-MNIST. 70, 20, 5 and 5 clients in each cluster, respectively. Last two columns present means and standard deviations over the clusters. Best mean score in bold.

	CIFAR-10					
Method	0°	180°	350°	10°	Mean	Std
DAC	56.34	49.51	55.04	54.67	53.89	2.33
DAC-var	**57.23**	**49.63**	**55.57**	**54.68**	**54.28**	2.54
DAC - $\hat{s}_{ij}$	57.12	46.45	53.77	55.92	53.31	4.14
Random	58.20	46.50	55.93	56.07	54.12	4.52
PENS	57.18	40.56	54.71	55.60	52.01	5.97
Oracle	58.37	49.99	39.28	39.67	46.79	7.92
	Fashion-MNIST					
DAC	**75.08**	**74.95**	**73.03**	**74.33**	**74.35**	0.81
DAC-var	74.48	74.06	72.58	73.45	73.64	0.71
Random	73.14	54.41	71.02	72.52	67.77	7.75
PENS	74.62	42.03	73.11	73.86	65.91	13.79
Oracle	75.78	76.39	77.99	77.77	76.98	0.92

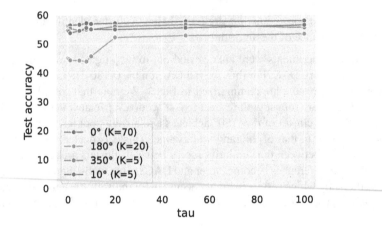

Fig. 3. Test accuracy of DAC on rotated CIFAR-10 as a function of τ. The random seed was fixed to the same value for all experiments.

6   Results on Label Shift

In this section, we present the results for experiments on label shift. This has not been studied in any of the previous works, although [9] hypothesize that PENS also should work in this setting. We study CIFAR-10, and create two different clusters using the labels: one cluster based on the animal classes (bird, cat, deer, dog, frog and horse) and one cluster based on the vehicle classes (airplane, automobile, ship and truck). We consider 100 clients, 60 in the animal cluster and 40 in the vehicle cluster. We thus have both heterogeneities in terms of cluster sizes, but also a larger distributional difference between the clusters as compared to the rotated covariate shift experiments.

The results are summarized in Table 3. We start by noting that the vehicles cluster is an easier task than the animals cluster since the oracle achieves a higher test accuracy on the vehicles cluster (56.93% vs 41.15%). We observe that both DAC and DAC-var outperform the random baseline and PENS on average, and in particular perform well on the vehicles cluster. PENS manages to perform relatively well on the animals cluster, but fails at the vehicles cluster - even performing worse than the random baseline and local training. We hypothesize that this is due to a noisy cluster assignment from the PENS neighbour identification step. Since DAC does not have any hard cluster assignments, it has the possibility to communicate with any client in the network, as opposed to PENS. This is visualised in Fig. 4, which presents a heatmap over communications between clients for different algorithms (the number of times client x communicates with client y). The x and y axes represent client ID:s, which are sorted with the first 40 belonging to the vehicles cluster and the last 60 to the animals cluster. We observe that DAC manages to identify clusters well, whereas PENS is much noisier.

Moreover, we see that there are horizontal artefacts for DAC in Fig. 4a. This is most likely due to the sampling getting stuck in exploiting a few clients with a high probability. Meanwhile, this is avoided for DAC-var as seen in Fig. 4b, which has a more smooth transition going from exploration in early phases to exploitation in late phases

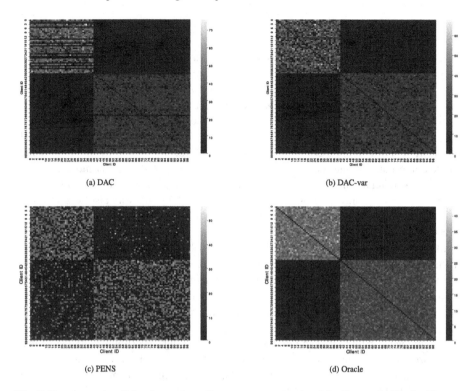

(a) DAC

(b) DAC-var

(c) PENS

(d) Oracle

Fig. 4. Heatmaps visualising how often client x communicates with client y during the T communication rounds for the label shift experiment on **CIFAR-10**. The x and y axes represent client IDs, which are sorted (0–39: vehicles, 40–99: animals).

Table 3. Test accuracies for label shift on **CIFAR-10**. 60 clients in 'animal' cluster, and 40 clients in 'vehicle' cluster. Best mean score in bold.

Method	Vehicles	Animals	Mean
DAC-var	**71.13**	**37.46**	**54.29**
DAC	70.92	37.14	54.03
Random	54.91	40.35	47.63
PENS	49.11	36.49	42.80
Local	51.10	35.11	43.11
Oracle	73.64	47.49	60.56

of the communication rounds. It is interesting to note that despite this, the difference in performance between DAC and DAC-var is very small.

7 Conclusions

Decentralized learning is a paradigm shift in modern deep learning, as data is increasingly becoming more distributed in the world due to data collection methods and privacy concerns. We present a novel algorithm named *Decentralized adaptive clustering (DAC)* for learning personalized deep nets on distributed non-iid data. Our method efficiently finds how clients in a peer-to-peer network should collaborate to solve their own local learning tasks. By sampling using a similarity metric, DAC identifies beneficial *soft* clusters and leverages clients that have similar learning tasks, while at the same time keeping data private. Our experimental results show that DAC is more efficient in finding beneficial communication patterns than previous works, as it is not limited to hard cluster assignments. Furthermore, our results show that this also leads to better performance in terms of test accuracy on image classification tasks experiencing covariate and label shift.

In this work, we have assumed that data cannot be shared due to privacy reasons. At the same time, we assume that model parameters (or equivalently, gradients) can be communicated. Previous works have shown that information about the training data can be reconstructed using gradients [3]. We leave this as an interesting open question to study in our framework for future work, which is compatible with methods such as differential privacy.

Finally, we conclude that in our decentralized learning experiments label shift is a much harder problem than covariate shift. We hypothesize that this is due to aggregating models trained on widely different data distributions, which is detrimental to federated averaging. The clients thus experience so-called *client drift* where the model parameters drift far away from each other in parameter space. This is further enhanced by the fact that all clients in our experiments start with differently initialized models. This aligns well with conclusions from previous works which have shown that the same initial parameters are important for federated averaging [8]. Although our proposed method DAC manages to solve the problem better than both the random and local baselines, we see the problem of how to efficiently aggregate models as an interesting research question going forward.

References

1. Blot, M., Picard, D., Cord, M., Thome, N.: Gossip training for deep learning (2016). https://doi.org/10.48550/ARXIV.1611.09726, https://arxiv.org/abs/1611.09726
2. Boyd, S., Ghosh, A., Prabhakar, B., Shah, D.: Randomized gossip algorithms. IEEE Trans. Inf. Theory **52**(6), 2508–2530 (2006). https://doi.org/10.1109/TIT.2006.874516
3. Geiping, J., Bauermeister, H., Dröge, H., Moeller, M.: Inverting gradients-how easy is it to break privacy in federated learning? Adv. Neural Inf. Process. Syst. **33**, 16937–16947 (2020)
4. Ghosh, A., Chung, J., Yin, D., Ramchandran, K.: An efficient framework for clustered federated learning. Adv. Neural Inf. Process. Syst. **33**, 19586–19597 (2020)
5. Kairouz, P., et al.: Advances and open problems in federated learning. Found. Trends® Mach. Learn. **14**(1–2), 1–210 (2021)
6. Kempe, D., Dobra, A., Gehrke, J.: Gossip-based computation of aggregate information. In: 44th Annual IEEE Symposium on Foundations of Computer Science, 2003. Proceedings, pp. 482–491. IEEE (2003)

7. Krizhevsky, A., Hinton, G., et al.: Learning multiple layers of features from tiny images (2009)
8. McMahan, B., Moore, E., Ramage, D., Hampson, S., Arcas, B.A.: Communication-efficient learning of deep networks from decentralized data. In: Artificial Intelligence and Statistics, pp. 1273–1282. PMLR (2017)
9. Onoszko, N., Karlsson, G., Mogren, O., Listo Zec, E.: Decentralized federated learning of deep neural networks on non-iid data. arXiv preprint arXiv:2107.08517 (2021)
10. Ormándi, R., Hegedűs, I., Jelasity, M.: Gossip learning with linear models on fully distributed data. Concurr. Comput. Pract. Exp. **25**(4), 556–571 (2012). https://doi.org/10.1002/cpe.2858, https://doi.org/10.1002%2Fcpe.2858
11. Vapnik, V.: The Nature of Statistical Learning Theory. Springer science & business media, Berlin, Heidelberg (1999). https://doi.org/10.1007/978-1-4757-3264-1
12. Xiao, H., Rasul, K., Vollgraf, R.: Fashion-mnist: a novel image dataset for benchmarking machine learning algorithms. arXiv preprint arXiv:1708.07747 (2017)

Sketch to Skip and Select: Communication Efficient Federated Learning Using Locality Sensitive Hashing

Georgios Kollias[(✉)], Theodoros Salonidis, and Shiqiang Wang

IBM T. J. Watson Research Center, Yorktown Heights, NY, USA
{gkollias,tsaloni,wangshiq}@us.ibm.com

Abstract. We introduce a novel approach for optimizing communication efficiency in Federated Learning (FL). The approach leverages sketching techniques in two complementary strategies that exploit similarities on the data transmitted during the FL training process to identify opportunities for skipping expensive communication of updated models in training iterations, and dynamically select subsets of clients hosting diverse models. Our extensive experimental investigation on different models, datasets and label distributions, shows that these strategies can massively reduce downlink and uplink communication volumes by factors order of $100\times$ or more with minor degradation or even increase of the accuracy of the trained model. Also, in contrast to baselines, these strategies can escape suboptimal descent paths and can yield smooth non-oscillatory accuracy profiles for non-IID data distributions.

1 Introduction

Communication efficiency is a crucial issue in Federated Learning (FL), especially when large deep learning models are employed. Existing techniques for reducing the computation and communication overhead of FL focus on selecting a small fraction of clients in each FL training round or transmitting compressed models instead of original models. However, most of these techniques are either based on a simple randomized procedure, such as random client selection [3], or approaches such as magnitude-based gradient compression [13]. These methods do not take data characteristics into account and ignore the fact that data at clients are often non-independent and/or non-identically distributed (non-IID). This causes issues such as low accuracy or bias as useful data on certain clients tends to be largely ignored by the FL training process. In addition, as we empirically show in this chapter, random client selection can also cause instabilities in the convergence process for non-IID distributions.

Therefore, a largely open question is: *how to design communication efficient FL training procedures that are data-aware and can incorporate characteristics of non-IID data distribution?* We address this problem in this work. The core idea is to compute sketches of useful information obtained during the FL process, and use these sketches to determine when to share the model parameter vector or the gradient between server and clients and which clients to select. The benefit of this approach is that the sketches capture important knowledge related to data distributions and progress of local model updates, which is not possible using existing techniques.

R. Goebel et al. (Eds.): FL 2022, LNAI 13448, pp. 72–83, 2023.
https://doi.org/10.1007/978-3-031-28996-5_6

Our main contributions are as follows:

- We introduce a novel predicate that decides the proximity of models hosted at different nodes of an FL system, in a communication efficient way. The predicate is a communication skipping mechanism: if two remote models are approximately "close" do not share them. We implement this predicate based on Locality Sensitive Hashing (LSH) sketching techniques.
- We propose and implement a new method for client selection in FL that leverages sketching combined with clustering.
- We integrate our techniques in an FL simulation framework and evaluate their performance through extensive training experiments over six configurations of real datasets and data distributions and different parameters. We observe massive (order $100\times$) downlink and uplink communication savings over state of the art baselines without classification accuracy degradation. In some cases we obtain improvements in *both* accuracy and communication. For some non-IID data distributions we also demonstrate that in contrast to baselines, our client selection method avoids convergence issues such as fluctuations in accuracy during training.

2 Related Work

Communication efficiency is an extensively studied topic in general distributed learning from a theoretical point of view. It has also been addressed in applications such as distributed learning for data centers and more recently in the context of FL. In this section, we will focus on techniques that have been applied to FL context and are most related to this work.

Local Updating Methods. Local updating methods aim to reduce the total number of communication rounds by doing more computations. The most commonly used method for FL is Federated Averaging (FedAvg) [19], a method based on averaging local stochastic gradient descent (SGD) updates. FedAvg reduces communication overhead by doing multiple local SGD updates in parallel per communication round. FedProx improves upon FedAvg for the case of heterogeneous data [17]. The number of FedAvg SGD updates in these techniques is typically fixed and not adaptive to changing data. This can create divergence issues (if set too high) or high communication overhead (if set too low). The work of [24] proposes adaptive techniques for deciding the number of local SGD updates and frequency of communication to server. However, it does not exploit data similarities between clients and server and across clients.

FL Training using Model Compression. There exist several approaches which perform FL training using compressed model parameters or gradients in order to reduce communication overhead, at the potential expense of accuracy. These schemes use different compression techniques such as forcing the updating models to be sparse and low-rank or performing quantization with structured random rotations [13]. In [16], Li et. al. proposed DiffSketch which compresses transmitted messages via sketches to achieve communication efficiency and privacy benefits. For independent and identically distributed (IID) *MNIST* data with a large number of clients, they show high communication benefits, but these come at the expense of accuracy. Most approaches reduce overhead on the uplink direction from clients to server. The work in [4] uses lossy compression and dropout to reduce server-to-device downlink communication. In FetchSGD [21] the clients sketch their gradients using Count Sketch [5], which is a randomized data structure, before transmitting to the server. In [7] they similarly leverage count sketches for compression but under distributed differential privacy (DP) via secure aggregation (SecAgg).

Our approach significantly differs from the above approaches. It does not perform FL training based on compressed model parameters. Instead, it uses a special type of sketches based on LSH to decide on client selection and transmission of non-compressed model parameters. Thus, the goal is to minimize communications while using the necessary non-compressed data to maintain high accuracy by exploiting data similarities during the training process. In addition the above approaches typically demonstrate communication reduction but may yield significant accuracy loss. In contrast, our approach can yield massive communication overhead reduction (up to 100×) for non-IID distributions with minimal or zero accuracy loss. Our approach is also based on a generic sender/receiver predicate and is directly applicable to both uplink and downlink directions. It is also orthogonal to the existing compression-based training schemes and can be used in conjunction with them for further communication gains, if desirable.

Client Selection Methods. Client selection methods seek to reduce the number of participating clients. FedAvg uses random selection [3] which is used predominantly in FL settings in practice. There exist also works which select subset of clients based on device resource requirements [12,20,23]. These techniques do not consider data characteristics. The investigation in [10] proposes a data-aware client selection approach that is similar to ours at a high level. This approach involves hierarchical clustering of the clients based on a similarity metric on the gradients and sampling from these clusters. However, it incurs massive communication overhead during the clustering step because it requires all clients to send to the server their gradients (which have the same high dimensionality of model parameters). In contrast, in our sketch-to-select approach we use sketches of the model parameters which incur very low communication overhead in the clustering step. In addition, our sketch-to-skip strategy reduces communication overhead on both uplink and downlink by skipping client model updates to server and server global model transmission to the clients, respectively.

3   Methods

We leverage sketching techniques for informing our decisions of *when* to communicate model parameters and *which* clients to compute with. In particular, we vectorize the learning parameter tensors of a local model snapshot during training and compute a locality sensitive hash of the concatenation of vectors. For a locality sensitive hashing function $h(\cdot)$ and starting vectors a and b, their hashes $h(a)$ and $h(b)$ are also vectors of reduced size, with the interesting property that they are close with high probability if a and b are close. This property motivates us to consider using such "short" hashes instead of the full model parameter tensors, when we need to *decide* whether two models, hosted at distributed agents, are approximately close (i.e. "similar") or not: agents compute, exchange and compare their "short" model hashes and then decide whether to communicate and share the actual models. This is a *communication efficient, model proximity predicate* and we use its Boolean output in two types of strategies:

1. **Sketch-to-Skip** skip sending the model snapshot, at execution points FL would normally send, when the predicate indicates that the model snapshot at the receiver side is "close".
2. **Sketch-to-Select** select a subset of computing clients that host models that are not "close" to each other.

3.1 Sketch-Based Communication Skipping: Sketch-to-Skip

Our model proximity protocol uses a generic sender/receiver predicate and unlike most existing FL communication efficiency techniques, it can be applied to both uplink (clients to server) and downlink (server to clients) directions. Also it is a one-comparison protocol: projects and compares the projections. It is also modular in the sense that alternative sketching methods can be plugged-in: the work by [9] is particularly relevant as they also minimize the distortion in l_2 norm.

Our model proximity predicate referred to as lsh in the sequel, is based on randomized projections (sketching) of *flattened* (i.e. vectorized and concatenated) model parameter tensors. Let a and b, with d elements each, be the flattened tensors of the model paremeters at the perspective sender and receiver sides, which we wish to compare. In lsh, the sender generates k random vectors $r_1, r_2, \ldots, r_k$, uniformly sampled from $(-1, 1)$ for given seed s and with d elements each. The vectors are organized in a $k \times d$ projection matrix that multiplies (projects) a to a k element vector h_a. The sender sends the seed s and the sketching dimension k to the receiver so that it can generate an identical projection matrix, similarly compute a projection h_b of its b and send h_b to the sender. Finally the sender computes the relative norm difference of the two sketched vectors $\|h_a - h_b\|_2 / \|h_b\|_2$: if this is smaller than the threshold parameter of this protocol, then the sender skips sending its a.

Communication Savings. The potential for communications savings is very high. When the proximity protocol decides that communication should be skipped (based on the lsh threshold parameter) only the hash of size k will have been sent instead of the full model of size d. As an example, the models in our experiments have hundreds thousands of parameters ($d = 238,510$ parameters for the FCNN model and $d = 555,178$ for the CNN model). The proximity protocol uses a vector of dimension $k = 100$. This can potentially yield dramatic communication savings of the order of $\frac{k}{d}$, i.e. 0.04% for FCNN and 0.02% for CNN when communication is skipped. We will quantify this potential in the experiments section.

Computation Complexity. The computation of the hashes involves two steps. At the beginning of training iterations, at each client, a projection matrix is constructed which requires $O(dk)$ flops; this cost is amortized over all iterations. Then, for each iteration, this matrix is used to project the local model vector of size d at each agent, which also requires $O(dk)$ flops, since this is dense matrix vector multiplication (matvec). The work by [1,8] can further reduce the complexity in generating the projection matrix or projecting the vectors, which according to [13] can be considered negligible compared to the computational complexity of local SGD training iterations within FL.

3.2   Sketch-Based Client Selection: `Sketch-to-Select`

We introduce a "data-aware" scheme for client selection, where "data" corresponds to *sketches* of flattened model parameter tensors across all clients. As the last stage in iterations marked for updating the subset of selected clients (including c out of all n clients available), all n clients sketch their flattened model parameters and upload their resulting sketched vectors to the server. Then the server clusters the n sketched vectors into c clusters and randomly samples one vector per cluster. Clients for which their sketched vector was sampled are added to the new subset of selected clients.

The intention behind this scheme is the inclusion of clients hosting as diverse model parameters as possible. Parameters which are "close" will have their sketches being "close" and thus most probably they will land in the same cluster. This also means that selecting one representative model from each of c clusters - for a budget of c selected clients total - maximizes coverage of the distributed model parameter space distribution.

For sketching, we utilize the same type of randomized projection matrices as in `lsh`. We use ubiquitous Lloyd's algorithm [18] for clustering our n vectors (of k elements each, k the sketching dimension) into c clusters; also `k-means++` [2] for initializing the coordinates of its c centroids. Interestingly, `k-means++` has a analogous objective to what we are trying to do: build a set of centroids that are as far as possible from each other. So it becomes quite natural to use it for cluster initialization.

For the client slection iterations, the computation complexity for projecting is $O(dk)$ flops per client; at server side, Lloyd's algorithm incurs an overhead of $O(nckr)$ flops, where r is the number of rounds for centroid updates. Also, the communication complexity for uplink communication of the sketches is $O(nk)$.

3.3   Sketch to Skip and Select FL Algorithm

The FedAvg FL training algorithm [19] consists of multiple rounds, where each round consists of the following steps: Running SGD model updates locally at the clients for E iterations. Then randomly selecting a subset of the clients to upload their updated model parameters to the server. The server aggregates the parameters of the clients by taking their mean and sends the updated global model to all clients.

Our *Sketch to Skip and Select FL* training algorithm is shown in Algorithm 1. At a high level it is based on two ideas for modifying FedAvg as follows.

The first idea is to perform model updates (uploading local client models, aggregation, downloading global server model) only if local client models are sufficiently different than the global server model. This is achieved using the `sketch-to-skip` strategy between server and clients, performing skip if the model of *all* selected clients is close to the global model at the server. When model updates are skipped, no client selection takes place. This approach can be seen in Algorithm 2.

The second idea is to use `sketch-to-select` data-aware scheme instead of FedAvg random client selection: Once the selected clients are able to upload their models, a new client selection can occur using our data-aware `sketch-to-select` algorithm. This is performed by all clients sending their model sketches to the server, the server clustering clients based on the sketches, and then selecting randomly a client from each cluster. The sketch-to-select strategy takes into account the clients' data heterogeneity issue as opposed to the FedAvg random client selection strategy which is oblivious to it. This approach can be seen in Algorithm 3.

More specifically, Algorithm 1 executes in multiple rounds $0, \ldots, T-1$. Each round starts with the `sketch-to-skip` Algorithm 2: the server sends the sketch of its global model to the clients; the clients update their model parameters by performing E local SGD steps, compare the updated model sketches with the global model sketch and send to server the outcome of the comparison; if *all* client models have not deviated from the global server model by more than δ, then the server decides to skip the uplink update, aggregation and downlink update steps (lines 13, 17, 21 in Algorithm 1, respectively) and client selection step (line 19 in Algorithm 1).

Client selection (`sketch-to-select` Algorithm 3) occurs at each $j*u$-th round, where u is a parameter and $j = 0, 1, \ldots$, provided that skip does not occur on that round.

Algorithm 1. Sketch to Skip and Select FL

1: **Input:** number of all clients N, number of clusters C, number of rounds T, number of local updates E, learning rate η, skip step threshold δ, sketching dimension k, set of client selection update steps $\mathcal{U}_T = \{0, u, 2u, \ldots, \lfloor \frac{T}{u} \rfloor u\}$

2: **At server:**

3: Initialize model parameters $\bar{\mathbf{w}}^0$ and set of selected clients $\mathcal{S}_0 = [N]$

4: Transmit $\bar{\mathbf{w}}^0$ to all clients $i \in \mathcal{S}_0$

5: **for** $t = 0, \ldots, T - 1$ **do**

6:     Execute `Sketch-to-Skip` strategy (Algorithm 2)

7:     **At clients:**

8:     **for** each client $i \in \mathcal{S}_t$ in parallel **do**

9:         *Comment:* `skip` *received as in Algorithm 2*

10:         **if** value of `skip` received from server is `True` **then**

11:             Skip this round t: continue to round $t + 1$

12:         **else**

13:             Transmit local model $\mathbf{w}_i^t$ to the server

14:         **end if**

15:     **end for**

16:     **Server update:**

17:     $\bar{\mathbf{w}}^{t+1} \leftarrow \frac{1}{|\mathcal{S}_t|} \sum_{i \in \mathcal{S}_t} \mathbf{w}_i^t$

18:     **if** $t \in \mathcal{U}_T$ **then**

19:         Execute `Sketch-to-Select` strategy (Algorithm 3)

20:     **end if**

21:     Server broadcast $\bar{\mathbf{w}}^{t+1}$ to all clients

22: **end for**

---

4 Experiments

4.1 Experimental Setup

Datasets and Data Distributions at Different Nodes. We experiment with three datasets: the original MNIST (referred to as *MNIST-O*) [15], Fashion-MNIST (referred to as *MNIST-F*) [25] and CIFAR-10 [14]. We consider two different ways of distributing the data into different nodes for each of the datasets. In Case 1, each data sample is

---

Algorithm 2. `Sketch-to-Skip` strategy

1: **At server:**
2: $\bar{\mathbf{h}}^t \leftarrow$ Flatten and sketch global model $\bar{\mathbf{w}}^t$; $\bar{\mathbf{h}}^t \in \mathbb{R}^k$
3: Transmit $\bar{\mathbf{h}}^t$ to all clients $i \in \mathcal{S}_t$
4: **At clients:**
5: **for** each client $i \in \mathcal{S}_t$ in parallel **do**
6:     $\mathbf{w}_{i,t}^0 \leftarrow \bar{\mathbf{w}}^t$
7:     **for** $j = 0, \ldots, E-1$ **do**
8:         $g_i(\mathbf{w}_{i,t}^j) \leftarrow \nabla f_i(\mathbf{w}_{i,t}^j)$
9:         $\mathbf{w}_{i,t}^{j+1} \leftarrow \mathbf{w}_{i,t}^j - \eta g_i(\mathbf{w}_{i,t}^j)$
10:    **end for**
11:    $\mathbf{w}_i^t \leftarrow \mathbf{w}_{i,t}^E$
12:    $\mathbf{h}_i^t \leftarrow$ Flatten and sketch local model $\mathbf{w}_i^t$; $\mathbf{h}_i^t \in \mathbb{R}^k$
13:    `skip`$_i \leftarrow$ `False`
14:    **if** $\|\bar{\mathbf{h}}_i^t - \bar{\mathbf{h}}^t\|_2 / \|\bar{\mathbf{h}}^t\|_2 < \delta$ **then**
15:        `skip`$_i \leftarrow$ `True`
16:    **end if**
17:    Transmit `skip`$_i$ to server
18: **end for**
19: **At Server:**
20: `skip` $\leftarrow$ `False`
21: **if** `skip`$_i$ is `True` for *all* $i \in \mathcal{S}_t$ **then**
22:    `skip` $\leftarrow$ `True`
23: **end if**
24: Transmit `skip` to all clients $i \in \mathcal{S}_t$

---

randomly assigned to a node, thus each node has uniform (but not full) information. In Case 2, all the data samples in each node have the same label[1]. This represents the case where each node has non-uniform (non-IID) information, because the entire dataset has samples with multiple different labels.

Models. For *MNIST-O* and *MNIST-F* we train deep fully connected neural network (FCNNs) and for *CIFAR-10* deep convolutional neural networks (CNNs).[2] We use stochastic gradient descent (SGD) for training FCNNs and CNNs. The loss function is cross-entropy on cascaded linear and non-linear transforms [11].

Training and Control Parameters. For local training at each client, we use a static learning rate of $\eta = 0.05$ for *MNIST-O* and *MNIST-F* and $\eta = 0.01$ for *CIFAR-10*. The mini-batch size is $B = 100$. We train for $T = 1000$ rounds. We simulate a client-

---

[1] When there are more labels than nodes, each node may have data with more than one label, but the number of labels at each node is no more than the total number of labels divided by the total number of nodes rounded to the next integer.

[2] The FCNN has 3 layers with the following structure: 784×300 Fully Connected $\rightarrow 300 \times 10$ Fully Connected $\rightarrow$ Softmax. The CNN has 9 layers with the following structure [22]: $5 \times 5 \times 32$ Convolutional $\rightarrow 2 \times 2$ MaxPool $\rightarrow$ Local Response Normalization $\rightarrow 5 \times 5 \times 32$ Convolutional $\rightarrow$ Local Response Normalization $\rightarrow 2 \times 2$ MaxPool $\rightarrow 2048 \times 256$ Fully connected $\rightarrow 256 \times 10$ Fully connected $\rightarrow$ Softmax.

Algorithm 3. `Sketch-to-Select` strategy

1: **At clients:**
2: $\bar{\mathbf{h}}_i^t \leftarrow$ All clients $i \in [N] \setminus \mathcal{S}_t$ flatten and sketch their local models $\mathbf{w}_{i,t}$
3: All clients $i \in [N]$ transmit their local model sketches $\bar{\mathbf{h}}_i^t$ to the server
4: **At server:**
5: Server computes clusters $\mathcal{A}^t := \{\mathcal{A}_1^t, \dots, \mathcal{A}_C^t\}$ from $\bar{\mathbf{h}}_i^t, i \in [N]$ using Lloyd's algorithm with k-means++ initialization
6: Server samples $\mathcal{S}_t \in [N]$ by drawing one client from each cluster $\mathcal{A}_i^t, i \in [C]$ uniformly at random
7: Server broadcasts $\bar{\mathbf{w}}^{t+1}$ to sampled clients

---

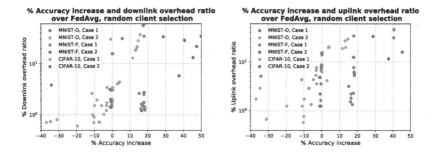

Fig. 1. Overhead ratio for downlink (left panel) and uplink (right panel) communication (vertical axis) vs accuracy increase (horizontal axis). Baseline is `FedAvg` with random client selection.

server FL system of $N = 50$ clients using synchronous $E = 1$ steps of distributed gradient descent [6] and select $C = 10$ (out of the 50) clients for the client selection runs. Selected clients are then elected every $u = 100$ iterations (frequency of client selection) for all applicable cases. For the sketching dimension k, we use the values of 100 and 10 for sketch-based communication skipping and client selection, respectively.

Comparison Baseline. We compare our methods against FedAvg [19] with the same training and control parameters (η, E, B, T, N, C) as above.

Metrics. We collect downlink and uplink communication volumes during training and the accuracy value at its end, for all attempted combinations and setup parameters (proximity primitives, thresholds and client selection intervals when in client selection mode). Then we compute the *percent relative error* $100 * (x - y)/y\%$ for the accuracy (where x is the classification accuracy of our method and y of the comparison baseline), also referred as *accuracy increase* and the *percent ratio* $100 * x/y$ for the downlink and uplink communication volumes (where x refers to our method and y to the comparison baseline), also referred to as *overhead ratio*[3].

---

[3] A positive (negative) *accuracy increase* means that our method attains better (worse) accuracy than the baseline, by the indicated percent, so *the more positive the better*. Similarly 1%, 5%, 10%, 50% *overhead ratio* values correspond to 100×, 20×, 10×, 2× communication savings compared to baseline, respectively: *the smaller the better*, with the baseline at 100%.

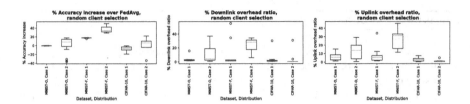

Fig. 2. Box plots for accuracy increase (left panel) and overhead ratio for downlink (middle panel) and uplink (right panel) communication for various dataset and distribution combinations as in Fig. 1. Baseline is `FedAvg` with random client selection.

4.2 Results

Figure 1 depicts the communication savings (overhead ratio) vs. accuracy increase obtained with our proximity primitive and client selection strategies, with respect to the `FedAvg` with random client selection baseline, for various parameter settings of our strategies on the 6 configurations. We observe that for each configuration there exist several parameter settings that yield very low uplink/downlink overhead ratios (10% or much lower) and small negative (-5%) or positive accuracy increase.

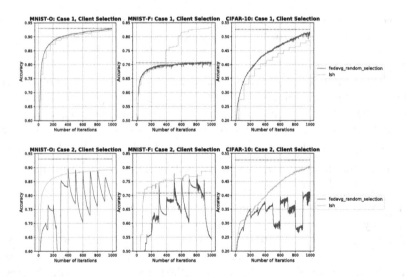

Fig. 3. Classification accuracy with client selection: Case 1 (top row); Case 2 (bottom row).

Figure 2 shows boxplot statistics for accuracy increase, downlink and uplink overhead ratio for each configuration in Fig. 1. We observe that the median overhead ratio across the six configurations ranges between $[0.21\%, 28.28\%]$ ($[476x, 3.5x]$ savings) for downlink and $[0.57\%, 31.25\%]$ ($[175x, 3.2x]$ savings) for uplink communication. Median accuracy increase ranges between $[-6.47\%, 34.22\%]$ across the 6 configurations. For example, in CIFAR-10 Case 2 configuration, the median overhead ratio (across all `lsh` parameter settings we used) for downlink is 0.21% (476x savings) and for uplink 0.57% (175x savings) while median accuracy increase is 5.6%.

Figure 3 compares the accuracy profiles of our approach for a selected parameter set and FedAvg with random client selection baseline for each of the 6 configurations. In 5/6 configurations our approach yields higher accuracy and in CIFAR-10, Case 1 it is tracking closely the baseline accuracy. A few more interesting observations are in place.

Our Approach Exhibits a Step-wise Accuracy Evolution. This is due to skipping sharing model parameters during some iterations until the models become different enough to resume sharing. Essentially the number of steps equals the number of total iterations minus the number of iterations where communication was skipped.

Random Client Selection Accuracy Profiles are "Oscillatory" for Case 2 Distribution (Fig. 3, Bottom Row.) Random client selection will select clients without taking into account the latent affinity in the local models for some of the labels. In contrast, our client selection will group affine clients and select a single representative from the group, thus ensuring that affine clients will not be selected for the same selection interval (in the limit: avoid repetition of samples) and save their spot for inclusion of models that are not close (in the limit: include new samples). Therefore, our sketch-based client selection results in stable accuracy profiles for these cases and this reflects the crucial role of clustering as a mechanism to diversify.

MNIST-F **Gets Significant Accuracy Boost in Addition to Communication Savings (Middle Panes in Fig. 3.)** Effectively, sketching seems to be providing a mechanism to escape suboptimal descent paths during training for some datasets.

5   Conclusions

Sketching has been used in FL to compress model representations prior to sending, with the intention to directly mix the compressed representation into the computation of the model update at the receiving side [13]. In our work, different sketches based on locality sensitive hashing are used in completely orthogonal and indirect ways: to decide whether communicating the model should occur in the first place and which clients to engage in the computation. We have empirically demonstrated that this app-roach can massively reduce downlink and uplink communication volumes by factors order of $100\times$ or more with minor degradation or even increase of the accuracy of the trained model. We also empirically identified cases where, in contrast to the baseline, our strategies provide a mechanism to escape suboptimal descent paths and can yield smooth accuracy profiles for non-IID data distributions.

References

1. Ailon, N., Chazelle, B.: Approximate nearest neighbors and the fast johnson-lindenstrauss transform. In: Proceedings of the Thirty-Eighth Annual ACM Symposium on Theory of Computing, pp. 557–563 (2006)

2. Arthur, D., Vassilvitskii, S.: k-means++: the advantages of careful seeding. In: Proceedings of the Eighteenth Annual ACM-SIAM Symposium on Discrete Algorithms, pp. 1027–1035. Society for Industrial and Applied Mathematics (2007)

3. Bonawitz, K., et al.: Towards federated learning at scale: system design. In: Systems and Machine Learning (SysML) Conference (2019)

4. Caldas, S., Konečny, J., McMahan, H.B., Talwalkar, A.: Expanding the reach of federated learning by reducing client resource requirements. arXiv preprint arXiv:1812.07210 (2018)

5. Charikar, M., Chen, K., Farach-Colton, M.: Finding frequent items in data streams. In: Widmayer, P., Eidenbenz, S., Triguero, F., Morales, R., Conejo, R., Hennessy, M. (eds.) ICALP 2002. LNCS, vol. 2380, pp. 693–703. Springer, Heidelberg (2002). https://doi.org/10.1007/3-540-45465-9_59

6. Chen, J., Monga, R., Bengio, S., Jozefowicz, R.: Revisiting distributed synchronous sgd. In: International Conference on Learning Representations Workshop Track (2016). https://arxiv.org/abs/1604.00981

7. Chen, W.N., Choquette-Choo, C.A., Kairouz, P.: Communication efficient federated learning with secure aggregation and differential privacy. In: NeurIPS 2021 Workshop Privacy in Machine Learning (2021)

8. Clarkson, K.L., Woodruff, D.P.: Low-rank approximation and regression in input sparsity time. J. ACM (JACM) **63**(6), 1–45 (2017)

9. Datar, M., Immorlica, N., Indyk, P., Mirrokni, V.S.: Locality-sensitive hashing scheme based on p-stable distributions. In: Proceedings of the Twentieth Annual Symposium on Computational Geometry, pp. 253–262 (2004)

10. Fraboni, Y., Vidal, R., Kameni, L., Lorenzi, M.: Clustered sampling: low-variance and improved representativity for clients selection in federated learning. In: Proceedings of the International Conference on Machine Learning, 18–24 July 2021

11. Goodfellow, I., Bengio, Y., Courville, A., Bengio, Y.: Deep Learning, vol. 1. MIT press, Cambridge (2016)

12. Jin, Y., Jiao, L., Qian, Z., Zhang, S., Lu, S., Wang, X.: Resource-efficient and convergence-preserving online participant selection in federated learning. In: IEEE International Conference on Distributed Computing Systems (ICDCS) (2020)

13. Konečnỳ, J., McMahan, H.B., Yu, F.X., Richtárik, P., Suresh, A.T., Bacon, D.: Federated learning: Strategies for improving communication efficiency. In: NeurIPS Workshop on Private Multi-Party Machine Learning (2016)

14. Krizhevsky, A.: Learning multiple layers of features from tiny images. Technical report, University of Toronto (2009)

15. LeCun, Y., Bottou, L., Bengio, Y., Haffner, P.: Gradient-based learning applied to document recognition. Proc. IEEE **86**(11), 2278–2324 (1998)

16. Li, T., Liu, Z., Sekar, V., Smith, V.: Privacy for free: Communication-efficient learning with differential privacy using sketches. arXiv preprint arXiv:1911.00972 (2019)

17. Li, T., Sahu, A.K., Zaheer, M., Sanjabi, M., Talwalkar, A., Smith, V.: Federated optimization in heterogeneous networks. In: Machine Learning and Systems (MLSys) Conference (2020)

18. Lloyd, S.: Least squares quantization in PCM. IEEE Trans. Inf. Theory **28**(2), 129–137 (1982)

19. McMahan, B., Moore, E., Ramage, D., Hampson, S., Arcas, B.A.: Communication-efficient learning of deep networks from decentralized data. In: Artificial Intelligence and Statistics, pp. 1273–1282 (2017)

20. Nishio, T., Yonetani, R.: Client selection for federated learning with heterogeneous resources in mobile edge. In: IEEE International Conference on Communications (ICC), pp. 1–7 (2019)

21. Rothchild, D., et al.: FETCHSGD: communication-efficient federated learning with sketching. In: International Conference on Machine Learning, pp. 8253–8265. PMLR (2020)

22. Tensorflow: Convolutional neural network (CNN) (2020). https://www.tensorflow.org/tutorials/images/cnn

23. Wang, H., Kaplan, Z., Niu, D., Li, B.: Optimizing federated learning on non-iid data with reinforcement learning. In: IEEE Conference on Computer Communications (INFOCOM), pp. 1698–1707 (2020)

24. Wang, S., et al.: Adaptive federated learning in resource constrained edge computing systems. IEEE J. Sel. Areas Commun. **37**(6), 1205–1221 (2019)

25. Xiao, H., Rasul, K., Vollgraf, R.: Fashion-mnist: a novel image dataset for benchmarking machine learning algorithms. arXiv preprint arXiv:1708.07747 (2017)

Fast Server Learning Rate Tuning for Coded Federated Dropout

Giacomo Verardo$^{(\boxtimes)}$ ⓘ, Daniel Barreira, Marco Chiesa ⓘ, Dejan Kostic ⓘ,
and Gerald Q. Maguire Jr. ⓘ

KTH Royal Institute of Technology, Stockholm, Sweden
{verardo,barreira,mchiesa,dmk,maguire}@kth.se

Abstract. In Federated Learning (FL), clients with low computational power train a common machine model by exchanging parameters via updates instead of transmitting potentially private data. Federated Dropout (FD) is a technique that improves the communication efficiency of a FL session by selecting a *subset* of model parameters to be updated in each training round. However, compared to standard FL, FD produces considerably lower accuracy and faces a longer convergence time. In this chapter, we leverage *coding theory* to enhance FD by allowing different sub-models to be used at each client. We also show that by carefully tuning the server learning rate hyper-parameter, we can achieve higher training speed while also reaching up to the same final accuracy as the no dropout case. Evaluations on the EMNIST dataset show that our mechanism achieves 99.6% of the final accuracy of the no dropout case while requiring 2.43× less bandwidth to achieve this level of accuracy.

Keywords: Federated Learning · Hyper-parameters tuning · Coding Theory

1 Introduction

In recent years, stricter regulations such as GDPR [20] have been introduced to preserve data privacy for end users; therefore, standard Machine Learning (ML) tasks, which require collecting information at centralized locations such as data-centers cannot be implemented without violating users' privacy. At the same time, the number of mobile phones has consistently grown and is estimated to reach 8.8 billion in 2026 [10]. For this reason, Federated Learning (FL) [18] has been proposed to train machine learning models *without* collecting private data from users' devices. In FL, a parameter server broadcasts a global ML model to low powered devices (clients), which in turn perform training over their own datasets. The model updates are sent from the clients to the server, which aggregates them and may start another FL round. Even in case of highly heterogeneous client datasets, it has been demonstrated that the model converges [17].

FL poses strict requirements both in terms of the amount of *bandwidth* required for exchanging models and the *computational* and *memory* resources required to perform training on large models on the clients' devices. The size of a model could be hundreds of MB [8]. Clients must download such large models using their available (often heterogeneous) bandwidth, use processing and memory resources to train on the model on

R. Goebel et al. (Eds.): FL 2022, LNAI 13448, pp. 84–99, 2023.
https://doi.org/10.1007/978-3-031-28996-5_7

their data, and re-transmit the updated models to the FL servers; therefore, optimizing the bandwidth and computational overheads of running an FL session has become a topic of crucial importance.

Splitting a common, global model between clients and training it collaboratively has become imperative to reduce both memory and computational demands of an FL session. Federated Dropout (FD) is a technique that holds great promise to decrease the resource utilization of FL by pruning activations in the neural network, thus decreasing the number of variables to be exchanged and trained at the device side. Unlike standard centralized Dropout [24], where different dropped models are used at each training step, in FD a global model is divided into sub-models which are trained locally and then merged into an updated global model. Federated Dropout is orthogonal to message compression techniques, such as quantization [2] or sparsification [3], which also mitigate bandwidth overheads but do not reduce the computational power and memory needed at the client side.

Reaping the benefits of FD is not easy as it entails solving two main challenges:

- **Low accuracy.** FD learning may result in *lower accuracy* than traditional FL [7]. Intuitively, partially overlapping sub-models per client may improve performance. Recently it has been shown that selecting random sub-models for each client device may lead to better final accuracy [27]. However, it is not clear how sub-models should be selected, nor which is the orthogonality level which produce the optimal accuracy. Moreover, merging the sub-models into a new global model is a challenging task since it depends on their overlapping.
- **Slow convergence.** Although FD requires less bandwidth per round compared to traditional (no-dropout) FL, there is no guarantee that FD will converge rapidly. If FD requires significantly more rounds than FL to achieve high accuracy, then the promised bandwidth benefits would vanish.

We propose novel techniques to improve the accuracy of FD *without* losing the inherent bandwidth savings offered by FD (*i.e.*, by improving convergence speed). To tackle the above challenges, we explore the following two ideas:

- *Applying coding theory for sub-model selection.* Building upon the idea of sending different models to different clients during one FD round, we deterministically compute sub-models and then examine whether they perform better than random sub-models. We draw inspirations from *coding theory* (specifically, from the Code Division Multiple Access (CDMA) problem where orthogonal codes enable simultaneous communication channels *without* interference). We employ Gold codes [11] and Constant Weight Codes (CWC) [5] as masks to drop units and create different sub-models. The intuition is that selecting sub-models using these mechanisms will produce higher accuracy than random selection.
- *Adaptive server learning rate.* We experimentally observe that the convergence speed of an FD session depends on a critical parameter called *server learning rate*, which determines how the weight updates from the clients are incorporated into the trained model. Thanks to the inherent bandwidth savings of FD, we propose to search for the best server learning rate at the beginning of an FD session. A key challenge is to avoid consuming all of the bandwidth saved due to FD when performing this search.

Based on the above ideas, we design a mechanism called Coded Federated Dropout (CFD), which we incorporate alongside existing state-of-the-art FL systems, such as FedAdam [21] and FedAvg [18]. By evaluating on the EMNIST62 dataset, we show that CFD increases the final accuracy of the trained models while preserving the bandwidth savings of FD. In summary, our contributions are:

1. We are the first to leverage coding theory to carefully select the sub-models used in each FL round.
2. We show that the optimal server learning rate in a traditional FL session differs from that of an FD session.
3. We design a technique to *quickly* search for the best server learning rate. Our evaluation shows that we can identify good learning rates in just hundreds of rounds.
4. We show that CFD with Gold Codes achieves *comparable accuracy* to no-dropout FL with 2.43× *less bandwidth* on the EMNIST dataset.
5. We show that minimizing the "cross-correlation" metric in Gold Codes produces better final accuracy than maximizing the "minimal distance" metric of CWC codes.

The main system parameters used throughout the rest of the chapter and the related notation are summarised in Table 5.

2   Background

Federated Learning. An FL session is composed of one parameter server and multiple clients. At the beginning of an FL round, the server broadcasts a common global model $w_k^{(t)}$ to a fraction of the clients. At round t, each client k trains for a customizable number of epochs E and returns the update $\Delta w_k^{(t)}$ from the previously received weights:

$$\hat{w}_k^{(t)} = w_k^{(t)} - \eta_l \nabla_w L(w, D_k) \tag{1}$$

$$\Delta w_k^{(t)} = \hat{w}_k^{(t)} - w_k^{(t)} \tag{2}$$

where $L(w, D_k)$ is the employed loss function, which depends on the model weights and the client dataset D_k. When employing Federated Averaging (FAVG, [18]), the originally proposed aggregation method, the parameter server computes new weights by averaging the updates and adding them to the previous global model:

$$w^{(t+1)} = w^{(t)} + \eta \sum_{j \in S(t)} p_j \Delta w_j^{(t)} \tag{3}$$

$$p_j = \frac{|D_j|}{\sum_{j \in S(t)} |D_j|} \tag{4}$$

For FAVG, η is set to 1.0, whereas it can be different for other aggregation mechanisms.
Federated Dropout One of the major issues of FL is the communication overhead. FD improves bandwidth efficiency by randomly dropping connections between adjacent neural network layers. Unlike standard dropout [24], FD is not employed as a regularisation tool. Instead, FD keeps a fixed percentage α of activations, thus producing a

sub-model with a $(1 - \alpha)^2$ parameters fraction of fully connected networks. The sub-model is trained at the client-side, while the aggregation procedure only involves those nodes that have been kept. Moreover, the required computational power and memory at the client are reduced. However, although the benefits in bandwidth efficiency are remarkable, the same set of weights is trained at each client per round.

In [4], the authors suggest adapting the selection of dropped nodes based on the loss for each client; however, they state that this approach is unsuitable for FL since it wastes too much memory at the server. Therefore, they propose an alternative technique which employs a single sub-model for all clients, which degrades convergence rate and final accuracy. In contrast to random dropout [27], we propose to use coding theory for mask selection to enhance the orthogonality of sub-models by producing different dropping masks for each client. Hence, we allow partially disjoint sub-models per clients per round to improve both convergence time and final accuracy for the same α.

Code Division Multiple Access. Multiple access techniques address the problem of having multiple users communicate via a shared channel. Time and frequency division multiple access respectively splits the channel in time and frequency between users. In contrast, CDMA assigns a different code to each user and allows each of them to use the whole channel. If the codes are sufficiently orthogonal, the inter-user interference is low and transmission occurs with negligible error rate. CDMA has been extensively used in satellite [25] and mobile communication [15]. Gold [11] and Kasami [14] codes are examples of families of sequences designed for orthogonality.

Adaptive Federated Optimization. [21] have proven that using a different learning rate for each parameter during aggregation can greatly improve FL model convergence. They propose 3 aggregation methods (FedAdam, FedAdagrad, and FedYogi), which replaces (3). Here we describe only the FedAdam algorithm, which performs well in all the datasets:

$$\boldsymbol{\Delta}^t = \beta_1 \cdot \boldsymbol{\Delta}^{t-1} + (1 - \beta_1) \cdot \sum_{j \in S(t)} p_j \Delta \boldsymbol{w}_j^{(t)} \tag{5}$$

$$\boldsymbol{v}^{(t)} = \beta_2 \cdot \boldsymbol{v}^{(t-1)} + (1 - \beta_2) \cdot \boldsymbol{\Delta}^{(t)^2} \tag{6}$$

$$\boldsymbol{w}^{(t+1)} = \boldsymbol{w}^{(t)} + \eta \frac{\boldsymbol{\Delta}^{(t)}}{\sqrt{\boldsymbol{v}^{(t)}} + \tau} \tag{7}$$

where β_1, β_2 and τ are hyper-parameters. The key insight is that training variables which have been trained less in the previous rounds will improve convergence. For this reason, v_t stores an indication of how much variables have been trained and is used to independently scale each component of the next update $\boldsymbol{\Delta}^{(t)}$. However, the proposed optimization techniques require expensive hyper-parameters tuning and therefore a considerable amount of time, which might not be available in a FL session.

Other adaptive mechanisms have been proposed to correct the client drift due to the statistical heterogeneity in the clients datasets. [13] employ variance reduction, but this requires too much information to be stored server-side. [16] propose a trade-off between fairness and robustness of the global model.

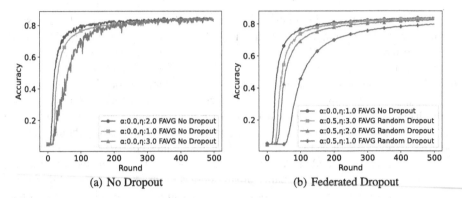

Fig. 1. Increasing the server learning rate η to 3.0 is beneficial for random FD with different sub-models per client, while it is detrimental for the no dropout case.

3 Methodology

This section describes the proposed Coded Federated Dropout (CFD) method which performs both tuning of the server learning rate η (Sect. 3.1) and the selection of the sub-models sent to the clients (Sect. 3.2).

3.1 Fast Server Learning Rate Adaptation

Similarly to centralized ML, increasing the server learning rate may lead to faster convergence, but further increasing the learning rate causes the objective function to diverge [28]. Figure 1(a) empirically confirms that this is also the case for no-dropout FL where a high server learning rate of $\eta = 3$ exhibits worse convergence than with $\eta = 2$. This result is based on the EMNIST62 dataset with more details in Sect. 4. Interestingly, Fig. 1(b) shows that in FD with random sub-models increasing the server learning rate to 3 leads to faster convergence. Moreover, a higher server learning rate in FD produces less oscillations in the accuracy across rounds compared to the no dropout case. This shows that the "best" server learning rate for FD may differ from the no-dropout case.

We propose a fast server learning rate adaptation method, which can also be extended to other parameters. At the beginning of training, we run Algorithm 1, which requires n_a adaptation steps. In each step (line 2), multiple FL sessions are launched in parallel from the same parameter server with different server learning rates $\mathbb{H}$ and, in general, different clients subsets per round. We start our search using three η values during the first adaptation step (line 1) and reduce it to two server learning rates in the following adaptation steps (line 14). The goal of this search (lines 4 to 12) is to find the server learning rate that reaches a preconfigured accuracy target γ (lines 8–9) in the minimum number of rounds r^* (line 5). More specifically, in each round r, the server collects both the gradient update Δw_k^t and the accuracy of the model for each training client in the round (line 6). Then, it computes the average of the median training accuracy $\overline{\gamma}$ in the last q FL rounds (line 7). The median operation is performed in order to

---

Algorithm 1. Fast server learning rate adaptation

Input: $w^0, \{D_k \forall k \in \{1, ..., T\}\}$
Parameter: $\gamma^*, q, n_a, \eta_0, \Delta\eta$
Output: η^*

1:    $\mathbb{H} \leftarrow \{\eta_0, \eta_0 - \Delta\eta, \eta_0 + \Delta\eta\}$
2:    **for** $s = 0$ **to** n_a **do**
3:      **for** $\eta \in \mathbb{H}$ **parallel do**
4:        $r \leftarrow 0$
5:        **while** $r < r^*$ **do**
6:          $\overline{\gamma}^t, w^{(t+1)} \leftarrow \texttt{Round}(\{D_k\}, w^{(t)})$
7:          $\overline{\gamma} \leftarrow \frac{1}{q} \cdot \sum_{i=0}^{q-1} \overline{\gamma}^{t-i}$
8:          **if** $\overline{\gamma} \geq \gamma^*$ **then**
9:            $r^* \leftarrow r, \eta^* \leftarrow \eta$
10:           wait for parallel search to end; go to line 15
11:          **end if**
12:          $r \leftarrow r + 1$
13:        **end while**
14:      **end for**
15:      $\Delta\eta \leftarrow \frac{\Delta\eta}{2}$
16:      $\mathbb{H} \leftarrow \{\eta^* - \Delta\eta, \eta^* + \Delta\eta\}$
17: **end for**

---

avoid the impact of outliers (*i.e.*, clients with too high or low training accuracies), while the average operation over the last rounds avoids sudden spikes. If one server learning rate $\overline{\gamma}$ is higher than a predefined threshold γ^*, then we have found a new optimal server learning rate $\eta^* = \eta$ that requires the new minimum number of rounds $r^* = r$ to achieve the target accuracy (lines 8–9). For the next adaptation step, the new tentative server learning rates $\mathbb{H}$ are chosen near η^* (lines 15–16) and the next adaptation step is performed. An adaptation step may also end when all the FL sessions produce $r \geq r^*$ (line 5). Worth noting is that the search at lines 3 to 13 can be done in parallel to improve convergence speed.

This algorithm reduces the number of rounds compared to testing all possible server learning rates using full FL sessions. In particular, since sessions are aborted when $r \geq r^*$, the overhead introduced by each adaptation step is limited. Assuming the parallel search is synchronized round-by-round, the additional overhead in number of rounds of our algorithm is:

$$3 \cdot r_0^* + 2 \sum_{i=1}^{n_a} r_i^* - r^* \tag{8}$$

where r_i^* is the minimum number of rounds at the end of the adaptive step i. The first term accounts for the first adaptive step, the second terms for the following adaptive steps, and the third term for the spared training rounds when running the full simulation with $\eta = \eta^*$.

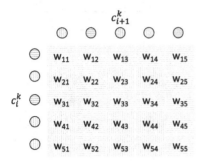

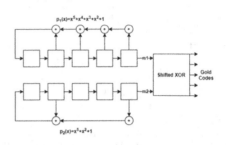

Fig. 2. Federated Dropout for masks $c_i^k=[0,1,0,1,1]$ and $c_{i+1}^k=[1,0,1,1,0]$ reduces the weights to be trained from 25 to 9.

Fig. 3. Gold code generation for two preferred feedback polynomials. The output is a set of $2^5 + 1 = 32$ sequences of length $2^5 - 1 = 31$.

Algorithm 1 selects the optimal η^* in terms of number of rounds to reach the target accuracy. The Round function at line 6 represents the underlying FL mechanism being used to compute the trained model, for instance, FAVG or FedAdam.

We argue that running full simulations to achieve the same level of granularity takes $T\times$ the number of rounds per simulation, where T is the number of tried server learning rates. This value is strictly greater than the bound provided by Eq. (8).

3.2   Coded Federated Dropout

We reduce the size of the model by dropping weights from each layer by associating to each client k and model layer i in the FL round a binary mask vector $c_i^k \in \mathbf{R}^{N_i}$. A unit is dropped or kept when the component c_{ij}^k is equal to 0 or 1 respectively. For adjacent fully connected layers (Fig. 2) the dropped weights can be straightforwardly obtained by eliminating rows and columns corresponding to the dropped units from the previous and following layer respectively. As in standard FD, we only drop a fraction α of nodes per layer i, which produces the same model size for all clients. For instance, in Fig. 2 we have $N_i = N_{i+1} = 5$ and $\alpha = 2/5$ and therefore only $N_i \cdot N_{i+1} \cdot (1-\alpha)^2 = 25 \cdot \frac{9}{25} = 9$ weights should be transmitted instead of $N_i \cdot N_{i+1} = 25$.

The problem to be solved is to obtain a matrix C_i per layer i with the following properties:

- each row of C_i is a codeword $c_i^k \in \mathbf{R}^{N_i}$; and
- the Hamming weight (*i.e.*, the number of ones in the codeword) of each row in C_i is equal to $N_i \cdot (1 - \alpha)$; and
- the number of rows in C_i is greater or equal than the number of clients per round M.

We consider 4 methods to compute C_i: (i) same random codeword for each client (baseline Federated Dropout), (ii) different random codeword for each client (proposed contemporaneously by [27]), (iii) Gold sequences, and (iv) CWCs. While the first two are straightforward, the other two provide different levels of orthogonality between the

Table 1. Preferred polynomial pairs for Gold codes generation.

Degree	Sequence length	Polynomial 1	Polynomial 2
5	31	$1 + x^2 + x^5$	$1 + x^2 + x^3 + x^4 + x^5$
6	63	$1 + x^6$	$1 + x^1 + x^2 + x^5 + x^6$
7	127	$1 + x^3 + x^7$	$1 + x^1 + x^2 + x^3 + x^7$
9	511	$1 + x^4 + x^9$	$1 + x^3 + x^4 + x^6 + x^9$
10	1023	$1 + x^3 + x^{10}$	$1 + x^2 + x^3 + x^8 + x^{10}$
11	2047	$1 + x^2 + x^5 + x^8 + x^{11}$	$1 + x^2 + x^{11}$

dropped models. Since sub-models are trained independently and then aggregated, having partially non overlapping sub-models reduces the impact of heterogeneous updates.

In CFD we exploit the different masks per client. At the beginning of each training round, we compute one matrix C_i for each layer i. Client k is assigned the k-th row from each C_i and the correspondent weights are extracted from the global model. If such a matrix is burdensome to be computed or if it would be the same after the generation process, then the rows and columns of the matrix are shuffled instead. In that way, the excess codewords can be employed when the number of rows of C_i is greater than M.

Applying coded masks to neural networks is not straightforward, since it requires different approaches according to the kind of employed layers. For *fully connected* layers, it is sufficient to apply dropout as in Fig. 2. For *convolutional* layers, we experimentally observed that dropping entire filters rather than individual weights achieves better performance. *Long Short-Term Memory* layers [12], which are composed of multiple gates, require that the same mask is employed for each set of weights.

After each sub-model has been trained, each weight in the global model is updated by averaging the contribution of each sub-model which contained that weight.

Gold Codes. Codewords orthogonality may be defined by means of cross-correlation. The correlation between two real binary sequences u^1 and u^2 of length L_u is a function of the shift l:

$$R(u_1, u_2, l) = \frac{1}{L_u} \sum_{j=1}^{L_u} u_j^1 \cdot u_{(j+l)mod L_u}^2 \tag{9}$$

$$u_j^1, u_j^2 \in \{-1, 1\} \quad \forall j = 1, ..., L_u$$

Gold codes are generated from two Linear Feedback Shift Registers (LFSR) with suitable feedback polynomials and initial conditions. The LFSRs produce two m-sequences, which are then circularly shifted and element-wise xored to produce all the sequences in the family. The size n_{LFSR} of the LFSR determines the code length $2^{n_{\text{LFSR}}} - 1$, the number of codewords in the set $2^{n_{\text{LFSR}}} + 1$, and the upper bounds for the maximum cross-correlation in the set:

$$\max_l \left| R(c_i^{k_1}, c_i^{k_2}, l) \right| = 2^{\lfloor (n_{\text{LFSR}}+2)/2 \rfloor} + 1 \tag{10}$$

$$\forall k_1, k_2 \in \{1, ...(2^{n_{\text{LFSR}}} + 1)\}, \quad k_1 \neq k_2$$

Algorithm 2. Constant Weight Code Generation

Input: N_i, M, α, t_{max}
Output: C_i

 1: Let $t = 0$.
 2: $d_{\min} = N_i, C_i = \{\}$
 3: $F_i = \{f \in \{0,1\}^{N_i} : w_h(f) = (1 - \alpha) \cdot N_i\}$, f added in lexicographic order
 4: Add random codeword from F_i to C_i
 5: **while** $t < t_{\max}$ **do**
 6:     $F_i = \{f \in F_i : d_h(f,c) \geq d_{\min} \forall c \in C_i\}$
 7:     **if** $|F_i| \neq 0$ **then**
 8:         Add first sequence from F_i to C_i
 9:     **else**
10:         $d_{\min} = d_{\min} - 2, C_i = \{\}$
11:         $F_i = \{f \in 0, 1_i^N : w_h(f) = (1 - \alpha) \cdot N_i\}$, f added in lexicographic order
12:         Add random codeword from F_i to C_i
13:     **end if**
14:     **if** $|C_i| = M$ **then**
15:         **return** C_i
16:     **end if**
17: **end while**
18: **return** C_i

After computing the sequences, we concatenate them as row vectors in matrix C_i, which will then have $2^{n_{\mathrm{LFSR}}} + 1$ rows and $2^{n_{\mathrm{LFSR}}}$ columns. For our experiments, we employ the preferred polynomials pairs listed in Table 1. The table also contains the correspondent length of the generated gold sequences. In order to have a suitable length for the model layers, we usually pad each resulting sequence with a 0 value after the longest run of zeros. Also note that Gold sequences with multiple of 4° are not supported. Figure 3 provides an example of the LFSR used to generate Gold codes of length 31.

Although Gold codes provide orthogonality, they have constraints on the size of C_i and α value, which can only be 50% since most Gold sequences are balanced (i.e., Hamming weight $2^{n_{\mathrm{LFSR}}-1}$). Please refer to [22] for details on constructions and properties of Gold codes and LFSR-generated sequences.

Constant Weight Codes. Another metric is the Hamming distance between two codewords u^1 and u^2, which is the number of ones in $u^1 \oplus u^2$:

$$d_h(u^1, u^2) = \sum_{j=1}^{L_u} u_j^1 \oplus u_j^2 \qquad (11)$$

We provide a method to create a matrix C_i with size $M \times N_i$ where, in order to improve orthogonality, the minimum Hamming distance between rows is maximized. CWC are a family of non-linear codes where each sequence has a fixed Hamming weight (*i.e.*, number of ones). CWC are flexible: they can provide sets of codewords with any cardinality, sequence length, and Hamming weight. We devise a variant of the

Table 2. Model summary. Total number of parameters is 6,603,710).

Layer Type	Output Shape	Param #	Activation	Hyper-parameters
Convolutional 2D	(–, 28, 28, 32)	832	ReLU	Num filters: 32 Kernel size: (5,5) Padding: Same
MaxPooling 2D	(–,14,14,32)	0	–	Pool size: (2,2) Padding: Valid
Convolutional 2D	(–, 14, 14, 64)	51264	ReLU	Num filters: 64 Kernel size: (5,5) Padding: Same
MaxPooling 2D	(–,7,7,64)	0	–	Pool size: (2,2) Padding: Valid
Flatten	(–, 3136)	0	–	
Dense	(–, 2048)	6424576	ReLU	Num units: 2048
Dense	(–, 62)	127038	–	Num units: 62

algorithm from [19] to generate M codewords with length N_i and weight $(1 - \alpha) \cdot N_i$ by maximizing the minimum distance. Starting from a random codeword, we iteratively select new sequences with a fixed distance from the current set. The sequences are added in lexicographic order. If the final set is not complete (i.e., a set of M sequences with weight $(1 - \alpha) \cdot N_i$ and length N_i does not exist for the given minimum distance), the required minimum distance is decremented and the selection procedure is performed again. The algorithm is described in 2, where we identify C_i as a set of codewords instead of a matrix.

4 Evaluation

We run our code in vanilla TensorFlow [1] and Python 3, since the major frameworks for FL do not support FD. In particular, although TensorFlow Federated [26] allows FD with the same dropping masks, it does not allow broadcast of different models to the clients (which we require for CFD). The generation algorithm for CWC was implemented in MATLAB. Training was performed on the EMNIST dataset [6,9] for character and digits recognition. We normalize the pixels in each image in the $[0, 1]$ interval and use a batch size of 10. We provide a description of the employed model in Table 2, which is *model C* from [23]. Each client optimizes the sparse categorical crossentropy loss with the SGD optimizer. We train the model for 500 rounds. We use four kinds of codes for CFD with dropout fraction $\alpha = 0.5$: random with same sub-model for each client (baseline FD), random with different sub-models, Gold and CWC. We experiment with two different server optimization methods (FAVG and FedAdam) and perform the fast server learning rate tuning for both of them. The FedAdam hyper-parameters β_1, β_2, and τ do not need to be tuned since it has been demonstrated that default values are usually enough to achieve good convergence [21].

Table 3. Selected η values for 10 simulations and different codes and aggregation algorithms.

	FedAdam				FAVG	
Server Learning Rate (Log10)→	−2.25	−2	−1.75	−1.5	0,25	0,5
α :0.0 Fedadam No Dropout	0%	30%	60%	10%	100%	0%
α :0.5 Random Fedadam	0%	20%	30%	**50%**	0%	**100%**
α :0.5 CWC FedAdam	0%	10%	40%	**50%**	0%	**100%**
α :0.5 Gold FedAdam	0%	0%	**80%**	20%	0%	**100%**
α :0.5 Fedadam + Baseline FD	**50%**	50%	0%	0%	**70%**	30%

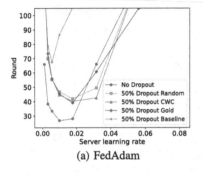
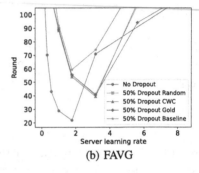

(a) FedAdam   (b) FAVG

Fig. 4. The dropout approaches require a higher η in order to reach the minimal number of rounds for the target accuracy.

**The Fast Server Learning Rate Tuning Algorithm Achieves Consistent Optimal.
η values across many simulations.** We run 10 training sessions for each coded approach with target accuracy $\gamma^* = 20/62$ (which is 20 times the random accuracy) and showcase the results in Table 3 (highest probability is in bold). Whereas for FAVG the selected η is the same for all simulations (except for the baseline FD), FedAdam produces higher variability. However, the differences between the different selected η^* amounts to a maximum of 0.5 in log scale for each code.

The Optimal Server Learning Rate in a Traditional FL session is Greater than that of an FD Session, Especially When a Different Sub-model Per Client is Employed.
We experiment with 10 simulations with our tuning algorithm and keep track of the number of rounds to reach γ^* for each experimented η. Figure 4 shows the average number of rounds for each η for both FedAdam and FAVG and makes evident that the η producing the minimum number of rounds is greater for the coded approaches compared to the no dropout. Moreover, although the no dropout case is still the fastest one, the coded approaches achieve up to 1.5× speedup to reach γ^* compared to the dropout baseline, thus improving convergence time.

Our Tuning Mechanism Saves Communication Resources Compared to Running Full FL Sessions with Different Values of η. We compute the number of additional rounds as in Eq. 8 and report the results in Table 4. In FedAdam$_{10}$, γ^* is 10 times the

Table 4. Average number of additional rounds for different codes.

	No Drop	Rand	CWC	Gold	FD
FedAdam$_{20}$	154.9	262.5	248.6	259.3	456.3
FAVG$_{20}$	166.4	393.0	383.1	387.9	479.3
FedAdam$_{10}$	140.7	219.2	225.6	211.9	351.2

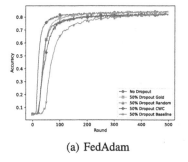

(a) FedAdam

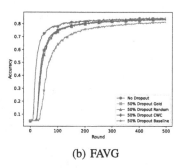

(b) FAVG

Fig. 5. Average test accuracy of FedAdam and FAVG for 5 simulations with the selected η^* from Table 3. Coded Federated Dropout with Gold codes and FedAdam improves convergence rate and final accuracy compared to random, CWC and baseline FD approaches.

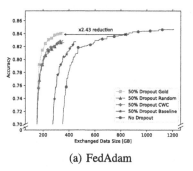

(a) FedAdam

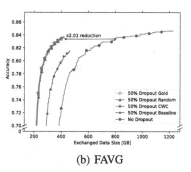

(b) FAVG

Fig. 6. Reachable test accuracy for FedAdam and FAVG given the amount of exchanged bytes in a FL session. Coded Federated Dropout with Gold codes and FedAdam reaches the same level of final accuracy as no dropout while reducing bandwidth usage by $2.43\times$.

random accuracy (10/62) instead of 20. The overhead is directly dependent on the convergence speed of the model. Consequently, the no dropout case requires the least overhead and the baseline FD the most. Still, the additional number of rounds is much lower than running multiple full FL sessions. For both FedAdam and FAVG, our tuning algorithm tests 10 η values. Therefore, running full sessions would require $500 \cdot (10 - 1)$ additional rounds. We point out that decreasing the accuracy threshold γ^* to 10/62 notably reduces the additional number of rounds (FedAdam$_{10}$). The best selected η is only sightly influenced by changing γ^*, thus demonstrating that tuning the threshold value is much easier than tuning η directly.

Table 5. Adopted notations and principal symbols.

Symbol	Description	Value
N_i	Number of units in model layer i	See Table 2
T	Number of total clients	3400
M	Number of clients per round	35
α	Dropout fraction for FD	0.5
η_l	Client learning rate	0.035
E	Training epochs per client	1
η	Server learning rate	See Sec. 3.1
β_1	Momentum parameter for FedAdam	0.90
β_2	Momentum parameter for FedAdam	0.99
τ	Adaptivity degree for FedAdam	0.001
$w^{(t)}$	Server weights at round t	–
$w_k^{(t)}$	Initial client k weights at round t	–
$\hat{w}_k^{(t)}$	Final client k weights at round t	–
D_k	Dataset for client k	–
$\{\xi\}_k^{(t)}$	Set of batches for client k at round t	–
$L(.)$	Client loss function	–
$S(t)$	Set of clients selected at round t	–
c_i^k	Binary mask for client k and layer i	–
c_{ij}^k	Component j of c_i^k	–
C_i	Codes Matrix per layer i	–
n_{LFSR}	Size of the LFSR	See Tab. 1
$R(u_1, u_2, l)$	Correlation between u_1 and u_2 for shift l	–
$d_h(u^1, u^2)$	Hamming distance between u_1 and u_2	–
$w_h(u)$	Hamming weight of u	–
γ^*	Target accuracy	$\frac{20}{62}$ or $\frac{10}{62}$
γ_k^t	Training accuracy for client k at round t	
$\overline{\gamma}^t$	Median training accuracy at round t	–
$\overline{\gamma}$	Average of $\overline{\gamma}^t$ at round t	–
q	Rounds number to compute $\overline{\gamma}$	–
n_a	Number of adaptation steps	3
η^*	Best server learning rate	See Tab. 3
$\Delta\eta$	Log distance between tentative η values	–
$\Delta\eta_0$	Initial $\Delta\eta$	1
$\mathbb{H}$	Set of tentative η values	–
r	Current round number	–
r^*	Best round number to reach γ^*	–
r_i^*	Best round number to reach γ^* at step i	–

Gold Codes Outperform Other FD Approaches for FedAdam and Achieve 99.6% of the Final Accuracy of the no Dropout Case While Saving > 2× bandwidth. Figure 5 shows the average test accuracy of simulations run with the previously selected η^* values. While the benefits of using Gold codes or CWC is negligible in terms of final accuracy compared to random for FAVG, FedAdam plus Gold codes produces higher convergence speed. Moreover, Gold FedAdam reaches 99.6% of the final accuracy of the no dropout case while saving almost $1 - (1-\alpha)^2 = 75\%$ of the bandwidth per round. The best result is achieved by FAVG without dropout (84.1% accuracy) when averaging over the last 100 rounds, while Gold codes achieve 83.8% for FedAdam, which is the 99.6%. Conversely, CWC does not perform well for FedAdam, achieving even worse performance than random codes. Regarding the overall bandwidth, we measure the size of the exchanged sub-models and compute the amount of gigabytes needed to reach a certain test accuracy. Figure 6 shows the reduction in overall bandwidth when CFD is employed with the selected η^* values. Gold codes plus FedAdam reduces the bandwidth needed to reach the maximum test accuracy by 2.43× compared to no dropout, while CFD plus FAVG by 2.01×.

Minimizing Cross-Correlation Instead of Maximizing Minimal Distance Provides Greater Sub-model Orthogonality. Figure 5 and 6 show that Gold codes always outperform CWC. Therefore, codes built by minimizing cross-correlation produce higher final accuracy and convergence rate than the ones obtained by maximizing the minimum distance. Nevertheless, optimizing any of the two metrics outperforms the baseline for federated dropout for both FedAdam and FAVG.

5   Conclusion and Future Works

We have presented a fast server learning rate tuning algorithm for Federated Dropout and shown considerable reduction on the number of rounds to assess the optimal η^*. Moreover, we have shown that convergence rate and final accuracy of models trained in a FL session are improved when using coding theory to carefully perform Federated Dropout. Specifically, CFD with Gold sequences paired with an optimization mechanism such as FedAdam can achieve up to the same accuracy of the no dropout case, with 2.43× bandwidth savings. However, Gold codes have specific lengths and Hamming weights, so they are not flexible enough, while CWC does not improve performance compared to random dropout. Hence, future work will investigate further sequences from coding theory for FD.

Acknowledgements. This research work was conducted with funding awarded by the Swedish Research Council for the project "Scalable Federated Learning" with registration number 2021-04610. This publication is based upon work supported by the King Abdullah University of Science and Technology (KAUST) Office of Research Administration (ORA) under Award No. ORA-CRG2021-4699.

References

1. Abadi, M., et al.: Tensorflow: a system for large-scale machine learning. In: 12th USENIX Symposium on Operating Systems Design and Implementation (OSDI'16), pp. 265–283 (2016). https://www.usenix.org/system/files/conference/osdi16/osdi16-abadi.pdf
2. Alistarh, D., Grubic, D., Li, J., Tomioka, R., Vojnovic, M.: QSGD: communication-efficient SGD via gradient quantization and encoding (2017)
3. Alistarh, D., Hoefler, T., Johansson, M., Khirirat, S., Konstantinov, N., Renggli, C.: The convergence of sparsified gradient methods (2018)
4. Bouacida, N., Hou, J., Zang, H., Liu, X.: Adaptive federated dropout: improving communication efficiency and generalization for federated learning (2020)
5. Brouwer, A., Shearer, J., Sloane, N., Smith, W.: A new table of constant weight codes. IEEE Trans. Inf. Theory 36(6), 1334–1380 (1990). https://doi.org/10.1109/18.59932
6. Caldas, S., et al.: Leaf: a benchmark for federated settings (2019)
7. Caldas, S., Konecný, J., McMahan, H.B., Talwalkar, A.: Expanding the reach of federated learning by reducing client resource requirements. CoRR abs/1812.07210 (2018). http://arxiv.org/abs/1812.07210
8. Chollet, F.: Keras. https://github.com/fchollet/keras (2015)
9. Cohen, G., Afshar, S., Tapson, J., van Schaik, A.: EMNIST: an extension of MNIST to handwritten letters (2017)
10. Ericcson: Mobile subscriptions shifting towards 5g. https://www.ericsson.com/en/mobility-report/reports/june-2021 (2021)
11. Gold, R.: Optimal binary sequences for spread spectrum multiplexing (corresp.). IEEE Trans. Inf. Theory 13(4), 619–621 (1967). https://doi.org/10.1109/TIT.1967.1054048
12. Hochreiter, S., Schmidhuber, J.: Long short-term memory. Neural Comput. 9(8), 1735–1780 (1997)
13. Karimireddy, S.P., Kale, S., Mohri, M., Reddi, S.J., Stich, S.U., Suresh, A.T.: Scaffold: stochastic controlled averaging for federated learning (2021)
14. Kasami, T.: Weight distribution formula for some class of cyclic codes. Coordinated Science Laboratory Report no. R-285 (1966)
15. Lee, W.: Overview of cellular CDMA. IEEE Trans. Veh. Technol. 40(2), 291–302 (1991). https://doi.org/10.1109/25.289410
16. Li, T., Hu, S., Beirami, A., Smith, V.: Ditto: fair and robust federated learning through personalization. In: Meila, M., Zhang, T. (eds.) Proceedings of the 38th International Conference on Machine Learning. Proceedings of Machine Learning Research, vol. 139, pp. 6357–6368. PMLR (2021). https://proceedings.mlr.press/v139/li21h.html
17. Li, X., Huang, K., Yang, W., Wang, S., Zhang, Z.: On the convergence of fedavg on non-iid data (2020)
18. McMahan, H.B., Moore, E., Ramage, D., Hampson, S., y Arcas, B.A.: Communication-efficient learning of deep networks from decentralized data (2017)
19. Montemanni, R., Smith, D.H.: Heuristic algorithms for constructing binary constant weight codes. IEEE Trans. Inf. Theory 55(10), 4651–4656 (2009). https://doi.org/10.1109/TIT.2009.2027491
20. Parliament, T.E.: The council of the European union: reform of EU data protection rules. https://gdpr-info.eu/ (2018)
21. Reddi, S., et al.: Adaptive federated optimization (2020)
22. Sarwate, D., Pursley, M.: Crosscorrelation properties of pseudorandom and related sequences. Proc. IEEE 68(5), 593–619 (1980). https://doi.org/10.1109/PROC.1980.11697
23. Springenberg, J.T., Dosovitskiy, A., Brox, T., Riedmiller, M.: Striving for simplicity: the all convolutional net (2015)

24. Srivastava, N., Hinton, G., Krizhevsky, A., Sutskever, I., Salakhutdinov, R.: Dropout: a simple way to prevent neural networks from overfitting. J. Mach. Learn. Res. **15**(1), 1929–1958 (2014)
25. Taaghol, P., Evans, B., Buracchini, E., De Gaudinaro, G., Lee, J.H., Kang, C.G.: Satellite umts/imt2000 w-cdma air interfaces. IEEE Commun. Mag. **37**(9), 116–126 (1999). https://doi.org/10.1109/35.790970
26. Tensorflow.org: Tensorflow federated. https://www.tensorflow.org/federated (2017)
27. Wen, D., Jeon, K.J., Huang, K.: Federated dropout - a simple approach for enabling federated learning on resource constrained devices (2021)
28. Zeiler, M.D.: Adadelta: An adaptive learning rate method (2012)

FedAUXfdp: Differentially Private One-Shot Federated Distillation

Haley Hoech[1], Roman Rischke[1], Karsten Müller[1],
and Wojciech Samek[1,2,3]

[1] Department of Artificial Intelligence, Fraunhofer Heinrich Hertz Institute,
10587 Berlin, Germany
haley@haleyhoech.com,
{roman.rischke,karsten.mueller,wojciech.samek}@hhi.fraunhofer.de
[2] Department of Electrical Engineering and Computer Science,
Technische Universität Berlin, 10587 Berlin, Germany
[3] BIFOLD – Berlin Institute for the Foundations of Learning and Data,
10587 Berlin, Germany

Abstract. Federated learning suffers in the case of non-iid local datasets, i.e., when the distributions of the clients' data are heterogeneous. One promising approach to this challenge is the recently proposed method FedAUX, an augmentation of federated distillation with robust results on even highly heterogeneous client data. FedAUX is a partially (ϵ, δ)-differentially private method, insofar as the clients' private data is protected in only part of the training it takes part in. This work presents a *fully differentially private* modification, termed FedAUX*fdp*. To specify the amount of noise in the applied Gaussian mechanism, we further contribute an upper bound on the l_2-sensitivity of regularized multinomial logistic regression. In experiments with deep networks on large-scale image datasets, FedAUXfdp with strong differential privacy guarantees performs significantly better than other equally privatized SOTA baselines on non-iid client data in just a single communication round. Fully privatizing the FedAUX modification results in a negligible reduction in accuracy at all levels of data heterogeneity.

Keywords: Federated Learning · Differential Privacy · Federated Distillation · Non-IID Data · Heterogeneous Data · Regularized Empirical Risk Minimization

1 Introduction

Federated learning (FL) is a form of decentralized machine learning, in which a global model is formed by an orchestration server aggregating the outcome of training on a number of local client models without any sharing of their private training data [20]. Interest in federated learning has increased recently for its privacy and communication-efficiency advantages over centralized learning on mobile and edge devices [15,26]. A classical mechanism for model aggregation in FL is federated averaging (FedAVG), where the locally trained models are weighted proportionally to the size of the local dataset. In each communication round of federated averaging, weight updates of the clients' local models are sent to the orchestration server, averaged by the server, and the average is sent back to the federation of clients to initialize the next round of training [20].

Federated ensemble distillation (FedD), an often even more communication-efficient and accurate alternative to FedAVG, uses knowledge distillation to transfer knowledge from clients to server [5,12,18,25]. In FedD, clients and server share a public dataset auxiliary to the clients' private data. The clients communicate the output of their privately trained models on the public distillation dataset to the server, which uses the average of these outputs as supervision for the distillation data in training the global model. In comparison to federated averaging, federated ensemble distillation offers additional privacy, as direct white box attacks are not possible for example, and allows combining different model architectures, making it appealing in an Internet-of-Things ecosystem [3,16,17].

FedAUX is an augmentation of federated distillation, which derives its success from taking full advantage of the AUXiliary data. FedAUX uses this auxiliary data for model pretraining and relevance weighting. To perform the weighting, the clients' output on each data point of the distillation dataset is individually weighted by a measure of similarity between that distillation datapoint and the client's local data, called a 'certainty score'. Weighting the outputs by the scores prioritizes votes from clients whose local data is more similar to the auxiliary/distillation data.

A major challenge of federated learning is performance when the distributions of the clients' data are heterogeneous, i.e. performance on "non-iid" data, as is often the circumstance in real-world applications of FL [13]. FedAUX overcomes that challenge, performing remarkably more efficiently on non-iid data than other state-of-the-art federated learning methods, federated averaging, federated proximal learning, Bayesian federated learning, and federated ensemble distillation. For example on MobilenetV2, FedAUX achieves 64.8% server accuracy, while even the second-best method only achieves 46.7% [24].

Despite its privacy benefits, federated distillation still presents a privacy risk to clients participating [22]. Data-level, local differential privacy protects the clients' data by limiting the impact of any individual datapoint on the model and quantifies the privacy loss associated to participating in training with parameters (ϵ, δ). Both governments and private institutions are increasingly interested in securing their data using differential privacy.

Each client in the FedAUX method trains two models on their local dataset. In [24], only the scoring model is privatized, leaving the classification model exposed. The clients' data is accordingly only protected with differential privacy in part of the training it participates in. In this work, we add a local, data-level (ϵ, δ)-differentially private mechanism for this second model and appropriately modify the FedAUX method to apply said mechanism. We thereby contribute a 'fully' privatized version of FedAUX. Full differential privacy here is used as a way of describing our contribution of privacy over the original FedAUX method. Additionally, we give an upper bound on the l_2-sensitivity of regularized multinomial logistic regression to specify the amount of noise in the applied Gaussian mechanism. See Sect. 4.2 for background on differential privacy.

In results with deep neural networks on large scale image datasets at an $(\epsilon = 0.6, \delta = 2 * 10^{-5})$-level of differential privacy we compare fully differentially private FedAUXfdp with two privatized baselines, federated ensemble distillation and federated averaging in a single communication round. FedAUXfdp outperforms these baselines dramatically on the heterogeneous client data. Our method modifications achieve better results than FedAUX in a single communication round and we see a negligible reduction in accuracy of applying this strong amount of differential privacy to the FedAUX modification.

Section 3 outlines the original FedAUX method, Sect. 4 explains our modification including our privacy mechanism as well as background on differential privacy, and Sect. 5 details the experimental set-up and highlights important results.

2   Related Work

FedAUXfdp modifies the semi-differentially private FedAUX method presented in [24]. For a discussion of works related to the non-privacy aspects of FedAUX, we hence refer interested readers to [24].

The authors of [7] introduced differential privacy and [14] established local differential privacy. Differential privacy bounds were greatly improved with the introduction of the moments accountant in [1].

In addition to quantifying privacy loss, differential privacy protects provably against membership inference attacks [6,28], in which an adversary can determine if a data point participated in the training of a model. Membership inference attacks can pose a privacy threat, for example, if participation in model training could imply a client has a particular disease or other risk factor. Alternatives for protecting privacy in general include secure multi-party computation or homomorphic encryption, though neither protect against membership inference attacks [28]. Others have combined local differential privacy and federated averaging on homogeneous data, notably [8,21]. In [2], federated averaging is performed with differential privacy on both iid and non-iid data with robust results. Even in the non-iid data setting, each client still sees a substantial number of data points from each class. We provide robust results on far more heterogeneous client data distributions. [30] requires a lot more rounds and also has a much larger degradation of accuracy for a given level of privacy. While [29] combined federated model distillation with differential privacy, they only attain robust results on non-iid data when the client and distillation data contains the same classes. One-shot FL, where the client models perform just a single round of communication was presented by [9]. The authors in [33] also combine distillation with one-shot FL.

Our one-shot federated distillation approach uses model distillation to transfer the learning outcome in form of softlabels for a public distillation dataset. [33]

use dataset distillation, a concept introduced in [31], to design a communication-efficient and privacy-preserving one-shot FL mechanism.

3 FedAUX

3.1 Method

In FedAUX, there are two actors, the clients and the orchestration server. Each client, $i = 1, \ldots, n$, has its own private, local, labeled dataset D_i. Auxiliary to the client data is a public, unlabeled dataset D_{aux}. The auxiliary data is further split into the negative data D^-, used in training the certainty score models, and the distillation data $D_{distill}$, used for knowledge distillation.

There are three types of models, the clients' scoring models, the clients' classification models, and the server's global model, which can all be decomposed into a feature extractor h and linear or logistic regression classification head. Whether the full model or just the classification head is trained varies by model and we outline this next. In FedAUX four kinds of training are conducted (See Fig. 1):

1. **Feature extractor.** Unsupervised pretraining with the public auxiliary data D_{aux} on the server to obtain the feature extractor, h_0, which is sent to the clients and initialized in all their models as well as the server's.
2. **Scoring model heads.** Supervised training of the scoring model classification heads s_i of all clients, in combination with the frozen feature extractor h_0 to generate scoring models $f_i = s_i \circ h_0$. Each training is a binary logistic regression on the extracted features of their private local data and the public negative data $h_0(D_i \cup D^-)$.
3. **Classification models.** Supervised training of the clients' full classification models $g_i = c_i \circ h_i$, consisting of a feature extractor h_i (initialized with h_0 from the pretraining) and linear classification head c_i, on their local datasets D_i.
4. **Server model.** Supervised training of the server's full model S, consisting of a feature extractor h (initialized with h_0 from the pretraining) and linear classification head. The server calculates an initial weight update of the clients' average class model weight updates from their training round. For the server's training, the input data X is the unlabeled $D_{distill}$ and the supervision Y a $(|D_{distill}| \times n_{classes})$-dimensional matrix of the softlabel output of the class model $g_i(D_{distill})$, weighted by a certainty score for each distillation datapoint. The certainty scores are the output of the (ϵ, δ)-differentially privatized scoring model on the distillation data $f_i(D_{distill})$, measures of similarity between each distillation data point and the client's local data. Each entry in Y is:

$$\frac{\sum_i f_i(x) \cdot g_i(x)}{\sum_i f_i(x)}, \text{ for } x \in D_{distill}. \tag{1}$$

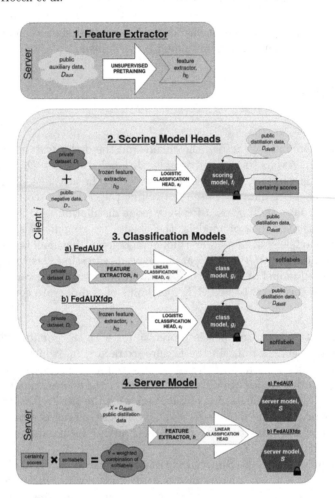

Fig. 1. Overview of FedAUX and FedAUXfdp training. Models secured with differential privacy indicated with black locks.

3.2 Privacy

Participating in the training of the scoring classification heads and classification models presents a privacy risk to the private data of the clients. In FedAUX, the scoring heads are sanitized using an (ϵ, δ)-differentially private sanitization mechanism. FedAUX's mechanism for privatizing the scoring model is based on freezing the feature extractor and using a logistic classification head. As the feature extractor was trained on public data, only sanitizing this head is required to yield a differentially private model. Further, using the L-BFGS optimizer in sci-kit learn's logistic regression guarantees finding optimal weights for the logistic regression heads. In FedAUXfdp we privatize the classification models in a similar fashion. This thereby makes the server model learned in FedAUXfdp fully differentially private, as discussed in Sect. 4, with the specific privacy mechanism outlined in Sect. 4.2.

4   FedAUXfdp

In the fully differentially private version of FedAUX, we adapt the training of the classification and server models as follows. Rather than training the full client models, we freeze the feature extractors and train only the classification heads using a multinomial logistic regression on extracted features of the client's local dataset D_i. As communicating model updates to the server poses a privacy threat, we no longer initialize the server with the averaged weight update of the clients. Accordingly, step three in the process is changed as follows:

3. **Classification model.** Supervised training of the classification model heads c_i of the clients, combined with the frozen feature extractor h_0, to generate class models $g_i = c_i \circ h_0$. Each is a multinomial logistic regression on the extracted features of their private local data $h_0(D_i)$. See Fig. 1.

As with the scoring models in the original FedAUX, freezing the feature extractors, which have been trained on public data, allows us to make the models differentially private by simply sanitizing the classification heads. Again, we opt for logistic classification heads because the L-BFGS optimizer in sci-kit learn's logistic regression guarantees convergence to globally optimal weights of the logistic regression.

We formulate the training of these classifiers as regularized empirical risk minimization problems.

4.1   Regularized Empirical Risk Minimization

Let $\boldsymbol{\beta} := (\boldsymbol{\beta}_1^T, \ldots, \boldsymbol{\beta}_C^T)^T \in \mathbb{R}^{C(p+1)}$ with $\boldsymbol{\beta}_k := (\beta_{k,0}, \ldots, \beta_{k,p})^T \in \mathbb{R}^{p+1}$ be the vector of trainable parameters of the regularized multinomial logistic regression problem with C classes

$$\min_{\boldsymbol{\beta}} J(\boldsymbol{\beta}, h, D) = \frac{1}{|D|} \sum_{i=1}^{|D|} -\log(p_{y_i}(h(\mathbf{x}_i))) + \frac{\lambda}{2}\|\boldsymbol{\beta}\|_2^2 \qquad (2)$$

with softmax function

$$p_{y_i}(\boldsymbol{\beta}, h(\mathbf{x}_i)) = \frac{\exp(\boldsymbol{\beta}_{y_i}^T h(\mathbf{x}_i))}{\sum_{k=1}^C \exp(\boldsymbol{\beta}_k^T h(\mathbf{x}_i))}$$

for a labeled data point $(\mathbf{x}_i, y_i)$ from a dataset D.

Thereby, $h(\mathbf{x}_i) \in \mathbb{R}^{p+1}$ is an extracted feature vector with the first coordinate being a constant for the bias term $\beta_{k,0}$, and $y_i \in \{1, \ldots, C\}$ the corresponding class label. We assume w.l.o.g. that

$$\|h(\mathbf{x})\|_2 \leq 1. \qquad (3)$$

To fulfill this assumption, we normalize the input features for the logistic regression problem as follows

$$\tilde{h}(\mathbf{x}) := h(\mathbf{x}) \left(\max_{\mathbf{x} \in D} \|h(\mathbf{x})\|_2 \right)^{-1}. \tag{4}$$

4.2   Privacy

We privatize the classification models using (ϵ, δ)-differential privacy. Informally, differential privacy anonymizes the client data in this context, insofar as with very high likelihood the results of the model would be very similar regardless whether or not a particular data point participates in training [7].

Definition 1. *A randomized mechanism $\mathcal{M} : \mathcal{D} \to \mathcal{R}$ satisfies (ϵ, δ)-differential privacy, if for any two adjacent inputs D_1 and D_2 that only differ in one element and for any subset of outputs $S \subseteq \mathcal{R}$,*

$$P[D_1 \in S] \leq \exp(\epsilon) P[\mathcal{M}(D_2) \in S] + \delta.$$

Definition 2. *For two datasets, D_1, D_2 differing in one data point, the l_2-sensitivity is*

$$\Delta_2(\mathcal{M}) := \max_{D_1, D_2 \in \mathcal{D}} \|\mathcal{M}(D_1) - \mathcal{M}(D_2)\|_2$$

We use the Gaussian mechanism, in which a specific amount of Gaussian noise is added relative to the l^2-*sensitivity* [7] and according to pre-selected ϵ and δ values.

Lemma 1 ([7]). *For $\epsilon \in (0, 1)$, $c^2 > 2 \ln(1.25/\delta)$, the Gaussian mechanism with parameter $\sigma \geq c\Delta_2(\mathcal{M})/\epsilon$ is (ϵ, δ)-differentially private.*

Sensitivity of the Classification Models. We contribute the following theorem for the l_2-sensitivity of regularized multinomial logistic regression (2), which generalizes a corollary from [4].

Theorem 1. *The l_2-sensitivity of regularized multinomial logistic regression, as defined in (2), is at most $\frac{2\sqrt{C}}{\lambda|D|}$.*

Proof. W.l.o.g. we set $h(\mathbf{x}) = \mathbf{x}$ in this proof and omit the argument h in the definition of J for ease of exposition. Let $D = \{(\mathbf{x}_1, y_1), \ldots, (\mathbf{x}_N, y_N)\}$ and $D' = (D \setminus \{(\mathbf{x}_N, y_N)\}) \cup \{(\mathbf{x}'_N, y'_N)\}$. That is, D and D' differ in exactly one data point. Furthermore, let

$$\boldsymbol{\beta}_1^* = \arg \min_{\boldsymbol{\beta}} J(\boldsymbol{\beta}, D) \tag{5}$$

$$\boldsymbol{\beta}_2^* = \arg \min_{\boldsymbol{\beta}} J(\boldsymbol{\beta}, D'). \tag{6}$$

The goal is to show that $\|\boldsymbol{\beta}_1^* - \boldsymbol{\beta}_2^*\|_2 \leq \frac{2\sqrt{C}}{\lambda N}$. We define

$$d(\boldsymbol{\beta}) := J(\boldsymbol{\beta}, D') - J(\boldsymbol{\beta}, D) \tag{7}$$
$$= \frac{1}{N} \left(l(\boldsymbol{\beta}, \mathbf{x}_N') - l(\boldsymbol{\beta}, \mathbf{x}_N) \right),$$

with the log-softmax loss function

$$l(\boldsymbol{\beta}, \mathbf{x}) := -\log(p_y(\boldsymbol{\beta}, \mathbf{x})) \tag{8}$$

for an arbitrary data point $(\mathbf{x}, y)$.

With

$$\nabla_{\boldsymbol{\beta}} \, l(\boldsymbol{\beta}, \mathbf{x}) = -\frac{\nabla_{\boldsymbol{\beta}} \, p_y(\boldsymbol{\beta}, \mathbf{x})}{p_y(\boldsymbol{\beta}, \mathbf{x})} \tag{9}$$

we obtain

$$\frac{\partial \, p_k(\boldsymbol{\beta}, \mathbf{x})}{\partial \, \boldsymbol{\beta}_k} = \frac{\exp(\boldsymbol{\beta}_k^T \mathbf{x}) \cdot \sum_{j \neq k} \exp(\boldsymbol{\beta}_j^T \mathbf{x})}{(\sum_j \exp(\boldsymbol{\beta}_j^T \mathbf{x}))^2} \mathbf{x} \tag{10}$$

$$\frac{\partial \, p_k(\boldsymbol{\beta}, \mathbf{x})}{\partial \, \boldsymbol{\beta}_{\ell \neq k}} = -\frac{\exp(\boldsymbol{\beta}_k^T \mathbf{x}) \cdot \exp(\boldsymbol{\beta}_\ell^T \mathbf{x})}{(\sum_j \exp(\boldsymbol{\beta}_j^T \mathbf{x}))^2} \mathbf{x} \tag{11}$$

$$\frac{\partial \, l(\boldsymbol{\beta}, \mathbf{x})}{\partial \, \boldsymbol{\beta}_{k=y}} = \frac{\sum_{j \neq k} \exp(\boldsymbol{\beta}_j^T \mathbf{x})}{\sum_j \exp(\boldsymbol{\beta}_j^T \mathbf{x})} \mathbf{x} \tag{12}$$

$$\frac{\partial \, l(\boldsymbol{\beta}, \mathbf{x})}{\partial \, \boldsymbol{\beta}_{\ell \neq y}} = -\frac{\exp(\boldsymbol{\beta}_\ell^T \mathbf{x})}{\sum_j \exp(\boldsymbol{\beta}_j^T \mathbf{x})} \mathbf{x}. \tag{13}$$

Note, that the factors on the rhs of (12) and (13) have absolute values of at most 1. Hence, we can bound

$$\|\nabla_{\boldsymbol{\beta}} \cdot d(\boldsymbol{\beta})\|_2 = \frac{1}{N} \|\nabla_{\boldsymbol{\beta}} \, l(\boldsymbol{\beta}, \mathbf{x}_N') - \nabla_{\boldsymbol{\beta}} \, l(\boldsymbol{\beta}, \mathbf{x}_N)\|_2 \tag{14}$$
$$\leq \frac{1}{N} \left(\|\nabla_{\boldsymbol{\beta}} \, l(\boldsymbol{\beta}, \mathbf{x}_N')\|_2 + \|\nabla_{\boldsymbol{\beta}} \, l(\boldsymbol{\beta}, \mathbf{x}_N)\|_2 \right)$$
$$\leq \frac{1}{N} \left(\sqrt{C} \|\mathbf{x}_N'\|_2 + \sqrt{C} \|\mathbf{x}_N\|_2 \right)$$
$$\leq \frac{2\sqrt{C}}{N},$$

where the last inequality follows from assumption (3) that $\|\mathbf{x}\|_2 \leq 1$.

We observe that due to the convexity of $l(\boldsymbol{\beta}, \mathbf{x})$ in $\boldsymbol{\beta}$ and the 1-strong convexity of the l_2-regularization term in (2), $J(\boldsymbol{\beta}, D)$ is λ-strongly convex. Hence, we obtain by Shalev-Shwartz inequality [27]

$$\left(\nabla_{\boldsymbol{\beta}} \, J(\boldsymbol{\beta}_1^*, D) - \nabla_{\boldsymbol{\beta}} \, J(\boldsymbol{\beta}_2^*, D) \right)^T \left(\boldsymbol{\beta}_1^* - \boldsymbol{\beta}_2^* \right) \geq \lambda \|\boldsymbol{\beta}_1^* - \boldsymbol{\beta}_2^*\|_2^2. \tag{15}$$

Algorithm 1. Classification model training and privatization

---

for each client **do**

$\qquad \beta^* \rightarrow \operatorname{argmin}_\beta J(\beta, h, D)$

$\qquad \sigma^2 \rightarrow \frac{8C \ln(1.25\delta^{-1})}{\epsilon^2 \lambda^2 (|D|)^2}$

$\qquad \beta^* \rightarrow \beta^* + \mathcal{N}(0, I\sigma^2)$

end for

Moreover, by construction of $d(\beta)$,

$$J(\beta_2^*, D) + d(\beta_2^*) = J(\beta_2^*, D'). \tag{16}$$

By optimality of β_1^* and β_2^*, it holds

$$\begin{aligned} \mathbf{0} = \nabla_\beta \; J(\beta_1^*, D) &= \nabla_\beta \; J(\beta_2^*, D') \\ &= \nabla_\beta \; J(\beta_2^*, D) + \nabla_\beta \; d(\beta_2^*). \end{aligned} \tag{17}$$

Applying the Cauchy-Schwartz inequality finally leads to

$$\begin{aligned} \|\beta_1^* - \beta_2^*\|_2 \cdot \|\nabla_\beta \; d(\beta_2^*)\|_2 &\geq \left(\beta_1^* - \beta_2^*\right)^T \nabla_\beta \; d(\beta_2^*) \\ &= \left(\beta_1^* - \beta_2^*\right)^T \left(\nabla_\beta \; J(\beta_1^*, D) - \nabla_\beta \; J(\beta_2^*, D)\right) \\ &\geq \lambda \|\beta_1^* - \beta_2^*\|_2^2, \end{aligned} \tag{18}$$

which concludes the proof, since

$$\|\beta_1^* - \beta_2^*\|_2 \leq \frac{\|\nabla_\beta \; d(\beta_2^*)\|_2}{\lambda} \leq \frac{2\sqrt{C}}{\lambda N}. \tag{19}$$

We remark that in the binary case ($C = 2$) one regression head parameterized by $\beta \in \mathbb{R}^{(p+1)}$ suffices, resulting in an l_2-sensitivity of at most $\frac{2}{\lambda|D|}$.

Private Mechanism. Using Theorem 1 and the Gaussian mechanism, we get our (ϵ, δ)-differentially private mechanism for sanitizing the multinomial classification models as follows:

$$\mathcal{M}_{priv}(D) = \mathcal{M}(D) + \mathcal{N}(0, I\sigma^2), \text{ where}$$

$$\sigma^2 = \frac{8C \ln(1.25\delta^{-1})}{\epsilon^2 \lambda^2 |D|^2}$$

This leads to the overall training procedure for the classification models described in Algorithm 1.

4.3   Cumulative Privacy Loss

By the composability and post-processing properties of differentially private mechanisms [7], the cumulative privacy loss for an individual client's dataset in training of the server's model is equal to the sum of the loss of the scoring and classification models. The server model is (ϵ, δ)-differentially private, where

$$\epsilon = \epsilon_{scores} + \epsilon_{classes}$$
$$\delta = \delta_{scores} + \delta_{classes}$$

5   Experiments

We ran experiments on large-scale convolutional, ShuffleNet- [32], MobileNet- [23], and ResNet-style [10] networks, using CIFAR-10 as local client data and both STL-10 and CIFAR-100 as auxiliary data. Of the auxiliary data, 80% is used for distillation and 20% for unsupervised pretraining. The pretraining is done by contrastive representation learning using the Adam optimizer with a learning rate of 10^{-3}.

The number of clients is $n = 20$ and there is full participation in one round of communication. The training data is split among the clients using a Dirichlet distribution with parameter α as done first in [11] and later in [5,18]. With the lowest $\alpha = 0.01$, clients see almost entirely one class of images. With the highest $\alpha = 10.24$, each client sees a substantial number of images from every class. See also Table 1. We follow [24] in their selection of highlighted Dirichlet parameters α, who chose $\alpha = 2^n * 10^{-2}$, for $n \in \{0, 2, 4, 10\}$.

Table 1. Ranked percentage of data coming from the three largest classes for each level of data heterogeneity

Class	$\alpha = 0.01$	$\alpha = 0.04$	$\alpha = 0.16$	$\alpha = 10.24$
First	94.5%	75.3%	56.8%	15.1%
Second	5.2%	16.6%	22.3%	13.6%
Third	0.3%	5.6%	10.1%	12.0%

We find the optimal weights of the class model logistic regressions using scikit-learn's LogisticRegression with the L-BFGS [19] optimizer. For baselines, we chose Federated Ensemble Distillation (FedD) and Federated Averaging (FedAVG), which we pretrain (+P) in the same fashion as FedAUXfdp. We also compare FedAUXfdp to FedAUX, but with a frozen feature extractor (+F) for consistency. In FedAUX+F, the clients' local models (linear classification heads) are trained for 40 local epochs. For FedAUX+F, FedAUXfdp, and FedD+P, the full sever model is trained for 10 distillation epochs using the Adam optimizer with a learning rate of $5 \cdot 10^{-5}$ and a batch size of 128. For FedAVG+P, the average of the weights of the clients' logistic regressions is used as a classification head on top of the frozen feature extractor on the server.

For privacy, we chose $(\epsilon = 0.1, \delta = 10^{-5})$ for the scores and unless otherwise mentioned $(\epsilon = 0.5, \delta = 10^{-5})$ for the classes. We choose regularization parameter $\lambda = 0.01$ for both the certainty score and class models unless otherwise mentioned.

Table 2. Server model inference accuracy of **FedAUXfdp as compared to FL baselines** with pretraining. All methods cumulative privacy loss ($\epsilon = 0.6, \delta = 2e-05$).

Model	Method	$\alpha = 0.01$	$\alpha = 0.04$	$\alpha = 0.16$	$\alpha = 10.24$
ShuffleNet	FedAVG+P	46.0± 0.4	56.7± 6.6	67.5± 3.5	74.1 ± 1.4
	FedD+P	41.8 ± 4.4	54.7 ± 5.0	68.8 ± 2.1	72.3 ± 1.6
	FedAUXfdp	**75.2 ± 1.1**	**74.6 ± 1.1**	72.3 ± 0.6	71.7 ± 1.3
MobileNetV2	FedAVG+P	47.2± 2.6	54.2± 5.5	65.6± 0.9	72.0 ± 0.6
	FedD+P	43.7 ± 1.8	52.2 ± 4.6	67.0 ± 1.7	70.8 ± 0.2
	FedAUXfdp	**72.8 ± 0.4**	**72.0 ± 1.2**	70.8 ± 0.2	69.4 ± 0.8

As shown in Table 2, on both ShuffleNet and MobileNetv2 architectures FedAUXfdp significantly outperforms baselines in the most heterogeneous settings ($\alpha = 0.01, 0.04$). While the baselines undergo a steady reduction in accuracy as client data heterogeneity increases, FedAUXfdp is even improving. As data heterogeneity increases fewer classes per client result in the addition of less noise, see Theorem 1.

Table 3. FedAUXfdp server model inference accuracy at **various levels of class differential privacy** (ϵ, δ) and **comparison to FedAUX+F** server model inference accuracy. Scoring model privacy for all methods ($\epsilon = 0.1, \delta = 1e-05$).

Model	Method	Class DP	$\alpha = 0.01$	$\alpha = 0.04$	$\alpha = 0.16$	$\alpha = 10.24$
ShuffleNet	FedAUX+F	None	64.8 ± 1.1	64.9 ± 0.5	67.7 ± 0.8	73.4 ± 0.1
	FedAUXfdp	None	76.1 ± 0.3	75.6 ± 0.4	75.2 ± 0.5	75.4 ± 0.1
	FedAUXfdp	(1.0, 1e-05)	75.7 ± 0.7	75.1 ± 0.7	74.6 ± 0.5	74.9 ± 0.2
	FedAUXfdp	(0.5, 1e-05)	75.2 ± 1.1	74.6 ± 1.1	72.3 ± 0.6	71.7 ± 1.3
	FedAUXfdp	(0.1, 1e-05)	60.8 ± 2.4	59.4 ± 5.8	33.9 ± 5.4	34.6 ± 3.0
	FedAUXfdp	(0.01, 1e-05)	36.3 ± 5.1	39.8 ± 7.5	12.6 ± 5.1	11.7 ± 3.5
MobileNetV2	FedAUX+F	None	60.1 ± 1.2	61.2 ± 1.8	63.7 ± 0.8	67.5 ± 0.0
	FedAUXfdp	None	73.0 ± 0.5	73.3 ± 0.6	73.2 ± 0.2	73.0 ± 0.1
	FedAUXfdp	(1.0, 1e-05)	73.0 ± 0.4	72.7 ± 1.0	72.7 ± 0.3	72.4 ± 0.0
	FedAUXfdp	(0.5, 1e-05)	72.8 ± 0.4	72.0 ± 1.2	70.8 ± 0.2	69.4 ± 0.8
	FedAUXfdp	(0.1, 1e-05)	66.4 ± 3.3	53.1 ± 12.9	38.9 ± 4.4	34.9 ± 3.3
	FedAUXfdp	(0.01, 1e-05)	44.4 ± 6.8	28.7 ± 5.1	16.6 ± 5.8	11.5 ± 0.8

Table 3 shows the impact on the server model accuracy from the method modifications and from different levels of privacy in FedAUXfdp. The method modifications (FedAUXfdp without the class differential privacy) are an all-around improvement in accuracy over FedAUX+F, especially on non-iid client data. The logistic classification heads outperform the linear ones in a single communication round. For FedAUXfdp with no class differential privacy the results are nearly constant as opposed to FedAUX+F, where one sees the usual improvement as iid-ness increases.

Privatizing FedAUXfdp at additional epsilon-delta values of $(0.5, 10^{-5})$ results in nearly no reduction in accuracy over FedAUXfdp with no class model privacy. Only at $\epsilon = 0.1$ we see a drop in accuracy. With equal regularization, the additional differential privacy impacts the models trained on the non-iid data distributions less than those trained on homogeneous data, again due to the class size term C in the l_2-sensitivity from Theorem 1.

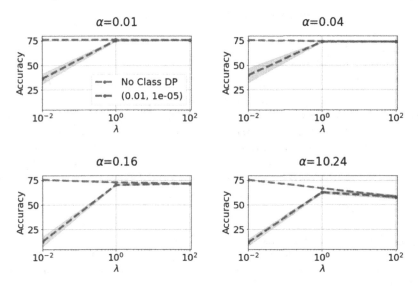

Fig. 2. Accuracy vs. regularization. Server model inference accuracy of FedAUXfdp on ShuffleNet with and without $(\epsilon = 0.01, \delta = 1e - 05)$ class model differential privacy at various levels of class model regularization λ.

The drop in accuracy of adding class differential privacy can be partially compensated for by increasing the regularization parameter λ of the client models' logistic regressions. Regularization reduces model variance and therefore the impact an individual datapoint has on the model. It thus affects the sensitivity of a differentially private mechanism as in the corollary from [4], which our sensitivity theorem generalizes. As shown in Fig. 2, on the ShuffleNet model architecture, increasing the regularization from $\lambda = 0.01$ to $\lambda = 1$ nearly eliminates the gap between the accuracy with and without $(\epsilon = 0.01, \delta = 10^{-5})$ class

Table 4. FedAUXfdp server model inference accuracy on ResNet8 with distillation data sharing 9/10 classes (STL-10) versus **entirely different distillation data classes** (CIFAR-100).

Distill Data	$\alpha = 0.01$	$\alpha = 0.04$	$\alpha = 0.16$	$\alpha = 10.24$
STL-10	77.2 ± 0.5	75.4 ± 1.0	74.7 ± 0.9	74.4 ± 0.8
CIFAR-100	70.4 ± 0.7	68.9 ± 1.8	67.6 ± 1.6	68.5 ± 1.9

model differential privacy at all levels of data heterogeneity α. The additional regularization does, however, reduce the accuracy of the model without the class differential privacy, moreso the more homogeneous the client data.

Table 4 shows results on ResNet with both STL-10 and CIFAR-100 as distillation data. STL-10 and CIFAR10 share 9/10 of the same classes, while CIFAR-100 has completely different classes. Even with distillation classes unmatching client classes, we still see robust results.

6   Conclusion

In this work, we have modified the FedAUX method, an augmentation of federated distillation, and made it fully differentially private. We have contributed a mechanism that privatizes respectably with little loss in model accuracy, particularly on non-iid client data. We additionally contributed a theorem for the sensitivity of l_2 regularized multinomial logistic regression. On large scale image datasets we have examined the impact of different amounts of differential privacy and regularization. Measuring the impact of federated averaging, distillation, and differential privacy on the attackability of the global server model would be an interesting investigation direction.

Acknowledgements. This work was partly supported by the German Ministry for Education and Research (BMBF) under Grants [BIFOLD (01IS18025A, 01IS18037I) and the European Union's Horizon 2020 research and innovation programme as grant [COPA EUROPE (957059)].

References

1. Abadi, M., et al.: Deep learning with differential privacy. In: Proceedings of the 2016 ACM SIGSAC Conference on Computer and Communications Security (CCS), pp. 308–318 (2016)
2. Adnan, M., Kalra, S., Cresswell, J., Taylor, G., Tizhoosh, H.: Federated learning and differential privacy for medical image analysis. Sci. Rep. **12**(1), 1953 (2022)
3. Chang, H., Shejwalkar, V., Shokri, R., Houmansadr, A.: Cronus: robust and heterogeneous collaborative learning with black-box knowledge transfer. arXiv preprint arXiv:1912.11279 (2019)
4. Chaudhuri, K., Monteleoni, C., Sarwate, A.D.: Differentially private empirical risk minimization. J. Mach. Learn. Res. **12**, 1069–1109 (2011)

5. Chen, H.Y., Chao, W.L.: FedDistill: Making bayesian model ensemble applicable to federated learning. arXiv preprint arXiv:2009.01974 (2020)
6. Choquette-Choo, C.A., Tramer, F., Carlini, N., Papernot, N.: Label-only membership inference attacks. In: Proceedings of the 38th International Conference on Machine Learning. PMLR, vol. 139, pp. 1964–1974 (2021)
7. Dwork, C., Roth, A.: The algorithmic foundations of differential privacy. Found. Trends Theor. Comput. Sci. 9(3–4), 211–407 (2014)
8. Geyer, R.C., Klein, T., Nabi, M.: Differentially private federated learning: a client level perspective. arXiv preprint arXiv:1712.07557v2 (2018)
9. Guha, N., Talwalkar, A., Smith, V.: One-shot federated learning. arXiv preprint arXiv:1902.11175 (2019)
10. He, K., Zhang, X., Ren, S., Sun, J.: Deep residual learning for image recognition. In: Proceedings of the IEEE Conference on Computer Vision and Pattern Recognition (CVPR), pp. 770–778 (2016)
11. Hsu, T.M.H., Qi, H., Brown, M.: Measuring the effects of non-identical data distribution for federated visual classification. arXiv preprint arXiv:1909.06335 (2019)
12. Itahara, S., Nishio, T., Koda, Y., Morikura, M., Yamamoto, K.: Distillation-based semi-supervised federated learning for communication-efficient collaborative training with non-iid private data. arXiv preprint arXiv:2008.06180 (2020)
13. Kairouz, P., McMahan, H.B., Avent, B., Bellet, A., Bennis, M.: Advances and open problems in federated learning. Found. Trends Mach. Learn. 14, 1–210 (2021)
14. Kasiviswanathan, S.P., Lee, H.K., Nissim, K., Raskhodnikova, S., Smith, A.: What can we learn privately? In: 2008 49th Annual IEEE Symposium on Foundations of Computer Science, pp. 531–540 (2008)
15. Li, Q., Wen, Z., He, B.: Federated learning systems: vision, hype and reality for data privacy and protection. arXiv preprint arXiv:1907.09693 (2019)
16. Li, X., Huang, K., Yang, W., Wang, S., Zhang, Z.: On the convergence of FedAvg on non-iid data. In: Proceedings of 8th International Conference on Learning Representations (ICLR). OpenReview.net (2020)
17. Li, Y., Zhou, W., Wang, H., Mi, H., Hospedales, T.M.: Fedh2l: federated learning with model and statistical heterogeneity. arXiv preprint arXiv:2101.11296 (2021)
18. Lin, T., Kong, L., Stich, S.U., Jaggi, M.: Ensemble distillation for robust model fusion in federated learning. In: Advances in Neural Information Processing Systems (NeurIPS), vol. 33 (2020)
19. Liu, D.C., Nocedal, J.: On the limited memory BFGS method for large scale optimization. Math. Program. 45(1–3), 503–528 (1989)
20. McMahan, B., Moore, E., Ramage, D., Hampson, S., y Arcas, B.A.: Communication-efficient learning of deep networks from decentralized data. In: Proceedings of the 20th International Conference on Artificial Intelligence and Statistics (AISTATS), pp. 1273–1282 (2017)
21. McMahan, B., Ramage, D., Talwar, K., Zhang, L.: Learning differentially private recurrent language models. In: Proceedings of the 8th International Conference on Learning Representations (ICLR) (2018)
22. Papernot, N., Abadi, M., Úlfar Erlingsson, Goodfellow, I., Talwar, K.: Semi-supervized knowledge transfer for deep learning from private training data. In: Proceedings of the 5th International Conference on Learning Representations (ICLR). OpenReview.net (2017)
23. Sandler, M., Howard, A.G., Zhu, M., Zhmoginov, A., Chen, L.: MobileNetV2: inverted residuals and linear bottlenecks. In: Proceedings of the IEEE Conference on Computer Vision and Pattern Recognition (CVPR), pp. 4510–4520 (2018)

24. Sattler, F., Korjakow, T., Rischke, R., Samek, W.: Fedaux: leveraging unlabeled auxiliary data in federated learning. In: IEEE Transactions on Neural Networks and Learning Systems (2021)
25. Sattler, F., Marban, A., Rischke, R., Samek, W.: CFD: Communication-efficient federated distillation via soft-label quantization and delta coding. IEEE Trans. Netw. Sci. Eng. **9**(4), 2025–2038 (2022)
26. Sattler, F., Müller, K.R., Samek, W.: Clustered federated learning: model-agnostic distributed multitask optimization under privacy constraints. IEEE Trans. Neural Netw. Learn. Syst. **32**(8), 3710–3722 (2021)
27. Shalev-Shwartz, S.: Online learning: theory, algorithms, and applications. Ph.D. thesis, Hebrew University (2007)
28. Shokri, R., Stronati, M., Song, C., Shmatikov, V.: Membership inference attacks against machine learning models. In: IEEE Symposium on Security and Privacy, pp. 3–18 (2017)
29. Sun, L., Lyu, L.: Federated model distillation with noise-free differential privacy. In: Proceedings of the Thirtieth International Joint Conference on Artificial Intelligence (IJCAI-21) (2021)
30. Triastcyn, A., Faltings, B.: Federated learning with bayesian differential privacy. In: 2019 IEEE International Conference on Big Data (Big Data), pp. 2587–2596 (2019)
31. Wang, T., Zhu, J.Y., Torralba, A., Efros, A.A.: Dataset distillation. arXiv preprint arXiv:1811.10959 (2018)
32. Zhang, X., Zhou, X., Lin, M., Sun, J.: ShuffleNet: an extremely efficient convolutional neural network for mobile devices. In: Proceedings of the IEEE Conference on Computer Vision and Pattern Recognition (CVPR), pp. 6848–6856 (2018)
33. Zhou, Y., Pu, G., Ma, X., Li, X., Wu, D.: Distilled one-shot federated learning. arXiv preprint arXiv:2009.07999 (2021)

Secure Forward Aggregation for Vertical Federated Neural Networks

Shuowei Cai[1] , Di Chai[1,2] , Liu Yang[1,2] , Junxue Zhang[1,2] , Yilun Jin[1] ,
Leye Wang[3] , Kun Guo[4] , and Kai Chen[1(✉)]

[1] iSING Lab, The Hong Kong University of Science and Technology,
Kowloon, Hong Kong
kaichen@cse.ust.hk
[2] Clustar, Nanshan, China
[3] Peking University, Beijing, China
[4] Fuzhou University, Fuzhou, China

Abstract. Vertical federated learning (VFL) is attracting much attention because it enables cross-silo data cooperation in a privacy-preserving manner. While most research works in VFL focus on linear and tree models, deep models (*e.g.*, neural networks) are not well studied in VFL. In this work, we focus on SplitNN, a well-known neural network framework in VFL, and identify a trade-off between data security and model performance in SplitNN. Briefly, SplitNN trains the model by exchanging gradients and transformed data. On the one hand, SplitNN suffers from the loss of model performance since multiply parties jointly train the model using transformed data instead of raw data, and a large amount of low-level feature information is discarded. On the other hand, a naive solution of increasing the model performance through aggregating at lower layers in SplitNN (*i.e.*, the data is less transformed and more low-level feature is preserved) makes raw data vulnerable to inference attacks. To mitigate the above trade-off, we propose a new neural network protocol in VFL called Security Forward Aggregation (SFA). It changes the way of aggregating the transformed data and adopts removable masks to protect the raw data. Experiment results show that networks with SFA achieve both data security and high model performance.

Keywords: Vertical federated learning · Split Neural network · Secure Forward aggregation

1 Introduction

Federated learning (FL) [8] is a new paradigm of collaborative machine learning with privacy preservation, and it could be categorized into several categories according to different data partition scenarios [16]. Among them, vertical federated learning (VFL) is defined as the scenario in which multiple participants hold the same entities but different features. Existing work has explored various

R. Goebel et al. (Eds.): FL 2022, LNAI 13448, pp. 115–129, 2023.
https://doi.org/10.1007/978-3-031-28996-5_9

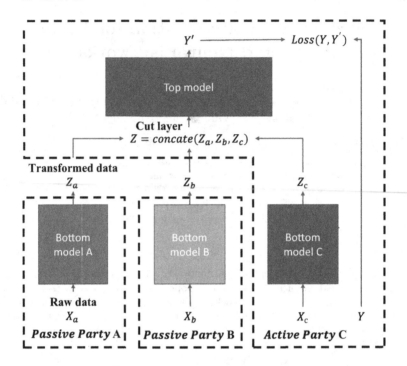

Fig. 1. Split neural network in VFL

types of VFL models, such as logistic regression [6,17] and decision trees [3]. However, the neural network is not well studied in the VFL scenario. Specifically, there is little analysis of data security and model performance in complex models like neural networks.

Split neural network (SplitNN) [14] is a framework able for neural networks in VFL. As shown in Fig. 1, the whole network is partitioned into a top model and several bottom models. Each VFL participant keeps a bottom model for transforming its raw data, and the transformed data are passed to the top model at the cut layer to make the prediction in each forward process. However, exchanging the transformed data between participants result in a trade-off between data security and model performance in SplitNN.

On the one hand, using the transformed data instead of the raw data for prediction will result in a loss of model performance because the transformed data contains only a part of the information in the raw data. According to the analysis in [12], a significant amount of low-level feature information is discarded while the raw data passes through the layers. This discarding information happens while the raw data passes through the bottom models of SplitNN, and it also transforms data from fine grain to coarse grain. For example, using the term "cheap baby products" to represent a classic cotton diaper from a famous brand.

However, this transformation increases the difficulty of the model's prediction because the model cannot capture the interaction between the discarded information, just like the classic "beer and diaper" relationship in data mining. A person who buys beer may be interested in diapers, but it's hard to say that a person who buys a drink will be interested in baby products. When two participants in SplitNN possess feature information like beer and diapers, low-level feature interaction loss happens, and it will decrease the model's performance.

On the other hand, the transformed data which are sent directly to the active party leaks information about the raw data. The passive party's raw data will be vulnerable to inference attacks if the transformed data contains too much information about it. As a result, it is inappropriate to increase the amount of information in the transformed data to improve the model's performance. Thus, we identify this trade-off, as the transformed data influences both the model performance and data security. It is impossible to achieve high model performance and high data security simultaneously in SplitNN.

Motivated by the above problem, we propose a method to mitigate this trade-off between data security and model performance. We consider that the direct exposure of the transformed data is improper, and the data protection by controlling the amount of information in the transformed data is hazardous. To this end, we proposed a Secure forward aggregation (SFA) protocol that can securely aggregate the bottom models' output without exposing the individual output from the bottom model. We modify the aggregation method at the cut layer and provide a removable mask to protect the passive party's transformed data and ensure raw data security. With SFA, we mitigate the trade-off and can achieve lossless performance compared to the centralized model with high security.

The main contributions of this work are summarized as follows:

- We evaluate the trade-off between the model performance and the security of raw data in SplitNN in vertical federated learning.
- We present a Secure forward aggregation protocol to protect the participant's transformed data while being lossless. With SFA, we can mitigate this trade-off and achieve both good model performance and high data security in neural networks in VFL.

2   Introduction

In this section, we first introduce splitNN, one of the most popular frameworks of neural networks in VFL. While noting the special designs for VFL in this architecture, we also analyze the trade-off between data security and model performance.

2.1   Background: SplitNN in VFL

As shown in Fig. 1, splitNN is a distributed network structure in VFL that support multiparty settings. The participants of SplitNN are categorized into the

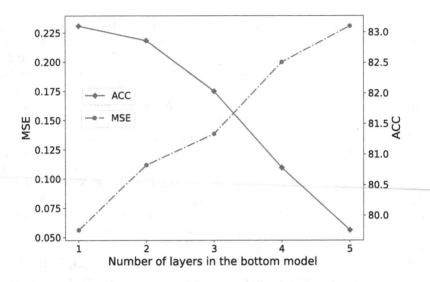

Fig. 2. Performance-security trade-off in splitNN

active party (participant with labels) and the passive party (participant without labels). Each passive party holds one bottom model for local data transformation. The active party holds both a bottom model and a top model and uses the top model to make predictions with the transformed data from all participants.

The forward process of SplitNN consists of three steps: 1) participants use their bottom models to transform the data, 2) passive parties send the transformed data to the active party, and 3) the active party will concatenate these transformed data, applies activation functions and feed it into the top model to get the prediction results. The layer which concatenates these transformed data is also called the cut layer. In the backward process, the active party will first update the top model normally and calculate the gradients of the embeddings. Then it will send the gradients of these embeddings to their owners to update their bottom models.

2.2 Trade-Off of SplitNN

The participant's raw data security is a primary concern in vertical federated learning. In SplitNN, one substantial information leakage is the transformed data directly sent to the active party. Those transformed data do not contain all raw data information because some low-level information is lost during the forward propagation. However, there is still a correlation between the transformed and original data. When the active party of SplitNN applies inference attacks like [11] to dig out the correlation, the raw data is able to be approximated.

Indeed, discarding more information from the transformed data is a way to improve data security in SplitNN. Increasing the number of layers in the bottom model is a feasible way to fulfill this. A higher bottom model will increase the complexity of the transformation and discard more low-level feature information from the transformed data, making raw data hard to reconstruct. However, the discarded low-level feature information in the transformed data is crucial to the model's performance. It contributes to the model performance in low-order feature interactions between participants. The connections between the bottom models are used to capture these low-level feature interactions, but they are missing in SplitNN.

Therefore, to further measure the relationship between data security and model performance in SplitNN, we use the generative regression network (GRN) in [11] to attack the SplitNN and generate approximation data to get close to the raw data. As shown in Fig. 2, the approximation data of GRN is far from the raw data when the number of layers in the bottom model is high, but the model performance drop significantly(*i.e.,* 3%). The model's performance is the best when there is only one layer in the bottom model. However, the restored data is closest to the raw data in this case, and the MSE between the approximation data and the raw data is only 0.055. Model performance and raw data security become the two ends of the scale in SplitNN. As a result, we urgently need a method to mitigate this trade-off.

3   Secure Forward Aggregation

3.1   Overview

In this section, we propose a novel protocol called Secure Forward aggregation (SFA) to protect the transformed data of the passive parties. It provides removable masks to passive parties, and the masks do not introduce noise into the computation of the model. SFA protocol is used at the topmost layer for the bottom models of all participants. It securely aggregates the bottom models' output values without exposing their true values using a summation operation with masks. In the mask generation of SFA, we securely share a part of the transformed data from the active party using homomorphic encryption and send it to the passive party. The shared result will be the mask that protects the passive party's output, and homomorphic encryption ensures that the active party knows nothing about the value of the mask. Therefore, the mask effectively protects the passive party's raw data without introducing noise into the training.

Different from methods like secure aggregation [1], secure forward aggregation can protect the passive party's input in the aggregate output even in the two-party scene. In SFA, we use a weight mask generated by the passive party and sent to the active party under homomorphic encryption to produce masks for the transformed data. The weight mask is seen as a part of the weight of the topmost layer of the active party's bottom model and is also used to prohibit the active party from knowing the actual output of its bottom model. Therefore, the active party cannot recover the passive party's input from the aggregated result. Moreover, SFA could be applied to multi-participant scenarios, allowing all passive parties to keep masks to protect their transformed data. With SFA, we can aggregate the transformed data securely regardless of the information it contains. Therefore, the trade-off between model and security is moderate, and we can train a model that both performs well and protects raw data perfectly.

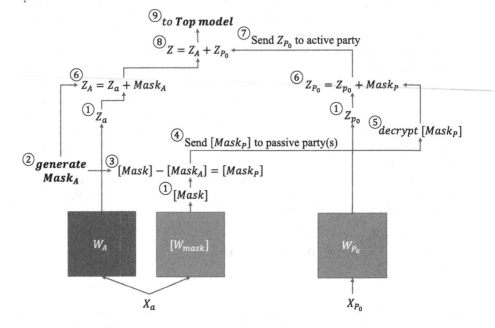

Fig. 3. Secure Forward Aggregation in two party scene

3.2 Aggregation Method

We sum the transformed data from the bottom models in SFA instead of concatenating them in SplitNN. The first reason is that the concatenate operation exposes the transformed data directly, increasing the difficulty of data protection. Moreover, the concatenate operation treats each neuron independently, but sum will not. So, the feature interaction will not be captured at the cut layer. Therefore, concatenation operation at the cut layer will indirectly increase the loss of data information by passing the transformed data through another layer for capturing feature interaction. As a result, we change the aggregation method at the cut layer from concatenating operation to a summation operation.

3.3 Training with Weight Mask

The algorithm of the Secure Forward Aggregation protocol is shown in Algorithm 1. During the initialization stage, one passive party will generate a weight mask

(W_{mask} in algorithm 1) and send it to the active party as a part of the weights in the topmost layer of the bottom model. This weight mask will be encrypted by Paillier homomorphic encryption [13] and sent to the active party. This weight mask will never be decrypted, and it will be used to generate masks for passive parties without letting the active party know.

Figure 3 shows the forward process and steps of secure forward aggregation in a two-party setting. A and P_0 are the active and passive parties; X_a and X_{p_0} here are the raw data or the values output from hidden units; W_A and W_B here are (part of) the weight of the topmost layer of the bottom model, $[W_{mask}]$ is the weight mask, and $[\cdot]$ represents homomorphic encryption. In the forward process of SFA, both parties will calculate Z_a and Z_{p_0} normally using W_A, X_a and W_{P_0}, X_{P_0}. Then, the active party will calculate $[Mask]$ using the encrypted value $[W_{mask}]$. Then, it will generate a random matrix $mask_A$ and subtract it from the mask and send the remaining part $[Mask_P]$ back to the passive party P_0. Then, P_0 will decrypt the result and obtain its mask. After that, the two parties add the mask onto their transformed data, and the passive party P_0 sends its masked transformed data to the active party for aggregation. Finally, the active party will sum these transformed data to obtain the final result Z.

Secure Forward Aggregation protocol can also protect the transformed data in a multiparty setting. If there is extra passive party other than party P_0, party P_0 will continue share the masks to other passive parties, calculate $Mask_{P_0} = Mask_P - \sum_{i=1}^{n} Mask_{P_i}$ and send the new mask $Mask_{P_i}$ to passive party P_i. In this way, the active party still knows nothing about the masks.

3.4   Removable Mask on Transformed Data

Unlike methods that follow differential privacy to generate noise to protect their intermediate result, the mask generated in the SFA protocol is a part of the original output. Therefore, the mask in SFA will not introduce noise to the aggregated value. It is because we regard the encrypted W_{mask} as a part of the weight for the active party, and the actual weight for the last layer in the bottom model of the active party should be $W_{A_{true}} = W_{mask} + W_A$. It is clear to see that the final output Z is the sum of the two party's transformed data:

$$Z = Z_A + \sum_{i=0}^{N} Z_{P_i} = Z_a + Mask_A + \sum_{i=0}^{N} (Z_{P_i} + Mask_{P_i})$$

$$= (W_A + W_{mask}) X_a + \sum_{i=0}^{N} W_{P_i} X_{P_i} \tag{1}$$

$$= W_{A_{true}} X_a + \sum_{i=0}^{N} W_{P_i} X_{P_i}$$

Algorithm 1. Secure forward aggregation

Participants Settings: Active party A, Passive party P_0, ($\{P_i | i = 1 \ldots n\}$ for other passive party in multiparty scene)

Input: Batch of raw data or embedding from hidden units hold by participants of VFL: X_a, X_{p_0} (X_{p_i} for other passive parties),

Output: Aggregated result Z

Initialization

1: Active party A generates weight matrix W_A, Passive party P_0 generates weight matrix W_{P_0}. (If there are other passive parties, they generate their own weight matrix W_{p_i})

2: Party P_0 generates HE key pair $\{sk_b, pk_b\}$. Generate weight matrix W_{mask}, encrypt it using sk_b and send the encrypted result $[W_{mask}]$ to party A.

Forward process

1: All parties obtain the next batch of data (or hidden units value from the layer below)

2: Party A calculates $Z_a = W_A X_a$ and $[Mask] = [W_{mask}]X_a$, Party P_0 calculates $Z_{p_0} = W_{P_0} X_{P_0}$. (Other passive parties calculate $Z_{p_i} = W_{P_i} X_{P_i}$)

3: Party A generates random matrix $Mask_A$, calculate $[Mask_P] = [Mask] - [Mask_A]$ and send it to party P_0.

4: Party P_0 decrypt $[Mask_P]$. (If there are other passive parties, P_0 generates random matrix $Mask_{P_i}$ and send it to party P_i and calculate: $Mask_{P_0} = Mask_P - \sum_i^n Mask_{P_i}$)

5: Party A calculates $Z_A = Z_a + Mask_A$, Party P_0 calculates $Z_{P_0} = Z_{p_0} + Mask_{P_0}$ and send it to party A (other passive parties calculate $Z_{P_i} = Z_{p_i} + Mask_{P_i}$ and send it to party A)

Backward process

1: Active party send the upper gradient to each participants

2: All participants use this gradient to update their bottom model. $[W_{mask}]$ in party A is kept unchanged.

We can see that $W_{A_{true}} X_a + \sum_{i=0}^{N} W_{P_i} X_{P_i}$ are the aggregated result of all transformed data. The masks for passive parties are a part of $W_{A_{true}} X_a$. They are generated by the encrypted weight mask $[W_{mask}]$ and shared using a random matrix, and added back to the final aggregated result. In the backward process, the participants calculate the gradient normally, and all parties will add the gradients to the plaintext weight. During the whole training process, W_{mask} is kept unchanged. Therefore, we can consider it a noise initially added to the model weights. As the model is updated continuously, the impact of this noise will gradually fade away when doing gradient descends and updating the weights of the plaintext part.

3.5   Security Analysis

This subsection discusses the security of Secure Forward Aggregation in a semi-honest setting, which is the standard security assumption in federated learning.

We show that the transformed data are well protected in the Secure Forward Layer, and the passive parties cannot infer the data from the active party.

Passive Party's Data Security. In the SFA protocol, the transformed data Z_{p_i} for passive party B is protected by a mask $Mask_{P_i}$. The active party will only obtain the masked result, and it cannot distinguish the mask and the transformed data from the masked result. Even though it knows that $Mask$ is a transformation of X_b, there are infinite eligible values of $Mask$. Therefore, it is insufficient to infer the exact value of mask $Mask_P$ or $Mask_{P_i}$ and to further infer the passive party's raw data.

Active Party's Data Security. The active party's transformed data is secure because they are not sent outside. Though the passive party knows that $Mask$ is a transformation of X_b, it knows nothing about the random generated $Mask_A$. Therefore, the passive party cannot infer $Mask$ to perform further inference attacks, and the active party's data security is ensured.

3.6   Mitigate Trade-Off Using SFA

We have already shown that SFA ensures the security of the transformed data. Therefore, we can keep a shallow bottom model for better performance. When there is only one fully-connected layer in the bottom model, and the aggregate method is changed from concatenation to summation, the structure of the model is the same as the centralized neural network. Therefore, the performance degradation caused by the model architecture no longer exists.

Though the weight mask also impacts training, with reasonable settings, the initialized weights of the weight mask will not significantly impact the final results of the model. We initialize the weight mask using a uniform distribution bounded by $2/\sqrt{in\_features}$ and encrypt it, then send it to the active party. The weight generation of this weight mask follows [10], and it reduces the impact of the weight mask of model training and the final performance.

4   Experiment

In the experiment sections, extensive experiments are done to show how SFA can mitigate the trade-off between data security and model performance.

4.1   Experiment Setting

We use a neural network structure with six fully-connected layers to illustrate the performance of SFA on neural networks in VFL. We select SplitNN and a centralized model (all data are integrated for modeling) to compare a neural network with SFA (SFA-NN). We also fixed the number of hidden units of each

Table 1. Datasets descriptions

Datasets	Sector	News20	Amazon	FMNIST
Datasize	9619	$18,846$	$100,000$	$60,000$
Features	$55,197$	$173,762$	257	784
Labels	105	20	2	10

Table 2. Model performance on different datasets (ACC)

Datasets	Sector	News20	Amazon
Centralized	$91.28_{\pm 0.39}$	$83.63_{\pm 0.27}$	$77.46_{\pm 0.10}$
SplitNN	$86.43_{\pm 0.51}$	$79.76_{\pm 0.68}$	$72.86_{\pm 0.07}$
SFA-NN(ours)	$90.86_{\pm 0.30}$	$83.86_{\pm 0.32}$	$77.44_{\pm 0.10}$

layer for fair comparison and ran the experiment of model performance for ten trials to reduce randomness in training.

We fix the dropout to 0.3, batch size to 256, and apply batch normalization to train the model for 50 epochs in default. Then, we select the best learning rate from $\{1e-1, 1e-2, 1e-3, 1e-4, \dots\}$ with zero regularization coefficient for all experiments. The default participant number of VFL is set to two, and the features are partitioned equally for each participant. The bottom model height is set to 5 for SplitNN and 1 for SFA-NN in default for a fair comparison with the same level of security.

4.2 Dataset

We use four classification datasets to demonstrate the performance problem and the trade-off in SplitNN: Sector [2], news20 [9], Amazon electronic[1] and Fashion MNIST (FMNIST) [15] dataset.

We preprocessed these data to meet the requirement of the experiments of SplitNN. We used the TF-IDF algorithm to transform the news20 data into a sparse matrix for training. We use a trained Deep Interest network [18] to preprocess and transform 100,000 items in the Amazon electronic data into embeddings of 257 and treat them as data in model training. FMNIST is the dataset we demonstrate the security concerns in SplitNN, so we normalize the ranges of all feature values in it into (0, 1) as [11] for better demonstration.

The detailed descriptions of the data set after preprocessing are shown in Table 1.

4.3 Performance of SFA

We experiment and compare the performance of SplitNN and SFA-NN to show that our proposed method achieves good performance in high security. We also

---

[1] http://jmcauley.ucsd.edu/data/amazon/.

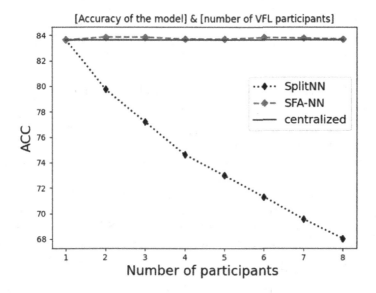

Fig. 4. Model performance in multiparty settings

use the Centralized model in this experiment, which refers to a model with a standard neural network structure trained by pooling all data together in a non-federal learning setting. Because the performance of federated learning models should be as close as possible to the model performance in the non-federal settings [16], we use it as the target of SFA-NN to evaluate its performance. This baseline can precisely reflect the ability of SFA-NN to reduce the performance gap between neural networks in VFL and centralized neural networks.

Model Performance Under Two-Party Setting. Table 2 shows the experiment result of SFA-NN in the two-party setting. The performance of SFA-NN is close to the centralized model and is significantly better than SplitNN. Although the weight mask of SFA impacts the model's training, it will not have a significant impact on the final performance of the model. The performance gap between SFA-NN and the centralized model is small, and for comparison, SplitNN's performance is low on these tasks, and SFA-NN's performance is significantly better than SplitNN.

Model Performance Under Multiparty Setting. One of the reasons that SplitNN has gained popularity is that it supports multiparty training conveniently. Pessimistically, the more participants there are, the more feature partitions between participants will result in more low-level feature interaction loss. Thus, a severe model performance decrease will happen in the multiparty scenario of SplitNN. As shown in Fig. 4, the model performance drops dramatically on the News20 dataset when the number of participants increases. But there is no such performance loss in SFA-NN, which shows that our method is effective in multiparty settings.

4.4   Trade-Off Between Security and Model Performance

In this experiment, we fix the total number of network layers and the number of neurons in each hidden layer. We then adjust the height of the cut layer and the height of the bottom model to observe the performance of the model and the security of the raw data. (the height of the top model decreases with the increase of the height of the bottom model and vice versa).

Figure 5(a) shows the model performance on the News20 dataset with the bottom model of different heights. When the height of the bottom model increase, the model performance of SplitNN drops gradually. SFA-NN also suffers from this performance loss. Though the summation operation for aggregation at the cut layer improves the model performance, the model performance of SFA-NN is only similar to SplitNN with one less layer in the bottom model. The performance problem due to the discarded information has not been fundamentally solved. This experiment shows the damage that excessive discarding of low-level information brings to the model performance. Reducing the number of layers will be an intuitive solution for those seeking higher model performance, but this brings threats to the raw data.

To evaluate the information leakage of the transformed data, we train models using FMNIST datasets to 88% accuracy with the length of the transformed data set to 256. Then, we use the generative regression network(GRN) [11] to attack the bottom model and reconstruct the raw data using the test dataset. GRN is the network to generate approximation data to approximate the passive party's raw data. We take the active party's data features and the passive party's transform data as the input to train the model. We train the GRN by minimizing the Mean Square Error(MSE) between the real transformed data and the transformed result of the approximation data. Because the transformed data z_{p_0} are not known by the active party in SFA-NN, we use two masked outputs, Z_P (attack-1) and $Z_P + mask_A$ (attack-2), to substitute the transformed data, and the protections of these two attacks are $Mask_{P_0}$ and $Mask$ respectively. We also use random values between 0–1 as a baseline of the attack to evaluate the attack method's performance and show the effectiveness of SFA's protection.

Figure 5(b) shows the attack result on the transformed data, and the MSE metric indicates the distance of the attack results from the raw data. We can see that the attack is effective on the transformed data when the number of layers in the bottom model is low. When the layer number increase, the effect of the attack decrease, but the model performance gets lower. However, the attack is ineffective when SFA is used. GRN cannot achieve a good approximation of raw data even if the bottom model has only one layer. In fact, the MSE distance of the approximation data always gets larger as the training proceeds when the two attack methods act on the SFA, suggesting that the attack on transformed data with SFA is infeasible. In conclusion, SFA can protect the raw data with low bottom model layers. We can use SFA to gather the information from multiple participants at a low layer of the neural network and improve the model's performance.

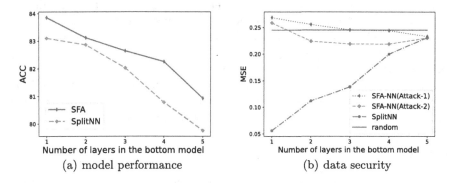

(a) model performance   (b) data security

Fig. 5. Trade-off between data security and model performance

5 Related Work

FDML [7] is another framework that supports neural networks in feature-partition settings with privacy-preservation. In FDML, each participant has an independent local model, and the final predictions of the model are obtained by summing the outputs of all local models. However, there is no direct connection between the local models of FDML, so it also suffers from a similar performance loss in SplitNN. This performance loss is also reflected in their experiments on neural networks.

Moreover, due to the design assumption that labels are shared among participants in FDML, researchers seldom focus on label security in this framework. In fact, the gradient at the top layer of FDML exposes the labels directly [5]. Leakage of data labels is unacceptable for vertical federal learning. Therefore, we do not include it as a baseline in VFL.

6 Conclusion

This work proposes a Secure Forward Aggregation protocol to mitigate the trade-off between model performance and data security in SplitNN in VFL. This protocol provides removable masks to protect the transformed data in SplitNN and aggregates the information from different parties better. Experimental results show that we achieve almost the same performance as the centralized model, and we can keep the raw data safe and resistant to attacks using SFA. We effectively mitigate the trade-off between model performance and data security in neural networks in VFL.

This work still has some limitations. On the one hand, SFA introduces partial homomorphic encryption to perform secure computations, increasing the computational effort. Nevertheless, there are ways to reduce time consumption. For example, we can reduce the multiplication calculation of the same ciphertext weight masks and plaintext data and accelerate computation using parallelism and hardware [4]. On the other, there is a lack of hyperparameters analysis about the weight mask on model training and data security. Also, the security analysis is limited to semi-honest settings, but it is hard to ensure in a real-world scenario. We will continue to improve this work from the perspective of algorithm design and then conduct a comprehensive analysis of the effectiveness of SFA. We will enhance this work in the future to achieve good efficiency while keeping the data security and model performance in neural networks in VFL.

References

1. Bonawitz, K., et al.: Practical secure aggregation for privacy-preserving machine learning. In: proceedings of the 2017 ACM SIGSAC Conference on Computer and Communications Security, pp. 1175–1191 (2017)
2. Chang, C.C., Lin, C.J.: LIBSVM: a library for support vector machines. ACM Trans. Intell. Syst. Technol. **2**(3), 1–27 (2011)
3. Cheng, K., et al.: SecureBoost: a lossless federated learning framework. IEEE Intell. Syst. **36**(6), 87–98 (2021)
4. Cheng, X., Lu, W., Huang, X., Hu, S., Chen, K.: HAFLO: GPU-based acceleration for federated logistic regression. arXiv preprint arXiv:2107.13797 (2021)
5. Fu, C., et al.: Label inference attacks against vertical federated learning. In: 31st USENIX Security Symposium (USENIX Security 2022). USENIX Association, Boston, MA (2022). https://www.usenix.org/conference/usenixsecurity22/presentation/fu
6. Hardy, S., et al.: Private federated learning on vertically partitioned data via entity resolution and additively homomorphic encryption. arXiv preprint arXiv:1711.10677 (2017)
7. Hu, Y., Niu, D., Yang, J., Zhou, S.: FDML: a collaborative machine learning framework for distributed features. In: Proceedings of the 25th ACM SIGKDD International Conference on Knowledge Discovery & Data Mining, pp. 2232–2240 (2019)
8. Kairouz, P., et al.: Advances and open problems in federated learning. Found. Trends Mach. Learn. **14**(1–2), 1–210 (2021)
9. Lang, K.: NewsWeeder: learning to filter netnews. In: Proceedings of the Twelfth International Conference on Machine Learning, pp. 331–339 (1995)
10. LeCun, Y., Bottou, L., Orr, G.B., Müller, K.-R.: Efficient backprop. In: Orr, G.B., Müller, K.-R. (eds.) Neural Networks: Tricks of the Trade. LNCS, vol. 1524, pp. 9–50. Springer, Heidelberg (1998). https://doi.org/10.1007/3-540-49430-8_2
11. Luo, X., Wu, Y., Xiao, X., Ooi, B.C.: Feature inference attack on model predictions in vertical federated learning. In: 2021 IEEE 37th International Conference on Data Engineering (ICDE), pp. 181–192. IEEE (2021)
12. Mahendran, A., Vedaldi, A.: Understanding deep image representations by inverting them. In: Proceedings of the IEEE Conference on Computer Vision and Pattern Recognition, pp. 5188–5196 (2015)
13. Paillier, P.: Public-key cryptosystems based on composite degree residuosity classes. In: Advances in Cryptology-EUROCRYPT (1999)

14. Vepakomma, P., Gupta, O., Swedish, T., Raskar, R.: Split learning for health: distributed deep learning without sharing raw patient data. arXiv preprint arXiv:1812.00564 (2018)
15. Xiao, H., Rasul, K., Vollgraf, R.: Fashion-MNIST: a novel image dataset for benchmarking machine learning algorithms. arXiv preprint arXiv:1708.07747 (2017)
16. Yang, Q., Liu, Y., Chen, T., Tong, Y.: Federated machine learning: concept and applications. ACM Trans. Intell. Syst. Technol. **10**(2), 1–19 (2019)
17. Zhang, Q., Gu, B., Deng, C., Huang, H.: Secure bilevel asynchronous vertical federated learning with backward updating. In: Proceedings of the AAAI Conference on Artificial Intelligence, vol. 35, pp. 10896–10904 (2021)
18. Zhou, G., et al.: Deep interest network for click-through rate prediction. In: Proceedings of the 24th ACM SIGKDD International Conference on Knowledge Discovery & Data Mining, pp. 1059–1068 (2018)

Two-Phased Federated Learning with Clustering and Personalization for Natural Gas Load Forecasting

Shubao Zhao, Jia Liu, Guoliang Ma, Jie Yang, Di Liu, and Zengxiang Li[✉]

Digital Research Institute, ENN Group, Beijing, China
{zhaoshubao,liujiaam,maguolianga,yangjiev,liudif,lizengxiang}@enn.cn

Abstract. Natural gas load forecasting is essential to retailers in terms of profit-making and service quality. In practice, a retailer has limited consumer load data to build an accurate prediction model. Federated learning enables retailers to train a global model collaboratively, without compromising data privacy. However, it could not behave well on all consumers due to their diversity, e.g., different load patterns. To address this data heterogeneity issue, we propose two-phased federated learning with cluster-based personalization (CPFL) for natural gas load forecasting. Firstly, a knowledge-based federated clustering is proposed to categorize similar consumers from different retailers into clusters in a privacy-preserving manner. Then, vanilla federated learning is adopted to pre-train a global model, leveraging all available data from retailers. Finally, the pre-trained model is fine-tuned and personalized to each cluster respectively, using an attention-based model aggregation strategy according to the contribution difference of individual consumers in the cluster. Comprehensive experiments are conducted using a real-world data set with 2000 consumers from eight retailers, and the results show our proposed CPFL framework outperforms the state-of-the-art personalized federated learning approaches for time-series forecasting.

Keywords: Federated learning · Load forecasting · Clustering

1 Introduction

Natural gas load forecasting [11,21] is essential to retailers in terms of profit-making (e.g., demand management, resource coordination, and pipeline network planning) and service quality (e.g., safety management, personalized contract and proactive scheduling). With the rapid development of AI technologies, complex deep learning models trained by large amounts of data extract time-series features and thus enable accurate forecasting. However, the retailer usually serves a certain number of consumers within a region or even a small city. Its data is likely insufficient to support a high-performance deep learning model. In addition, it is probable to deduce consumers' operation and business confidential information through their energy load. Retailers are committed to preserve consumers data privacy without sharing to any others. Consequently, reputable retailers are reluctant to upload data for centralized model training in practice.

© The Author(s), under exclusive license to Springer Nature Switzerland AG 2023
R. Goebel et al. (Eds.): FL 2022, LNAI 13448, pp. 130–143, 2023.
https://doi.org/10.1007/978-3-031-28996-5_10

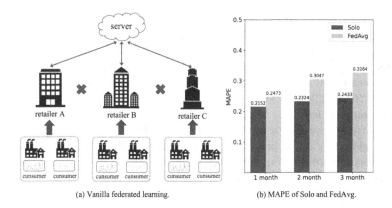

(a) Vanilla federated learning.   (b) MAPE of Solo and FedAvg.

Fig. 1. Vanilla federated learning leverages data from different retailers but could not address data heterogeneity issues among them. Experiments show that the federated model is even worse than the solo models trained using the data of individual consumers respectively.

A new AI paradigm federated learning (FL) is proposed in [12], which enables participants to jointly train a model without sharing their data. It has obtained great achievements in various industry domains, including healthcare, finance service and smart cities [23]. Recently, federated learning has also been used in load forecasting [3,6,17]. However, most FL application scenarios assume data from all participants are independent and identically distributed (IID). In real-world cases, this assumption is hard to be satisfied due to the diversity among participants. We conduct experiments with vanilla federated learning using federated average (FedAvg) model aggregation strategy on 2000 consumers. As shown in Fig. 1(b), the federated model trained by all available data performs even worse than individual models trained for each consumer.

In order to alleviate the impact of data heterogeneity and thus improving model performance, several personalized federated learning mechanisms have been proposed for various application domains including CV and NLP [18]. Specifically, in the time series forecasting field, Wang [20] propose to fine-tune the global federated model to personalized models for individual electricity consumers. Unfortunately, the very limited data of each consumer make the personalized model prone to bias and over-fitting. Moreover, a large number of models can also increase the management cost of the retailers. In addition, Guo [4] propose to build personalized federated models using similar data within the cluster only. However, this method could not fully exploit the advantages of federated learning as retailers' data out of the cluster are not used. Furthermore, the proposed similarity-based methods are data-driven without exploring the domain knowledge (e.g., time-series data processing and pattern recognition). Therefore, designing an effective personalized federated learning framework that can adapt to individual consumers properly remains crucial.

According to our domain knowledge, consumers from different retailers may have similar load patterns, for instance, if they are from the same region and/or the same industry sector. Therefore, a cluster of similar consumers who shares the same model could achieve higher prediction accuracy, while avoiding over-fitting and reducing management cost. From the other perspective, the data of consumers from different clusters may also be valuable especially for extracting low-level common features. In order to take advantage of both perspectives, we propose a two-phase cluster-driven personalized federated learning framework. Firstly, a global model is pre-trained using vanilla federated learning by lever-aging all available data from retailers. Then, the global model is fine-tuned for each cluster in a federated learning manner using its consumers' data from different retailers. In other words, consumers within the same cluster cooperated with each other to build a robust and accurate personalized model, while keeping their data within its retailer's sovereignty. Furthermore, consumers in the same cluster are not identical, and thus have different contributions to the person-alized model. Hence, an attention-based model aggregation strategy is adopted in the fine-tuning federated learning phase, considering different weights of con-sumers' local model updates. Experimental results on 2000 consumers from eight retailers show that our proposed framework outperforms the aforementioned personalized federated learning approaches [4, 20]. Moreover, the performance of our framework is less sensitive to the number of clusters, compared with other cluster-driven personalized approaches.

The main contributions of this work are as follows:

- A cluster-driven personalized federated learning for natural gas load forecast-ing is proposed to leverage all available data while considering their hetero-geneity.
- A knowledge-based federated clustering is proposed to categorize similar cus-tomers into clusters in a privacy-preserving manner, based on our industry domain knowledge and time-series data analytic experiences.
- A two-phased federated learning mechanism is proposed, enabling retailers to pre-training a global model and then fine-tuning it to personalized mod-els with respect to consumer clusters collaboratively in a federated learning manner.
- An attention-based model aggregation strategy is introduced in fine-tuning phase, to capture the contributions of individual consumers to the personal-ized federated model of their cluster.

The rest of this work is organized as follows. Section 2 reviews the related work on personalized federated learning especially for time-series forecasting. Section 3 introduces CPFL framework and technical details of each module. Section 4 reports experiments on a real-world dataset. Section 5 concludes this work.

2   Related Work

2.1   Time-Series Forecasting

Over the years, time series forecasting is a hot topic in both industry and academy communities. The continuous efforts could be classified into the following three groups with the increasing model complexity: 1) statistical approaches such as autoregressive integrated moving average(ARIMA) [14], 2) machine learning models such as XGBoost [9], 3) deep learning models such as LSTM [13] and transformer [22]. Complex deep learning models trained by large amounts of data could extract time series features automatically, and relieve the burden of time-consuming data pre-processing and feature engineering. However, in practice, a retailer serving parts of consumers within a region usually has insufficient data to train a high-performance deep learning model. Therefore, it is desirable to enable retailers to collaborate with each other to train AI models using their data in a secure way.

2.2   Federated Learning

With the emergence of Federated Learning [12], participants could jointly train a model by exchanging model updates instead of the raw data, reducing the risk of confidential information leakage. As society is more and more concerned with privacy protection, federated learning becomes popular in various applications. The most relevant studies [3, 19] to this work are apply federated learning to load forecasting with smart meter IoT data. Despite the popularity of FL, researchers have pointed out that the performance of vanilla FL models may degrade significantly, in the case that data from different participants could not satisfy IID assumption [1, 15, 16]. To address the issue, different model aggregation strategies (e.g., FedProx [10]) and Scaffold [8]) are proposed to replace classical federate averaging. Ji [7] proposed an attention-based model aggregation strategy considering different contributions of participant model updates to the global model. However, the aggregated global model could not obtain optimum performance for all participants due to high diversity. Consequently, it is still challenging to deploy FL models in real-world application scenarios.

2.3   Personalized Federated Learning

As data heterogeneity issue is very common in applications and critical to FL model performance, a number of researches are conducted in these few years [18] to address the issue. There are two research directions most relevant to our work. The first is to obtain a personalized FL model for individuals [2, 19]. In the healthcare sector, [2] propose a federated transfer learning framework that enables collaborations among large amounts of wearable devices, which aggregates device local models through federated learning and then obtains a personalized model through transfer learning. In the energy sector, [20] propose a personalized federated learning for individual consumer electricity load forecasting. The algorithm

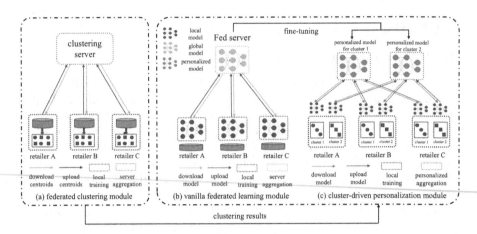

Fig. 2. The framework of cluster-driven personalized federated learning.

first trains a global federated model and then performs fine-tuning with each consumer's data to obtain its personalized model. The second is to obtain a personalized FL model for each cluster of similar individuals. In the health-care sector, [5] propose to cluster the distributed data into clinically meaningful communities and learnt one personalized model for each community. In the manufacturing sector, [4] propose a multi-task machinery fault diagnosis algorithm, according to the similarity of equipment IoT data features. In addition, [15] propose a clustered federated learning based on multi-task optimization.

The aforementioned personalized federated learning approaches are either prone to bias and over-fitting due to very limited data of individuals or could not fully utilize the valuable data from all participants. Instead, our proposed framework enables natural gas retailers to participate in two-phase federated learning, which could fully exploit federated learning advantages by leveraging all available consumer data without compromising their privacy and improve performance by fine-tuning the pre-trained model for each cluster according to different contributions of its consumers.

3   Method

Figure 2 illustrates two-phased federated learning with cluster-based personalization(CPFL) framework, which consists of the following three key functional modules:

- Knowledge-based federated clustering: categorizing customers into clusters in a privacy-preserving manner.
- Vanilla federated learning: pre-train a global federated model across retailers collaboratively.
- Cluster-based personalization: fine-tune the pre-trained global model for each cluster in a federated learning manner.

Our proposed framework has three important features to distinguish it from other personalized federated learning approaches for time-series forecasting in the literature. Firstly, a knowledge-based federated clustering categorizes consumers with similar load patterns into the same cluster, according to our industry domain knowledge and time-series data processing experiences. In addition, federated clustering is proposed to enable retailers to obtain global information for clustering consumers without compromising their privacy. Secondly, retailers participate in two-phase federated learning, pre-training global model by leveraging as much data as possible, and fine-tuning the model for each cluster to achieve a robust and accurate personalized model. Thirdly, we introduced an attention-based aggregation strategy in fine-tuning phase to consider the contribution difference of consumers to the cluster, for the purpose of improving performance further.

3.1 Knowledge-Based Federated Clustering

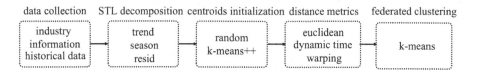

Fig. 3. The flowchart of knowledge-based federated clustering.

The goal of knowledge-based federated clustering is to categorize similar consumers into clusters without revealing the private data of retailers. The algorithm, as shown in Fig. 3, was developed based on our specific natural gas distribution domain knowledge (e.g., the seasonal pattern of domestic heating and manufacturing factories) and data scientists' experiences in time series data processing.

The algorithm takes historical natural gas consumption data and general information of different consumers into account. It decomposes the time series data through Seasonal and Trend decomposition using Loess (STL) and then clustering consumers based on the importance of these components. The federated clustering(k-means) module is shown in Fig. 2(a), supporting frequently used centroids initialization and distance metrics.

As shown in Algorithm 1, the cluster centroids of participants are initialized using random or k-means++ algorithms. Each participant updates local cluster centroids based on its consumers, using a k-means clustering algorithm. The server receives the cluster centroids from all the clients and aggregates them to obtain global cluster centroids. This process iterates many times until the model converges, i.e., the updates of cluster centroids are marginal.

Algorithm 1. Federated clustering algorithm

Input: The dataset $U = \{\pi_1, \pi_2, ..., \pi_p\}$ from p retailers, number of clusters k, initial cluster centroids C_i, local epochs L, and global epochs G.
Output: Cluster centroids $C = \{C_1, C_2, ..., C_k\}$ and labels.
1: Client initializes cluster centroids C and send to server.
2: **for** $g = 1, 2, ..., G$ **do**
3:     The server sends the cluster centroids C to the client.
4:     **for** $l = 1, 2, ..., L$ **do**
5:         Assign cluster label for each samples.
6:         Client update the cluster centroids using the formula (2).
7:     **end for**
8:     Client upload the cluster centroids to the server.
9:     Server update the cluster centroids using the formula (3).
10: **end for**

Suppose that training datasets from different retailers $U = \{\pi_1, \pi_2, ..., \pi_p\}$, where $\pi_l = \{x_1, x_2, ..., x_n\}$ denotes the data from retailer l, are partitioned into K clusters $C = \{C_1, C_2, ..., C_k\}$. The objective function of federated k-means can be formulated as:

$$J = \sum_{l=1}^{p}\sum_{j=1}^{k}\sum_{i=1}^{n} ||x_i^{(\pi_l)_j} - C_j||^2 \tag{1}$$

Here, $x_i^{(\pi_l)_j}$ denotes the training data in cluster centroid C_j and belonging to retailer π_l. $||x_i^{(\pi_l)_j} - C_j||^2$ denotes the distance from $x_i^{(\pi_l)_j}$ to C_j. Client and server update cluster centroids C_i of retailer π_l using formulates 2 and 3 respectively.

$$C_i^{\pi_l} = \frac{1}{|C_i^{\pi_l}|} \sum_{x \in C_i^{\pi_l}} x \tag{2}$$

$$C_i = \frac{1}{p} \sum_{C_i^{\pi_l} \in U} C_i^{\pi_l} \tag{3}$$

3.2   Two-Phase Federated Learning

The proposed CPFL is as shown in Fig. 2, adopting two-phases personalized federated learning as shown in Algorithm 2. A global federated model is first pre-trained across different retailers, using following objective function:

$$\arg\min_{w_g} L(w_g) = \sum_{\pi_l \in U}\sum_{x_i \in \pi_l} loss(f(x_i), y_i), \tag{4}$$

where $loss(f(x_i), y_i)$ denotes the loss function of the neural network. In this work, mean square error(MSE) is selected as the loss function. $f(x_i)$ denotes the forecast result and y_i denotes the ground truth. w_g denotes the parameters to be learned. p denotes the number of participators.

Algorithm 2. Two-phased federated learning

Input: Data from different retailers $U = \{\pi_1, \pi_2, ..., \pi_p\}$, results of federated k-means $C = \{C_1, C_2, ..., C_k\}$, global federated epochs G, personalized federated epochs L.

Output: Personalized federated learning for each cluster.

1: //Federated learning
2: **for** $g = 1, 2, ..., G$ **do**
3:     **for** $l = 1, 2, ..., p$ **do**
4:         Client π_l update model weights w_{π_l}.
5:     **end for**
6:     Server aggregates the model weights of each client to obtain global model weights w_g.
7: **end for**
8: //Cluster-based personalization
9: **for** $i = 1, 2, ..., k$ **do**
10:     Cluster C_i initializes personalized model weights w_{c_i} using w_g.
11:     **for** $j = 1, 2, ..., L$ **do**
12:         **for** $l = 1, 2, ..., p$ **do**
13:             Client π_l update model weights w_{π_l}.
14:         **end for**
15:         Server aggregates the model weights of each client to obtain personalized model weights w_{c_i}.
16:     **end for**
17: **end for**

The pre-trained global federated model is then fine-tuned to a personalized federated model for each cluster. Because consumers in the same cluster are considered similar, it realizes personalization in the form of federated learning instead of focusing only on the data of a specific consumer. The personalized federated model can effectively integrate useful knowledge from different consumers and meet the needs of privacy-preserving. The objective function is formulated as:

$$\arg\min_{w_{c_i}} L(w_{c_i}) = \sum_{\pi_l \in U} \sum_{c_i \in \pi_l} \sum_{x_i \in c_i} loss(f(x_i), y_i), \tag{5}$$

where w_{c_i} denotes the parameter of c_i to be learned.

3.3   Attention-Based Model Aggregation Strategy

Although we believe that consumers in the same cluster have similar load patterns, it is necessary to analyze the contributions of consumers to the personalized federated model in a more fine-grained manner. Because in a fine-grained view, they are still not similar. The forecasting performance of the personalized federated model may be sensitive to the number of clusters. If we can consider the contribution of different consumers to the personalized federated model in model aggregation, the sensitivity may be reduced. Ji [7] introduce an attention mechanism into the model aggregation and propose a Federated Attention(FedAtt) algorithm. The algorithm takes into account the distance between the client model and server model, so that the learned features of each client can be effectively selected to generate a better server model. Inspired by this, this section introduces the FedAtt algorithm for personalized model aggregation. We use euclidean distance to measure the distance between the local model and the personalized model. Suppose that cluster $C_i = \{x_1, x_2, ..., x_n\}$ has n consumers. At the t epoch, attention score can be expressed as $\alpha^t = \{\alpha_1^t, \alpha_2^t, ..., \alpha_n^t\}$. For consumer i, we calculate the euclidean distance between the local model and personalized model as follows:

$$d_i^t = ||w_i^{t+1} - w^t||^2 \tag{6}$$

The distance set between local model and personalized federated model can be expressed as $d_t = \{d_1^t, d_2^t, ..., d_n^t\}$. The attention score of i consumer on epoch t is as follows:

$$\alpha_i = d_i^t / \sum_{i=1}^{n} d_i^t \tag{7}$$

The personalized model weights update is as follows:

$$w^{t+1} = w^t - \sum_{i=1}^{n} \alpha_i(w^t - w_i^{t+1}) \tag{8}$$

4 Case Studies

4.1 Experimental Settings

A real-world dataset with natural gas monthly consumption of 2000 consumers from eight retailers is utilized in our experiments. These consumers come from different sector (e.g., Residential, Industrial and Commercial). Since those consumers may start natural gas service at different times, their load data cover the different lengths of time periods. To enable meaningful training, all consumers in the dataset have at least three years of load data. We choose the data from last year as the test set and the data before that as the train set for both knowledge-based federated clustering and personalized federated learning. MSE, MAE, and MAPE metrics are used to evaluate the performance of forecasting models with 1, 2 and 3 months forecasting horizons. In order to verify the performance advantages of our proposed CPFL framework, several model training methods are implemented and evaluated based on the aforementioned dataset, using the same LSTM network with a hidden layer and fully connected layer.

- Solo: train forecasting models for consumers individually.
- Centralized: collected data from all retailers and train a centralized model.
- FedAvg [12]: a vanilla federated learning among retailers using federated averaging model aggregation strategy.
- FedAtt [7]: federated learning among retailers using attention-based model aggregation strategy.
- PFL-Solo [20]: fine-tuning is used to personalize the global federated model for individual consumers.

- CFL [4]: train a personalized federated model for each cluster, without using data from other clusters.
- CPFL-Avg: our proposed CPFL framework, without attention-based aggregation strategy.
- CPFL-Att: our proposed CPFL framework, with attention-based aggregation strategy.

4.2 Forecasting Performance

Table 1. Performance comparison among algorithms with different forecasting horizons.

Methods	1 month			2 month			3 month		
	MSE	MAE	MAPE	MSE	MAE	MAPE	MSE	MAE	MAPE
Solo	0.0148	0.0919	0.2152	0.0170	0.0990	0.2324	0.0188	0.1037	0.2433
Centralized	0.0138	0.0883	0.1991	0.0181	0.1030	0.2308	0.0209	0.1118	0.2484
FedAvg	0.0155	0.0990	0.2473	0.0212	0.1180	0.3047	0.0238	0.1252	0.3264
FedAtt	0.0154	0.0987	0.2453	0.0208	0.1168	0.2995	0.0237	0.1249	0.3237
CFL	0.0130	0.0863	0.2018	0.0155	0.0955	0.2274	0.0168	0.0999	0.2396
PFL-Solo	0.0129	0.0851	0.2000	0.0158	0.0954	0.2262	0.0174	0.1000	0.2370
CPFL-Avg	0.0129	0.0848	0.1982	0.0151	0.0930	0.2212	0.0162	0.0968	0.2321
CPFL-Att	**0.0126**	**0.0834**	**0.1930**	**0.0148**	**0.0911**	**0.2137**	**0.0161**	**0.0956**	**0.2261**

Table 1 compares the performance of the aforementioned algorithms with different forecasting horizons. FedAvg and FedAtt perform even worse than Solo, although FL enables them to leverage all available data. The data heterogeneity makes them difficult to train optimum global federated models which are suitable for all consumers. Centralized model with access to all data outperforms FedAvg and FedAtt. CFL achieves better performance than Solo, Centralized, FedAvg and FedAtt, as it alleviates data heterogeneity to a certain extent through clustering. PFL-Solo achieves better performance than Solo, Centralized, FedAvg, FedAtt and CFL, as the pre-trained FL model fully leverages available data and data heterogeneity issue is alleviated by fine-tuning the pre-trained model for individual consumers. CPFL-Avg and CPFL-Att are our proposed algorithms without and with an attention-based model aggregation strategy respectively. Both of them outperform the aforementioned personalized FL algorithms, as our CPFL adopts two-phase FL leveraging all available data and fine-tuning personalized FL model to clusters lowering the risk of over-fitting. CPFL-Att outperforms CPFL-Avg, as it takes into account the contributions of different consumers to the personalized model in the fine-tuning and personalization phase.

4.3 Forecasting Performance Distribution

Figure 4 illustrates the advantages of CPFL-Att over Solo in terms of MAPE for 2000 consumers. The red circle represents the performance enhancement while

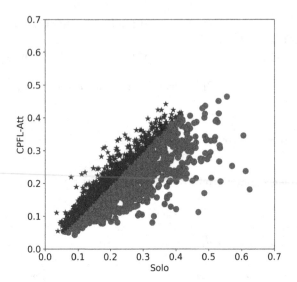

Fig. 4. MAPE of CPFL-Att against Solo.

the blue star represents the performance degradation after participating in our proposed federated learning framework using CPFL-Att algorithms. It is obvious that more consumers could achieve higher performance using CPFL-Att than Solo, and the extent of performance improvement is also more significant. Figure 5 reports the MAPE distribution of the Solo and CPFL-Att. The number of consumers with MAPE less than 0.2 increased significantly after participating CPFL-Att, while consumers with MAPE greater than 0.3 decreased significantly. In other words, CPFL-Att model enables more consumers achieve desirable forecasting accuracy, which is beneficial to both consumers and retailers for proper demand management and resource scheduling.

4.4 Performance on Different Number of Clusters

The number of clusters is one of the most critical parameters in cluster-driven approaches. With the increasing number of consumers in the same cluster, a better model generalization could be expected, but the data heterogeneity among many consumers may affect forecasting performance. Figure 6 reports forecasting performance (in terms of MAPE) of CFL, CPFL-Avg and CPFL-Att with different numbers of clusters. CFL uses data within the cluster only, and thus its performance is sensitive to the number of clusters. To the extreme, if the number of clusters is very small, the CFL performs similarly to vanilla federated learning. In contrast, if the number of clusters is very large, CFL performs similarly to Solo models. CPFL-Avg reports better performance than CFL. If the number of clusters is very large, the CPFL-Avg performs similarly to PFL-Solo. That is, fine-tuning the global model for each consumer. This could lead to bias and over-fitting. CPFL-Avg leverage all data from retailers and fine-tune

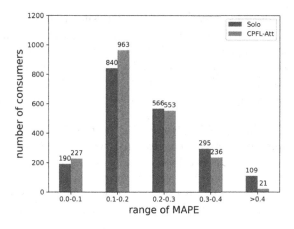

Fig. 5. MAPE distribution of our model and Solo.

a personalized model for each cluster but ignores the different contributions of consumers to the personalized model. CPFL-Att not only uses the data of all consumers but also takes into account the contribution of different consumers to the personalized model. This makes the model more robust and less sensitive to the number of clusters.

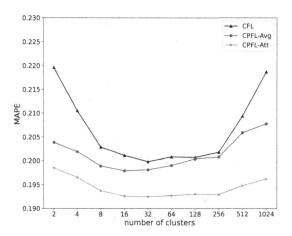

Fig. 6. MSE with different number of clusters.

5   Conclusion and Future Work

In this paper, we proposed a two-phased federated learning with cluster-based personalization (CPFL) framework for natural gas load forecasting. It enables retailers to work together to categorize their consumers into a number of clusters based on domain knowledge, and then train a personalized model for each cluster by two-phased federated learning, for the purpose of leveraging all available data and addressing data heterogeneity issues properly. According to our experiments based on a real-world dataset, the CPFL framework can achieve better performance than other personalized FL approaches recently proposed in the literature.

In the future, we will further improve the performance of the CPFL framework from multiple perspectives. For example, we will explore the feasibility of much larger deep learning networks (e.g., transformer) for datasets with more consumers and daily (or hourly) energy consumption. We may also consider the relationship among clusters to get the most valuable knowledge selectively (e.g., using graph neural network) for model performance enhancement.

References

1. Briggs, C., Fan, Z., Andras, P.: Federated learning with hierarchical clustering of local updates to improve training on non-IID data. In: 2020 International Joint Conference on Neural Networks (IJCNN), pp. 1–9. IEEE (2020)
2. Chen, Y., Qin, X., Wang, J., Yu, C., Gao, W.: FedHealth: a federated transfer learning framework for wearable healthcare. IEEE Intell. Syst. **35**(4), 83–93 (2020)
3. Fekri, M.N., Grolinger, K., Mir, S.: Distributed load forecasting using smart meter data: federated learning with recurrent neural networks. Int. J. Electr. Power Energy Syst. **137**, 107669 (2022)
4. Guo, S., Li, Z., Liu, H., Zhao, S., Jin, C.H.: Personalized federated learning for multi-task fault diagnosis of rotating machinery. arXiv preprint arXiv:2211.09406 (2022)
5. Huang, L., Shea, A.L., Qian, H., Masurkar, A., Deng, H., Liu, D.: Patient clustering improves efficiency of federated machine learning to predict mortality and hospital stay time using distributed electronic medical records. J. Biomed. Inform. **99**, 103291 (2019)
6. Husnoo, M.A., Anwar, A., Hosseinzadeh, N., Islam, S.N., Mahmood, A.N., Doss, R.: FedREP: towards horizontal federated load forecasting for retail energy providers. arXiv preprint arXiv:2203.00219 (2022)
7. Ji, S., Pan, S., Long, G., Li, X., Jiang, J., Huang, Z.: Learning private neural language modeling with attentive aggregation. In: 2019 International Joint Conference on Neural Networks (IJCNN), pp. 1–8. IEEE (2019)
8. Karimireddy, S.P., Kale, S., Mohri, M., Reddi, S., Stich, S., Suresh, A.T.: SCAFFOLD: stochastic controlled averaging for federated learning. In: International Conference on Machine Learning, pp. 5132–5143. PMLR (2020)
9. Li, P., Zhang, J.S.: A new hybrid method for China's energy supply security forecasting based on ARIMA and XGBoost. Energies **11**(7), 1687 (2018)
10. Li, T., Sahu, A.K., Zaheer, M., Sanjabi, M., Talwalkar, A., Smith, V.: Federated optimization in heterogeneous networks. Proc. Mach. Learn. Syst. **2**, 429–450 (2020)
11. Liu, J., Wang, S., Wei, N., Chen, X., Xie, H., Wang, J.: Natural gas consumption forecasting: a discussion on forecasting history and future challenges. J. Nat. Gas Sci. Eng. **90**, 103930 (2021)

12. McMahan, B., Moore, E., Ramage, D., Hampson, S., Arcas, B.A.: Communication-efficient learning of deep networks from decentralized data. In: Artificial Intelligence and Statistics, pp. 1273–1282. PMLR (2017)
13. Peng, S., Chen, R., Yu, B., Xiang, M., Lin, X., Liu, E.: Daily natural gas load forecasting based on the combination of long short term memory, local mean decomposition, and wavelet threshold denoising algorithm. J. Nat. Gas Sci. Eng. **95**, 104175 (2021)
14. Pradhan, P., Nayak, B., Dhal, S.K.: Time series data prediction of natural gas consumption using ARIMA model. Int. J. Inf. Technol. Manag. Inf. Syst. **7**(3), 1–7 (2016)
15. Sattler, F., Müller, K.R., Samek, W.: Clustered federated learning: model-agnostic distributed multitask optimization under privacy constraints. IEEE Trans. Neural Netw. Learn. Syst. **32**(8), 3710–3722 (2020)
16. Sattler, F., Wiedemann, S., Müller, K.R., Samek, W.: Robust and communication-efficient federated learning from non-IID data. IEEE Trans. Neural Netw. Learn. Syst. **31**(9), 3400–3413 (2019)
17. Taïk, A., Cherkaoui, S.: Electrical load forecasting using edge computing and federated learning. In: 2020 IEEE International Conference on Communications (ICC 2020), pp. 1–6. IEEE (2020)
18. Tan, A.Z., Yu, H., Cui, L., Yang, Q.: Toward personalized federated learning. In: IEEE Transactions on Neural Networks and Learning Systems (2022)
19. Wang, K., Mathews, R., Kiddon, C., Eichner, H., Beaufays, F., Ramage, D.: Federated evaluation of on-device personalization. arXiv preprint arXiv:1910.10252 (2019)
20. Wang, Y., Gao, N., Hug, G.: Personalized federated learning for individual consumer load forecasting. CSEE J. Power Energy Syst. (2022)
21. Wei, N., Li, C., Peng, X., Li, Y., Zeng, F.: Daily natural gas consumption forecasting via the application of a novel hybrid model. Appl. Energy **250**, 358–368 (2019)
22. Xu, J., Wang, J., Long, M., et al.: Autoformer: decomposition transformers with auto-correlation for long-term series forecasting. Adv. Neural. Inf. Process. Syst. **34**, 22419–22430 (2021)
23. Yang, Q., Liu, Y., Chen, T., Tong, Y.: Federated machine learning: concept and applications. ACM Trans. Intell. Syst. Technol. **10**(2), 1–19 (2019)

Privacy-Preserving Federated Cross-Domain Social Recommendation

Jianping Cai[1] , Yang Liu[2] , Ximeng Liu[1](✉) , Jiayin Li[1] , and Hongbin Zhuang[1]

[1] College of Computer and Data Science, Fuzhou University, Fuzhou 350108, China
snbnix@gmail.com
[2] Institute for AI Industry Research, Tsinghua University, Beijing 100084, China
liuy03@air.tsinghua.edu.cn

Abstract. By combining user feedback on items with social networks, cross-domain social recommendations provide users with more accurate recommendation results. However, traditional cross-domain social recommendations require holding both data of ratings and social networks, which is not easy to achieve for both information-oriented and social-oriented websites. To promote cross-domain social network collaboration among the institutions holding different data, this chapter proposes a federated cross-domain social recommendation (FCSR) algorithm. The main innovation is applying Random Response mechanism to achieve sparsely maintained differential privacy for user connections and proposing Matrix Confusion Method to achieve efficient encrypted user feature vector updates. Our experiments on three datasets show the practicality of FCSR in social recommendation and significantly outperforms baselines.

Keywords: Cross-Domain Social Recommendation · Federated Learning · Differential Privacy · Matrix Confusion Method · Random Response Mechanism

1 Introduction

Nowadays, recommendation systems are playing an essential role in modern business. It can accurately predict users' preferences and recommend items of interest to them, which undoubtedly brings excellent business value to websites that hold users' feedback. Besides users' feedback, the social connections of users have been proven to improve the quality of recommendations [8], which has attracted the attention of several studies [7,10,18] for cross-domain social recommendations. Unfortunately, user feedback and social networks are often not in the hands of one site. The information-oriented websites (IOW) that only hold users' feedback have to seek cooperation with social-oriented websites to improve the quality of recommendations. However, collaborative modeling is often not easy to implement. Most websites cannot freely share user information due to policy or privacy concerns, which leads to traditional centralized modeling techniques failing to be implemented due to a lack of necessary data.

Supported by the National Natural Science Foundation of China (project numbers 62072109 and U1804263).

Federated learning [21] (FL) has recently been shown to be a promising learning framework for facilitating collaborative modeling among multiple parties without sharing any raw training data. For cross-domain social recommendations, FL allows the information-oriented websites and the social-oriented websites to collaboratively build more accurate recommendation models without exposing their respective data. However, federated cross-domain social recommendations are currently facing the following multifaceted challenges. First, although some centralized social recommendation methods [7, 18] and purely federated recommendation algorithms [20] have been proposed, they cannot be directly applied to federated cross-domain recommendations. The key challenge is how to ensure the security of users' individual privacy in social networks. Second, FL requires applying privacy-preserving techniques to secure local data, but some techniques trade off at the cost of significant computational overhead, such as homomorphic encryption [16]. Since federated cross-domain social recommendations involve complex algebraic operations, achieving high enough computational efficiency while ensuring security is another important challenge we face. Besides, the sparsity of data is an essential characteristic of social recommendations [3]. Effectively exploiting the sparsity to achieve high efficiency is a fundamental problem faced in social recommendations.

In response to the challenges, our contributions in this chapter are as follows:

1) We propose a federated cross-domain social recommendation (FCSR) algorithm that treats the social-oriented website as a social services platform (SSP) and applies a FL framework to train social recommendation models without each participant's data.
2) We introduce a Random Response Mechanism to preserve individual privacy in SSP and design an efficient social network perturbation method, which avoids perturbing all possible social connections.
3) We propose a Matrix Confusion Method, which enables SSP to correctly update user feature vectors with high efficiency while the encrypted user feature vectors cannot be identified.
4) Facing the challenge of computing equations with large-scale sparse matrices, we propose a scheme to apply LU decomposition to improve the computational efficiency and study the impact of various decomposition strategies on the sparsity of the decomposed matrices.

2 Preliminaries

2.1 Social Recommendation System

Given a set of user ratings for items such as (u_i, v_j, r_{ij}), indicating that user u_i rates item v_j as r_{ij}, a typical recommendation system tries to predict the users' potential ratings for each item and then recommends items of interest to users from the predicted ratings.

To predict the ratings more accurately, collaborative filtering methods based on feature representations are widely used. The basic idea is to represent each user u_i and item v_j as feature vectors $\mathbf{u}_i$ and $\mathbf{v}_j$, respectively, and then train a model $\mathcal{M}$ such that the predicted rating $\widehat{r}_{ij} = \mathcal{M}(\mathbf{u}_i, \mathbf{v}_j)$ is as close as possible to the true rating r_{ij}.

The work close to ours is the cross-domain social recommendation approach proposed by [18]. The main idea is to build training models for user ratings from the information-oriented domain and social networks from the social-oriented domain separately, and then exchange the common users' (bridge users in [18]) feature vectors of both to achieve cross-domain social recommendation. However, the work only focuses on centralized learning, meaning rating data and social networks have to be aggregated together before learning. Unfortunately, users' ratings or social connections are often privacy-sensitive. The cross-domain social recommendation will not be achieved when data providers are reluctant to share data due to policy or commercial competition.

2.2 Vertical Federated Learning

As an emerging machine learning paradigm, FL can build a learning model exploiting distributed datasets of all participants without revealing private datasets [21]. There are three categories of FL, i.e., horizontal federated learning (HFL), vertical federated learning (VFL) and federated transfer learning (FTL).

VFL can mainly be applied in two or more different collaborating institutions, which hold heterogeneous user data, but some of the users involved are common. In the VFL scenario, participating institutions are assumed to be untrustworthy and attempt to mine others' privacy through the learning process. For data privacy and security reasons, the participants of VFL cannot directly exchange data. Some privacy security methods are applied to VFL to preserve each participant's privacy, such as homomorphic encryption [16], differential privacy [6], secure multi-party computation [1], and Diffie-Hellman Key Exchange [17].

2.3 Differential Privacy

Differential privacy (DP) [4] is a theoretically provable technique for protecting individual privacy and is widely used in Federated Learning. It protects individual privacy through data perturbation, defined as follows:

Definition 1 (ε-**Differential Privacy**). *Given two neighboring datasets $\mathcal{D}$ and $\mathcal{D}'$, a random algorithm $\mathcal{A}$ satisfies ε-DP if its all outputs $O \in \text{Range}\,(\mathcal{A})$ satisfies*

$$\Pr\left(\mathcal{A}\left(\mathcal{D}\right) = O\right) \leq e^{\varepsilon} \Pr\left(\mathcal{A}\left(\mathcal{D}'\right) = O\right). \tag{1}$$

Traditional DP mechanisms are mostly for continuous and discrete data, such as Laplace mechanism [5] for continuous data and Exponential mechanism [12] for discrete data. By studying the Rényi Differential Privacy [15], Mironov proposed a random response mechanism (RRM) [15] applicable to the binary release, which is defined as follows.

Definition 2 (**Random Response Mechanism**). *Given a function* $f : \mathcal{D} \mapsto \{0,1\}$, *RRM achieves* $\widetilde{f}\,(\mathcal{D})$ *satisfying ε-DP by*

$$\widetilde{f}\,(\mathcal{D}) = \begin{cases} f\,(\mathcal{D}) & \text{with probability } p \\ 1 - f\,(\mathcal{D}) & \text{with probability } 1 - p \end{cases}, \tag{2}$$

where $p = \frac{e^\varepsilon}{1+e^\varepsilon} \geq 0.5$.

In general, DP algorithm consists of several sub-algorithms. They satisfy the serial combination theorem [13] as follows.

Theorem 1 (Serial Combination). *Given k random algorithms $A_1, A_2, \ldots, A_k$ where A_i satisfies ε_i-DP, their combination satisfies $\left(\sum_{i=1}^{k} \varepsilon_i\right)$-DP.*

3   Problem Formulation

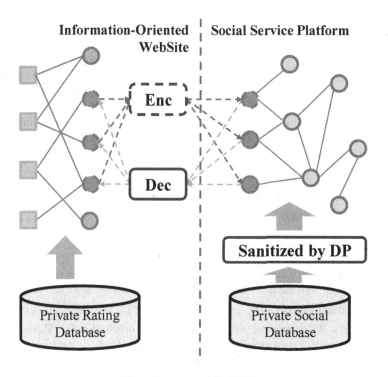

Fig. 1. System model of FCSR

3.1   System Model

The system model of our FCSR is shown in Fig. 1. In the system model, we consider two FL participants: the information-oriented website (IOW) and the social service platform (SSP).

IOW: IOWs hold a large amount of user feedback data by providing information services. Using these data, they can realize recommendation systems by user ratings.

IOW is the service requester, which initiates social service requests to SSP to improve recommendation quality.

SSP: SSP holds the users' social connections by providing social services. It is the service provider and is in charge of applying the privacy-preserving social relationships to improve the quality of the recommendation of collaborators.

As shown in Fig. 1, an IOW and SSP consist of a VFL system with two parties. They employ appropriate privacy security schemes to protect their respective local data. As a service requester, IOW encrypts the submitted data via encryption to ensure that SSP cannot obtain any available information. However, SSP cannot wholly hide its information as a service provider. Thus, we introduce DP to protect users' individual privacy in social networks.

3.2   Threat Model

In FCSR, SSP is considered to be semi-honest, i.e., SSP follows protocols to return the correct results, but actively try to learn the private information form the uploaded data. Meanwhile, we consider IOW as potentially malicious. IOW expects to mine users' social connections through machine learning or algebraic analysis. For this purpose, IOW may violate protocols by uploading some special constructed user features to capture users' social connections, or even directly invading SSP to illegally access the serving social network.

4   The Scheme of Federated Cross-Domain Social Recommendation

4.1   The Algorithm Framework

As shown in Fig. 1, our scheme consists of two parts: training the secure recommendation model on IOW and the individual privacy-secure social network service for SSP.

The rating data of IOW can be represented as the set $\mathcal{D}_r = \left\{ \left(u_i^{(k)}, v_j^{(k)}, r_{ij}^{(k)} \right) \right\}_{k=1}^m$ with m elements. We denote the set of users and items involved as $\mathcal{U}_r$, $\mathcal{V}_r$ respectively. Thus, IOW expects to train a group of user feature vectors $\{\mathbf{u}_i\}_{i \in \mathcal{U}_r}$ and a group of item feature vectors $\{\mathbf{v}_j\}_{j \in \mathcal{V}_r}$ to accurately predict the rating (u_i, v_j, r_{ij}) that are not in $\mathcal{D}_r$, where $\mathbf{u}_i, \mathbf{v}_j \in \mathbb{R}^{d \times 1}$, which are both d-dimensional feature column vectors.

In contrast, the social network data held by the SSP is represented as the set $\mathcal{D}_s = \left\{ \left(u_i^{(k)}, u_j^{(k)} \right) \right\}_{k=1}^n$ with n elements, where $\left(u_i^{(k)}, u_j^{(k)} \right)$ satisfying $u_i^{(k)} < u_j^{(k)}$ indicates that the user $u_i^{(k)}$ and $u_j^{(k)}$ are friends or know each other. Thus, the social network in SSP can be represented as an undirected graph $\mathcal{G}$. We denote the set of users involved in the social network as $\mathcal{U}_s$, which contains p_s users. The adjacency matrix of $\mathcal{G}$ can be denoted as $\mathbf{S}_{\mathcal{G}} \in \mathbb{R}^{p_s \times p_s}$, which satisfies

$$\mathbf{S}_{\mathcal{G}} = \begin{cases} 1 \text{ if } (u_i, u_j) \text{ or } (u_j, u_i) \in \mathcal{D}_s \\ 0 \text{ otherwise} \end{cases} \tag{3}$$

By Exp. (3), we know that $\mathbf{S}_\mathcal{G}$ is symmetric and contains only 0 or 1. Besides, in practical social networks, $\mathbf{S}_\mathcal{G}$ is usually highly sparse. The density of 1 can be expressed as

$$\rho_\mathcal{G} = \frac{n}{C_{p_s}^2} = \frac{\mathbf{1}^T \mathbf{S}_\mathcal{G} \mathbf{1}}{2C_{p_s}^2}, \tag{4}$$

where $C_{p_s}^2 = \frac{1}{2}p_s(p_s - 1)$, indicates the all possible social relationship pairs.

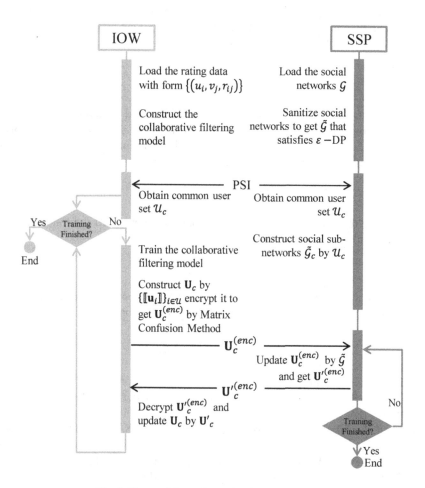

Fig. 2. The workflow of our algorithm framework

The federated cross-domain social recommendation should work on the common users between IOW and SSP. Thus, we denote the common users as the set $\mathcal{U}_c = \mathcal{U}_r \cap \mathcal{U}_s$. As the overall algorithmic workflow shown in Fig. 2, IOW trains a collaborative filtering model and obtains a group of user feature vectors of $\mathcal{U}_r$. And then, it submits the feature vectors $\{\mathbf{u}_i\}_{i \in \mathcal{U}_c}$ of common users to SSP and receives $\{\mathbf{u}'_i\}_{i \in \mathcal{U}_c}$ from SSP after updating by the social network. To describe the update of $\{\mathbf{u}_i\}_{i \in \mathcal{U}_c}$ more effectively, we stacks $\{\mathbf{u}_i\}_{i\in\mathcal{U}_c}$, $\{\mathbf{u}_i\}_{i\in\mathcal{U}_c}$ vertically and denote them as feature matrices $\mathbf{U}_c, \mathbf{U}'_c \in \mathbb{R}^{p_c \times d}$.

4.2 Learning of Social Networks with Differential Privacy

To learn user feature vectors by social networks, we adopt the semi-supervised learning method on graph proposed by [18]. It considers that if two users are strongly connected, they are more likely to have similar feature representations. Based on this consideration, two objective functions are proposed for optimizing $\mathbf{U}'_c$. One is the objective function for smoothness constraint, which is expressed as

$$f_1\left(\mathbf{U}'_c\right) = \frac{1}{2} \sum_{i,j\in\mathcal{U}_c} s_{ij} \left\| \mathbf{u}'_i/\sqrt{d_i} - \mathbf{u}'_j/\sqrt{d_j} \right\|^2, \tag{5}$$

where s_{ij} is the i-th row and j-column element of $\mathbf{S}_{\mathcal{G}_c}$ and d_i denotes the degree of user u_i. As shown in Fig. 2, $\mathbf{S}_{\mathcal{G}_c}$ is the adjacency matrix of sub-networks $\mathcal{G}_c$ involved the users in $\mathcal{U}_c$, i.e., a sub-matrix of $\mathbf{S}_{\mathcal{G}}$. Another objective function is to keep the consistency of the user feature representations, which is expressed as

$$f_2\left(\mathbf{U}'_c\right) = \frac{1}{2} \left\| \mathbf{U}'_c - \mathbf{U}_c \right\|^2_F. \tag{6}$$

Combining the above two objective functions, [18] developed the following optimization equation to obtain $\mathbf{U}'$, which is

$$\min_{\mathbf{U}'_c} f_1\left(\mathbf{U}'_c\right) + \mu f_2\left(\mathbf{U}'_c\right), \tag{7}$$

where $\mu > 0$ is a parameter to control the tradeoff between two objective functions. Since (7) is a quadratic equation, it has a closed-form solution as

$$\mathbf{U}'_c = \frac{\mu}{(2+\mu)} \left(\mathbf{I} - \frac{2}{(2+\mu)} \mathbf{D}^{-1/2} \mathbf{S}_{\mathcal{G}_c} \mathbf{D}^{-1/2} \right)^{-1} \mathbf{U}_c \tag{8}$$

where $\mathbf{D}$ is a diagonal matrix whose diagonal elements are consisted of $d_i, i \in \mathcal{U}_c$. Note that we corrected an error in [18] on computing $\mathbf{U}'_c$. Thus, our Exp. (8) is different from Exp. (15) in [18].

Since the calculation of $\mathbf{U}'_c$ involves $\mathbf{S}_{\mathcal{G}_c}$, unprotected $\mathbf{S}_{\mathcal{G}}$ will lead to leakages of users' social connections. Considering the characteristics of $\mathbf{S}_{\mathcal{G}}$, we adopt the random response mechanism (RRM) as Definition 2 to provide individual privacy guarantees. The process of obtaining the perturbed $\mathbf{S}_{\tilde{\mathcal{G}}}$ satisfying ε-DP is shown in Fig. 3.

In Fig. 3, we divide the perturbation process into two parts, satisfying ε_1-DP and ε_2-DP, respectively, where $\varepsilon_1 + \varepsilon_2 = \varepsilon$ by Theorem. 1. The first part satisfies ε_1-DP. Regarding all elements in $\mathbf{S}_{\mathcal{G}}$ above (or below) the main diagonal as a series of independent responses, we directly apply RRM on $\mathbf{S}_{\mathcal{G}}$ to achieve ε_1-DP. The element $\tilde{s}_{ij}$ of $\mathbf{S}_{\tilde{\mathcal{G}}}$ can be calculated by

$$\tilde{s}_{ij} = \begin{cases} s_{ij} & \text{with probability } p \text{ if } i < j \\ 1 - s_{ij} & \text{with probability } 1 - p \text{ if } i < j \\ \tilde{s}_{ji} & \text{otherwise} \end{cases}, \tag{9}$$

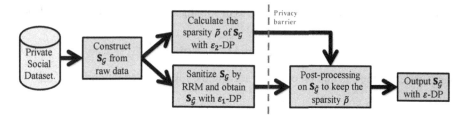

Fig. 3. Flowchart to Achieve ε-DP with RRM

where $p = \frac{e^{\varepsilon_1}}{1+e^{\varepsilon_1}}$.

Note that after sanitization, the density of $\mathbf{S}_{\mathcal{G}}$ will be changed. Denoting $\mathbf{S}_{\widetilde{\mathcal{G}}}$ as $\rho_{\widetilde{\mathcal{G}}}$, we have

$$\mathbb{E}\left(\rho_{\widetilde{\mathcal{G}}}\right) = \rho_{\mathcal{G}} p + (1 - \rho_{\mathcal{G}})(1 - p). \tag{10}$$

Since $\mathbf{S}_{\mathcal{G}}$ is highly sparse, even if p is close to 1, $\mathbb{E}\left(\rho_{\widetilde{\mathcal{G}}}\right)$ still changes dramatically. For example, $\rho_{\mathcal{G}}$ of FilmTrust is 0.34%. When $\varepsilon_1 = 5$, $p = 0.9933$ is close to 1 (only a tiny part of elements in $\mathbf{S}_{\widetilde{\mathcal{G}}}$ return fake responses). We calculate that $\mathbb{E}\left(\rho_{\widetilde{\mathcal{G}}}\right) = 1.01\%$, which is nearly twice more than the original $\rho_{\mathcal{G}}$. To keep the original density, we introduce the second perturbation process that satisfies ε_2-DP. It computes a noisy connection count $\tilde{n} = |\mathcal{D}_s| + Lap(1/\varepsilon_2)$ by Laplace mechanism and then computes $\tilde{\rho}_{\mathcal{G}}$ satisfying ε_2-DP by $\tilde{\rho}_{\mathcal{G}} = \tilde{n}/C_{p_s}^2$. Using $\tilde{\rho}_{\mathcal{G}}$, we can keep $\rho_{\widetilde{\mathcal{G}}}$ reach $\tilde{\rho}_{\mathcal{G}}$ by randomly adding or removing 1s in $\mathbf{S}_{\widetilde{\mathcal{G}}}$. It is post-processing and does not lead to any more privacy leakage [6]. Usually, we can allocate most of the privacy budget to ε_1, e.g., 99% of ε, because even if ε_2 is allocated a extremely small privacy budget, the deviation of $\rho_{\widetilde{\mathcal{G}}}$ is still not significant. For instance, $\varepsilon = 1$ and ε_1 is 50% of ε, we have $p = 0.62$ and $\rho_{\widetilde{\mathcal{G}}}$ of the dataset FilmTrust satisfying $(3.4 \pm 0.0074) \times 10^{-3}$. However, if ε_1 is changed to 99% of ε, we have $p = 0.73$ and $\rho_{\widetilde{\mathcal{G}}}$ satisfying $(3.4 \pm 0.37) \times 10^{-3}$, which shows that increasing the ratio of ε_1 can improve p up to 0.11 but the deviation of $\rho_{\widetilde{\mathcal{G}}}$ still remains in a small range.

4.3 Highly Efficient $\mathbf{S}_{\widetilde{\mathcal{G}}}$ Construction and Calculation for $\mathbf{U}_c'$

Since there is only a tiny part of elements in $\mathbf{S}_{\widetilde{\mathcal{G}}}$ return fake responses in general, it is unnecessary to traverse all possible connections and check whether they return a fake response. To construct $\mathbf{S}_{\widetilde{\mathcal{G}}}$ more efficiently, we first generate a random integer N_{fake} satisfying binomial distribution $\mathrm{B}\left(C_{p_s}^2, 1 - p\right)$ to denote the number of fake responses. And then, we randomly choose a group of $\left\{s_{ij}^{(t)}\right\}_{t=1}^{N_{fake}}$, $i < j$ to change their and the symmetric elements' values. Since the generation of N_{fake} is $O(1)$, the fake responses can be achieved by a random sampling algorithm [14]. Thus, the overall computational complexity of generating $\mathbf{S}_{\widetilde{\mathcal{G}}}$ is $O\left((1 - p + \rho_{\mathcal{G}})p_s^2\right)$, which is usually much lower than $O\left(p_s^2\right)$ of traversal.

In addition, Exp. (8) involves the process of solving an equation. Specifically, denoting

$$Q = I - \frac{2}{(2+\mu)} D^{-1/2} S_g D^{-1/2},\tag{11}$$

we can describe the calculation of U_c' as solving the following equation for U_c',

$$QU_c' = \frac{\mu}{(2+\mu)} U_c.\tag{12}$$

Solving equations is an algebraic calculation with high computational overhead. Even though $S_{\tilde{g}}$ is usually highly sparse, the traditional linear solution methods for sparse matrices cannot support large-scale social networks. Facing the challenge of solving large-scale sparse equations, we adopt LU decomposition to improve the computational efficiency of U_c'. Since Q is symmetric, we can express it as the following LU decomposition form

$$Q = PLL^T P^T,\tag{13}$$

where L is a lower triangular matrix; P is a permutation matrix. Since the multiplication with the permutation matrix P is equivalent to rearranging the elements of the matrix, the calculation of U can be equivalently converted into solving the equations about the triangular matrix twice after LU decomposition, i.e.,

$$LU_c^{(2)} = U_c^{(1)} \text{ and } L^T U_c^{(3)} = U_c^{(2)}.\tag{14}$$

where $U_c^{(1)} = \frac{\mu}{(2+\mu)} P^T U_c$, $U_c^{(3)} = P^T U_c'$. Compared to the regular sparse equations, solving equations on triangular matrices is far more efficient. Its computational overhead depends on the density of L. That is, fewer non-zero elements imply a smaller computational overhead.

Table 1. The Number of Non-zero Elements of **L** under Different Permutation Strategies for the Three Datasets

	FilmTrust	CiaoDVD	Epinions
PS.1	42, 672	4, 677, 004	Failed
PS.2	5, 236	564, 080	43, 108, 346
PS.3	**3, 115**	**232, 645**	**16, 030, 689**
PS.4	5, 070	839, 656	142, 441, 761

Our study shows that different permutation strategies during LU decomposition will result in different density of L. Here, we compared four different strategies, which are natural ordering (PS.1), minimum degree ordering on the structure of $Q^T Q$ (PS.2), minimum degree ordering on the structure of $Q^T + Q$ (PS.3), as well as approximate minimum degree column ordering (PS.4). As shown in Table 1, we test the density of L after LU decomposition with different strategies (PS.1 to PS.4) for the three classical datasets FilmTrust, CiaoDVD, and Epinions. The results show that L always has the least number of non-zero elements with PS.3, which means it is the most optimal LU decomposition strategy for social networks and can solve U_c' with the highest efficiency.

4.4 Privacy-Preserving User Feature Vector Update with Matrix Confusion Method

To avoid privacy leakage by directly uploading user features, IOW needs to encrypt them while maintaining computability before uploading. Completing the update efficiently of U_c without any privacy available to SSP is a critical challenge faced by federated cross-domain social recommendations. We propose Matrix Confusion Method according to the update of U_c, which enables the SSP to compute U'_c despite the inability to identify the received U_c.

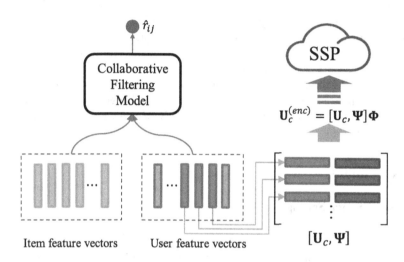

Fig. 4. Matrix confusion before uploading

As shown in Fig. 2, IOW encrypts U_c and obtains $U_c^{(enc)}$, and then replaces U_c by $U_c^{(enc)}$ to upload to SSP. As shown is Fig. 4, in our Matrix Confusion Method, $U_c^{(enc)}$ is constructed as the following step:

1) IOW randomly generates a matrix $\Psi \in \mathbb{R}^{p_c \times d}$ (the crimson vectors in Fig. 4) of the same shape as U_c and an invertible random matrix $\Phi \in \mathbb{R}^{2d \times 2d}$.
2) IOW stacks U_c and Ψ horizontally and then multiplies Φ right to obtain $U_c^{(enc)}$.
3) IOW uploads $U_c^{(enc)}$ to SSP.

Compared to the inefficient calculation on homomorphic encryption, our method only requires twice the calculation of unencrypted U_c to achieve the calculation on encrypted data. After SSP finishes calculating $U_c'^{(enc)}$, IOW can restore U'_c by the following step:

1) IOW multiply $U_c'^{(enc)}$ right by Φ^{-1} to get $[U'_c, \Psi']$.
2) IOW retain the first d columns of $[U'_c, \Psi']$ to obtain U'_c.

5 Security Analysis

The security consists of two aspects, i.e., the security of user features for IOW and the social network's security for SSP.

In our scheme, our Matrix Confusion Method avoids $\mathbf{U}_c$ from being identified while updating. Since IOW always keeps the random matrices $\mathbf{\Psi}$ and $\mathbf{\Phi}$ locally during the federated learning, SSP cannot infer the true value of $\mathbf{U}_c$ from the received $\mathbf{U}_c^{(enc)}$. Furthermore, our Matrix Confusion Method provides a non-analyzable guarantee for $\mathbf{U}_c$. Due to the randomness of $\mathbf{\Psi}$, stacking it horizontally with $\mathbf{U}_c$ and engaging in confusion destroys the properties originally held by $\mathbf{U}_c$. Attackers cannot analyze $\mathbf{U}_c^{(enc)}$ effectively, which ensures the security of the uploaded $\mathbf{U}_c$.

The security of social networks comes from the privacy guarantees provided by DP. As a proven DP method in [15], RRM provides sufficient security. Even if an attacker maliciously accesses $\widetilde{\mathcal{G}}$, he still cannot effectively infer individual privacy. Notice that our proposed DP approach provides static sanitized social networks for FL. Even if IOW requests updates for $\mathbf{U}_c$ multiple times, the privacy budget will not be consumed additionally. It prevents privacy leakage caused by IOW maliciously submitting multiple update requests.

6 Experiments

6.1 Experimental Setting

Table 2. The Number of Non-zero Elements of $\mathbf{L}$ under Different Permutation Strategies for the Three Datasets

	FilmTrust	CiaoDVD	Epinions
p_r	1,508	17,615	40,163
p_s	874	4,658	49,287
p_c	740	2,740	40,162
v_r	2,071	16,121	139,738
m	35,497	72,665	664,823
n	1,309	33,116	381,035

Notes. "p_r": the rated user number in IOW; "p_s": the social user number in SSP; "p_c": the common user number; "v_r": the item number in IOW; "m": the rating number in IOW; "n": the number of social connection pairs.

In this section, we evaluate the effectiveness of our proposed FCSR by experiments. The experiments run on a computer with Dual 4 Core 3.9 GHz AMD Ryzen CPU, 32

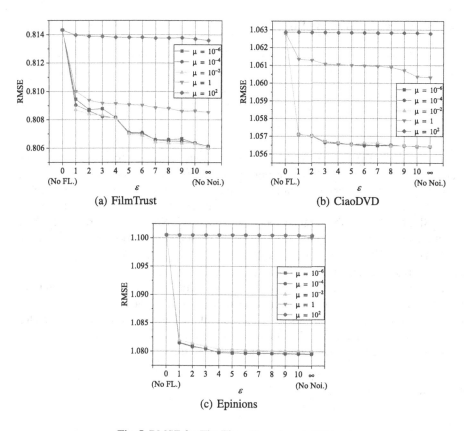

Fig. 5. RMSE for The Three Experimental Datasets

GB RAM and NVIDIA GeForce RTX 2080 Ti GPU. To fully evaluate our scheme, we experiment with three classic social recommendation datasets with different data scales, which are small-scale FilemTrust[1], medium-scale CiaoDVD[3], and large-scale Epinions[2]. Among them, Filmtrust comes from online film rating website which contains the social connections between users; The user ratings of CiaoDVD and Epinions are crawled from shopping websites and the social connections are constructed from the users' trust links. The details are shown in Table 2. We adopt NCF proposed by [9] as the recommended model of our FCSR and ε_1 and ε_2 are taken as 99% and 1% of ε. To test the generalizability of the training models, we randomly divide the rating data into a training set $\mathcal{D}_r^{(train)}$, and a test set $\mathcal{D}_r^{(test)}$ with a proportion of 9 : 1. Then, we perform multiple experiments on the same experimental parameters and take their average experimental results as our final experimental results.

---

[1] https://guoguibing.github.io/librec/datasets.html.
[2] https://www.cse.msu.edu/~tangjili/datasetcode/truststudy.htm.

6.2   Evaluation on Training Effect

We use RMSE on $\mathcal{D}_r^{(test)}$ as the evaluation metric to measure the learning effect of FCSR, which is calculated by

$$RMSE = \sqrt{\frac{1}{\left|\mathcal{D}_r^{(test)}\right|} \sum_{k \in \mathcal{D}_r^{(test)}} \left(r_{ij}^{(k)} - \hat{r}_{ij}^{(k)}\right)^2}. \tag{15}$$

The results in Fig. 5(a–c) test the impact of various privacy budgets ε and the social learning parameters μ on RMSE. In Fig. 5(a–c), we use the setting $\varepsilon = 0$ to indicate IOW trains the recommendation model independently without interacting with the SSP (non-FL scenario, i.e., No FL.), and $\varepsilon = \infty$ to indicate Federated learning without DP (i.e., SSP directly uses the original social networks, i.e., No Noi.). Figure 5(a–c) show that the cross-domain federation learning based on social networks effectively reduce the RMSE on $\mathcal{D}_r^{(test)}$. As ε increases, RMSE tends to increase overall, which means more accurate social networks will lead to more accurate predictions.

In addition, according to optimization (7), a smaller μ implies a higher weight of the smoothing constraint. In other words, the more significant the role of social network learning. Our experimental results show that smoothing constraints with higher weights (smaller μ) can reduce the RMSE more, indicating that enhancing the role of social networks in FL can effectively improve the learning effect.

6.3   Comparison with Existing Federated Schemes

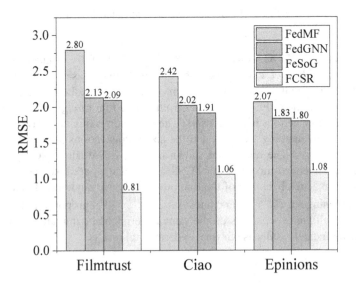

Fig. 6. RMSE for Dataset Epinions

We further compare our FCSR with the existing Federated recommendation, which are FedMF [2], FedGNN [19], and FeSoG [11]. Similarly, we use RMSE as the evaluation metric. The experimental results are shown in Fig. 6. Since FCSR introduces DP to protect individual privacy, we set $\varepsilon = 1$ facing the optimal case of μ in Fig. 5 to carry out the comparisons in Fig. 6. The results show that our proposed FCSR significantly improves the accuracy of existing federated schemes on all three datasets. The main reasons are as follows. First, we only apply DP on social networks instead of applying DP on both user feature vectors and social networks, as in [11]. It guarantees the introduction of FL will not produce worse results than recommendations without social networks. Second, FCSR requires only one perturbation to achieve ε-DP, which does not accumulate noise compared to the common gradient-based perturbations. In summary, FCSR is effective and practical.

7   Conclusions and Future Works

In this chapter, our proposed FCSR effectively supports the participants to collaboratively train better recommendation models with the private data maintained locally. Through security analysis, we ensure security during the FL process. Meanwhile, our experiments show that FCSR is an effective and practical algorithm. Currently, federated cross-domain social recommendations are a promising direction with substantial potential opportunities. In future works, we will concentrate on researching more effective federated cross-domain recommendation algorithms and overcoming challenges from security and efficiency.

References

1. Bogdanov, D., Laur, S., Willemson, J.: Sharemind: a framework for fast privacy-preserving computations. In: Jajodia, S., Lopez, J. (eds.) ESORICS 2008. LNCS, vol. 5283, pp. 192–206. Springer, Heidelberg (2008). https://doi.org/10.1007/978-3-540-88313-5_13
2. Chai, D., Wang, L., Chen, K., Yang, Q.: Secure federated matrix factorization. IEEE Intell. Syst. 36, 11–20 (2020). https://doi.org/10.1109/MIS.2020.3014880
3. Cui, J., Chen, C., Lyu, L., Yang, C., Li, W.: Exploiting data sparsity in secure cross-platform social recommendation. In: Advances in Neural Information Processing Systems, vol. 34, pp. 10524–10534 (2021)
4. Dwork, C., Kenthapadi, K., McSherry, F., Mironov, I., Naor, M.: Our data, ourselves: privacy via distributed noise generation. In: Vaudenay, S. (ed.) EUROCRYPT 2006. LNCS, vol. 4004, pp. 486–503. Springer, Heidelberg (2006). https://doi.org/10.1007/11761679_29
5. Dwork, C., McSherry, F., Nissim, K., Smith, A.: Calibrating noise to sensitivity in private data analysis. In: Halevi, S., Rabin, T. (eds.) TCC 2006. LNCS, vol. 3876, pp. 265–284. Springer, Heidelberg (2006). https://doi.org/10.1007/11681878_14
6. Dwork, C., Roth, A., et al.: The algorithmic foundations of differential privacy. Found. Trends Theor. Comput. Sci. 9(3–4), 211–407 (2014)
7. Fan, W., et al.: Graph neural networks for social recommendation. In: The World Wide Web Conference, pp. 417–426 (2019)
8. Guo, G., Zhang, J., Yorke-Smith, N.: Trustsvd: collaborative filtering with both the explicit and implicit influence of user trust and of item ratings. In: Proceedings of the AAAI Conference on Artificial Intelligence, vol. 29 (2015)

9. He, X., Liao, L., Zhang, H., Nie, L., Hu, X., Chua, T.S.: Neural collaborative filtering. In: Proceedings of the 26th International Conference on World Wide Web, pp. 173–182 (2017)

10. Liu, Y., Liang, C., He, X., Peng, J., Zheng, Z., Tang, J.: Modelling high-order social relations for item recommendation. IEEE Trans. Knowl. Data Eng. **34**, 4385–4397 (2020)

11. Liu, Z., Yang, L., Fan, Z., Peng, H., Yu, P.: Federated social recommendation with graph neural network. ACM Trans. Intell. Syst. Technol. **13**, 1–24 (2022). https://doi.org/10.1145/3501815

12. McSherry, F., Talwar, K.: Mechanism design via differential privacy, pp. 94–103 (2007). https://doi.org/10.1109/FOCS.2007.66

13. McSherry, F.D.: Privacy integrated queries: an extensible platform for privacy-preserving data analysis. In: Proceedings of the 2009 ACM SIGMOD International Conference on Management of Data, pp. 19–30 (2009)

14. Meng, X.: Scalable simple random sampling and stratified sampling. In: International Conference on Machine Learning, pp. 531–539. PMLR (2013)

15. Mironov, I.: Rényi differential privacy. In: 2017 IEEE 30th Computer Security Foundations Symposium (CSF), pp. 263–275. IEEE (2017)

16. Paillier, P.: Public-key cryptosystems based on composite degree residuosity classes. In: Stern, J. (ed.) EUROCRYPT 1999. LNCS, vol. 1592, pp. 223–238. Springer, Heidelberg (1999). https://doi.org/10.1007/3-540-48910-X_16

17. Raymond, J.F., Stiglic, A.: Security issues in the diffie-hellman key agreement protocol. IEEE Trans. Inf. Theory **22**, 1–17 (2000)

18. Wang, X., He, X., Nie, L., Chua, T.S.: Item silk road: recommending items from information domains to social users. In: Proceedings of the 40th International ACM SIGIR Conference on Research and Development in Information Retrieval, pp. 185–194 (2017)

19. Wu, C., Wu, F., Cao, Y., Huang, Y., Xie, X.: FedGNN: federated graph neural network for privacy-preserving recommendation. arXiv preprint arXiv:2102.04925 (2021)

20. Yang, L., Tan, B., Zheng, V., Chen, K., Yang, Q.: Federated Recommendation Systems, pp. 225–239 (2020). https://doi.org/10.1007/978-3-030-63076-8_16

21. Yang, Q., Liu, Y., Chen, T., Tong, Y.: Federated machine learning: concept and applications. ACM Trans. Intell. Syst. Technol. **10**, 1–19 (2019)

Author Index

R. Goebel et al. (Eds.): FL 2022, LNAI 13448, p. 159, 2023.
https://doi.org/10.1007/978-3-031-28996-5

Printed in the United States
by Baker & Taylor Publisher Services